ELECTIONS MATTER

Elections Matter

Ten Federal Elections that Shaped Australia

EDITED BY BENJAMIN T. JONES, FRANK BONGIORNO AND JOHN UHR

Elections Matter: Ten Federal Elections that Shaped Australia

© Copyright 2018 Benjamin T. Jones, Frank Bongiorno and John Uhr
All rights reserved. Apart from any uses permitted by Australia's Copyright Act 1968, no part of this book may be reproduced by any process without prior written permission from the copyright owners. Inquiries should be directed to the publisher.

Monash University Publishing
Matheson Library and Information Services Building
40 Exhibition Walk
Monash University
Clayton, Victoria 3800, Australia
www.publishing.monash.edu

Monash University Publishing brings to the world publications which advance the best traditions of humane and enlightened thought.

Monash University Publishing titles pass through a rigorous process of independent peer review.

www.publishing.monash.edu/books/em-9781925523157.html

ISBN: 9781925523157 (paperback)
ISBN: 9781925523164 (pdf)
ISBN: 9781925523171 (epub)

Series: Politics

Design: Les Thomas

Cover image by Les Thomas

 A catalogue record for this book is available from the National Library of Australia

Printed in Australia by Griffin Press an Accredited ISO AS/NZS 14001:2004 Environmental Management System printer.

 The paper this book is printed on is certified against the Forest Stewardship Council ® Standards. Griffin Press holds FSC chain of custody certification SGS-COC-005088. FSC promotes environmentally responsible, socially beneficial and economically viable management of the world's forests.

CONTENTS

Abbreviations vi

Author Biographies vii

Elections: Aren't They All the Same? xi
    Benjamin T. Jones

1. 1901: Getting the Job Done 1
    Marian Simms

2. 1910: Fisher Leads Labor to Victory 26
    John Uhr

3. 1929: The Patrician and the Orator 47
    Alex Millmow

4. 1940: What to Do in an Electoral Draw 68
    Benjamin T. Jones

5. 1954: Did Petrov Matter? 94
    Bridget Brooklyn

6. 1969: 'Our Politics Are No Longer Frozen' 116
    Richard Reid

7. 1987: Labor Makes It Three 137
    Frank Bongiorno

8. 1996: Lazarus Rises 161
    Jill Sheppard

9. 2001: Boats, Terror and Legacy 188
    Marija Taflaga

10. 2010: Another Hung Parliament 222
    Isobelle Barrett Meyering

Conclusion: A New Normal? 249
    Benjamin T. Jones

Appendix: How Australians Vote 252
    Michael Maley

Index 283

ABBREVIATIONS

ACT – Australian Capital Territory

ACTU – Australian Council of Trade Unions

AD – Australian Democrats

ALA – Australian Liberal Association

ALP – Australian Labor Party

ALPNC – Australian Labor Party Non-Communist

ANA – Australian Natives Association

ANU – Australian National University

CP – Country Party

FT – Free Trade Party

NAA – National Archives of Australia

NLA – National Library of Australia

NSW – New South Wales

SA – South Australia

UAP – United Australia Party

UWS – University of Western Australia

AUTHOR BIOGRAPHIES

Isobelle Barrett Meyering is a Research Fellow at Macquarie University. She works on the history of Australian feminism, gender politics and children's rights. Isobelle completed her PhD at UNSW Australia in 2017 and previously worked as a researcher at the Australian Domestic and Family Violence Clearinghouse from 2009 to 2013. She has also been a summer scholar at the Australian Museum of Democracy at Old Parliament House.

Frank Bongiorno is an award-winning author and professor of history at the Australian National University. His books include *The People's Party: Victorian Labor and the Radical Tradition 1875–1914* (1996), *The Sex Lives of Australians: A History* (2012) and *The Eighties: The Decade that Transformed Australia* (2015).

Bridget Brooklyn is a lecturer in Australian history and the history of feminism in the History and Political Thought discipline of the School of Humanities and Communication Arts, Western Sydney University. Her research interests are: Australian history of the nineteenth and twentieth centuries, including Australian imperial loyalty, eugenics and feminism. She is currently researching the life and work of conservative political activist and eugenicist Dr Mary Booth.

Benjamin Jones is a member of the School of History at the Australian National University. He is a historian specialising in republicanism and nationalism, Australian social and political history, public memory, and secularisation. His books include: *This Time:*

Australia's Republican Past and Future (2018), *Atheism for Christians* (2016), *Republicanism and Responsible Government* (2014), and *Project Republic* (2013).

Michael Maley spent more than 30 years as an election administrator before retiring in 2012 from the position of Special Adviser, Electoral Reform and International Services, Australian Electoral Commission (AEC). He has written and lectured extensively on elections and electoral administration, co-authored the revised edition of the International IDEA Handbook on Electoral Management Design, and originated the concept for the BRIDGE electoral administrators' course which has now been delivered in over 100 countries. He was awarded the Australian Public Service Medal in 2001, and the Joe C. Baxter Award of the International Foundation for Electoral Systems in 2015.

Alex Millmow is an associate professor in economics at Federation Business School, Federation University. His research interests include the economics of Joan Robinson, the making of the Australian economic profession and the role of economic ideas in steering public policy. Alex's latest work is *A History of Australasian Economic Thought* (2018). He is currently writing a biography of the Anglo-Australian economist Colin Clark. He is the current President of the History of Economic Thought Society of Australia (HETSA), a member of the Editorial Board of *Australian Universities Review* and is a council member of the Victorian Branch of the Economic Society of Australia.

AUTHOR BIOGRAPHIES

Richard Reid is a researcher in the School of Politics and International Relations at the Australian National University, where he lectures in British politics. He has published articles in the *Australian Journal of Public Administration*, *Asia-Pacific Journal of Public Administration*, *Parliamentary Affairs*, *Commonwealth and Comparative Politics*, and *British Politics*. He is currently Associate Editor of *International Political Science Review* and is a teaching fellow at the Australian Command and Staff College, Canberra. His interests are Australian and British political and military history, and contemporary Australian and British politics.

Marian Simms holds an adjunct chair at the University of Canberra and has held senior roles at the Australian Research Council, Deakin University, the University of Otago, and the Australian National University. Marian is a political scientist who has published widely on Australian and comparative politics and has edited books for the Centenary of Federation and the Centenary of Commonwealth Equal Franchise legislation. She served as editor of *Politics* (1988-90) and the *Australian Journal of Political Science* (2011-16). She was awarded a centenary medal in 2003.

Jill Sheppard is a lecturer in the School of Politics and International Relations at the Australian National University. Her research interests are elections and voting, political participation, and public opinion, particularly in Australia but also internationally. She is an investigator on several major survey studies of Australian public opinion and behaviour.

ELECTIONS MATTER

Marija Taflaga is an early career researcher at the Australian National University. Her major research interests are political parties and particularly the Liberal Party of Australia. Her research interests also include comparative Westminster parliaments and oppositions, the career paths of political elites, and Australian political history. Marija has undertaken research fellowships at the Australian Parliamentary Library and the Australian Museum of Democracy, Old Parliament House. She has also worked in the Federal Parliamentary Press Gallery as a researcher at *The Sydney Morning Herald* and *The Age*.

John Uhr is professor of political science in the School of Politics and International Relations at the Australian National University, where he established the Centre for the Study of Australian Politics. Among his recent books is *Political Leadership and Rhetoric*, written with Dr Adam Masters (Palgrave 2017).

ELECTIONS: AREN'T THEY ALL THE SAME?

Benjamin T. Jones

On 3 January 2013 Queensland premier Campbell Newman released a discussion paper questioning if voting at state level should be compulsory. This came nearly a century after Queensland distinguished itself in 1915 as the first jurisdiction in the British Empire to introduce compulsory voting. The response to Newman's plan was both immediate and scathing. Prime Minister Julia Gillard took to Twitter demanding he not 'make our democracy the plaything of cashed up interest groups'.[1] The deputy prime minister and treasurer, Wayne Swan, also condemned the 'absolutely stunning' suggestion.[2] Clive Palmer, a billionaire businessman soon to launch his own political party, also savaged the idea, noting 'The more people who participate in a democracy the better and it is good for the whole country if citizens accept the responsibility to vote'.[3] Newman was accused of trying to limit the public voice and was compared to former premier Joh Bjelke-Petersen and even the ultra-conservative Tea Party in the United States. The fierce backlash ensured the suggestion was never seriously pursued.

---

[1] Milanda Rout, 'Abolishing compulsory voting would take Queensland back to Joh era, says Wayne Swan', *Australian*, 3 January 2013.
[2] Ibid.
[3] 'Queensland's Newman Government may dump compulsory voting at state elections', *Courier-Mail*, 2 January 2013.

ELECTIONS MATTER

Optional voting had been briefly floated at the federal level nearly a decade earlier, following a parliamentary committee report on the electoral system in 2005. John Howard, who was prime minister at the time, said he personally supported the idea but felt the majority of Australians were committed to compulsory voting, which had been in place federally since 1924. He added: 'There are a lot of Liberals who are strongly in favour of the present system, and I think it is fair to say the party organisations on both sides of politics are in favour of the present system.'[4] Why is it that Australians are so attached to what is essentially a state repression of liberty? As John Hirst has noted, compulsory voting is 'the most distinctive feature of the Australian system', and numerous polls indicate a clear majority are in favour of it.[5] In the majority of developed nations, voting is a right that citizens can choose to exercise or not. American-style liberalism would find it anathema that the state would actively coerce free citizens into exercising a right. 'Is not a forced right an oxymoron?', reasons this school of thought.

When it comes to voting, Australia adheres to the civic republican ideal of communitarianism. This is part of an ancient intellectual tradition that values the common good of the community over individual good, and even individual rights. Like the citizens of ancient Athens who were compelled to attend the *Ekklēsia* (public assembly), civic republicans would argue that voting is a responsibility as well as a right. Many Australians would rather be at the beach, the pub, or just at home than in line at a polling station but it is overwhelmingly accepted that this is a civic duty (and compared to other possible

---

4   Stephanie Peatling, 'Howard rejects calls to end compulsory voting', *Sydney Morning Herald*, 5 October 2005.
5   John Hirst, *Sense and Nonsense in Australian History* (Melbourne: Black Inc, 2009), p.310.

civic responsibilities like compulsory military service, not a particularly onerous one). In the United States, the conservative satirist P.J. O'Rourke released a book with the humorous title *Don't Vote! It Just Encourages the Bastards*.[6] In Australia the opposite view was advanced in a now iconic political slogan. The Australian Democrats' early leader, Don Chipp, argued that the exact reason Australians needed to vote (for them) was to 'keep the bastards honest'. The message played well to the Australian electorate and the Democrats regularly held the balance of power in the federal Senate in the 1980s and 1990s.

Australia is one of the few democracies in the world to have compulsory voting. It is a major plank in the democratic system and one that ensures Australia has close to the highest proportional voter turnout in the world. Yet, despite this display of civic engagement and political participation, there is a popular view that elections do not really matter and that the two-party system presents only the illusion of choice. A joint poll conducted by the Australian National University (ANU) and Social Research Centre in 2014 found that only 43% of Australians felt it made a difference which party was in power.[7] At the 2013 federal election just under three quarters of young people aged 18-24 were enrolled to vote, despite their legal obligation to do so.[8] This equated to nearly half a million youths ignoring the law and their civic responsibility in this area. While the proportion of enrolled young people improved in 2016, they remained the largest absentee demographic with just half of 18 year olds registered

---

6   P.J. O'Rourke, *Don't Vote It Just Encourages the Bastards* (New York: Grove Press, 2011).
7   Margot O'Neill, 'Poll data reveals Australia's waning interest in politics, decline in support for democracy', *ABC News*, 12 August 2014.
8   Lucy Carter, '500,000 people aged 18 to 24 are not registered to vote', *ABC News*, 14 July 2013.

to vote.⁹ Various theories have been thrown up to explain this political disengagement, which extends beyond the established parties to a general disillusionment with democracy itself. A Lowy Institute poll in 2014 asked if 'democracy is preferable to any other kind of government'. Only 60% of adults and, incredibly, just 42% of young people, responded in the affirmative.¹⁰ In the aftermath of the 2016 election, the ANU's election study found that 40% of Australians were dissatisfied with their democracy (the highest level since the late 1970s). Just 30% of the 2800 responders took a detailed interest in the recent election campaign.¹¹

This book argues emphatically that elections *do* matter and that the Australian Westminster system of democracy has been remarkably successful in allowing voters to determine the national direction. Australia is one of the oldest continuing, and most stable, democracies in the world. Since the granting of responsible government to New South Wales in 1856, democracy has become part of the national Zeitgeist. Active political participation through voting was initially granted to men only but, beginning with South Australia in 1894, it was extended to women relatively quickly (although Aboriginal women and men were often excluded through both official and unofficial means into the 1960s). In 1902 Australia became the first place in the world to allow women both to vote and stand for parliament.

Throughout the twentieth century and beyond, elections have been seen as defining events. Despite the alleged similarities between

---

9   Stephanie Anderson, 'Election 2016: Hundreds of thousands of young voters missing from electoral roll, AEC says', *ABC News*, 23 May 2016.
10 Alex Oliver, *The Lowy Institute Poll 2014* (Sydney: Lowy Institute, 2014), p.3.
11 Henry Belot, 'Confidence in democracy hits record low as Australians "disaffected with political class"', *ABC*, 20 December 2016.

major parties, diverse leaders, policies and visions for the future have presented the electorate with genuine choice. The outcomes of federal elections have the potential to influence the lives of all Australians, whether they are engaged in the political process or not.

Australia's first federal election was held over two days on 29 and 30 March 1901. The result was a hung parliament with Edmund Barton, leader of the Protectionist Party, becoming the nation's first prime minister. The 2016 double dissolution was Australia's forty-fifth general election. While every election is important, some stand out as defining moments where the course of the nation was influenced or even determined. Some elections have had an impact well beyond the usual three-year cycle and have truly played a major part in forming the modern Australian nation. The fickle nature of Australia's electoral system has meant some prominent opposition leaders with a distinct vision never became prime minister despite strong support. Many contested policies were never implemented. Had key elections taken a different turn, Australia would probably have a different constitution, a different head of state, different health and education systems, and a different foreign policy approach. This book highlights ten elections of great importance to forming modern Australia, both socially and culturally.

Which federal election was the most important in Australian history? It is akin to the eternal pub discussions: was Essendon's 2000 squad the best footy team of all time? Is Margaret Court or Rod Laver Australia's greatest tennis player? Would you pick Glenn McGrath or Dennis Lillee to open your pace attack? There is no definitive answer and this work does not attempt to rank elections in terms of importance. The elections chosen for this collection will inevitably be contested and the editors and authors welcome the debates that may spring forth. This work is deliberately provocative in leaving out some of the more famous elections and including others that are less well remembered. The landmark Whitlam election of 1972, for instance, is a notable omission, with his 1969 loss discussed instead. Billy Hughes' emotion-charged, wartime election triumph of 1917 is absent but Andrew Fisher's comfortable 1910 victory is included. The message of this work is that elections can be important even when they seem relatively banal or routine in retrospect or at the time they were held. Further, this work suggests that it is not only the toppling of governments that is significant. In many cases, the retention of government has proved nation-forming. The case studies here represent a diverse selection of conservative and progressive victories, of opposition triumphs and government returns, all of which illustrate how elections matter, even when you think they don't.

Each of the authors in this collection discusses a federal election that significantly shaped the nation. The word 'shaped' has been strategically chosen. While it is not possible to measure empirically the importance of an election, each chapter explores the way elections mould national policy and identity, and chart a national direction. The significance lies not only with the winners but with the losers also. While 1949 was the election that began Robert Menzies' record-breaking, second period as prime minster, it was the 1954 contest that, at least in retrospect, eliminated the possibility of Herbert Vere 'Doc' Evatt becoming prime minister. How different might Australia be now if his occupancy of The Lodge, that had at one time seemed inevitable, eventuated? Or how different would the national story be if Kim Beazley had toppled John Howard in 2001, as many polls had suggested he was destined to do? The 2010 election is perhaps the most controversial inclusion as its ramifications are still being felt and considered. Mark Latham dismissed it in gendered language as a 'beauty contest' and urged voters to protest by leaving their ballot papers blank.[12] Would it have mattered if Tony Abbott assumed the prime ministership three years earlier? What would it have meant for Australia if the first female prime minster was removed at the public's first democratic opportunity?

This book is about far more than prime ministers and opposition leaders. It takes a holistic view of Australia's electoral system and explores the nuances that make these contests so significant. The division between preferential voting (using a method called the alternative vote) in the House of Representatives, and a mixture of proportional and preferential representation in the Senate (See Appendix), has unique ramifications for the fortunes of major and minor parties, and Independent candidates also. Similarly, the constitutional diktat that all six states receive equal Senate representation, despite the population disparity between them, has been a major influence at several elections. The emphasis here is on the broader social and cultural impact of elections, not just their immediate effect on the composition of parliament or the adoption of policy. Each chapter discusses why the particular election was so important and what the two (or more) visions being presented were. They explore what would have been the likely momentary and lasting consequences of a different result. The final significant question addressed is what these election results tell us about the Australian people. Elections reveal far more than policy concerns; they provide a snapshot of the values, hopes, and priorities of a people at any given moment.

---

12   Jamie Duncan, 'Latham's lash at leaders airs on Nine', *Sydney Morning Herald*, 15 August 2010.

ELECTIONS MATTER

Alfred Deakin, in his third spell as prime minister, opened the 1910 election campaign by informing voters that 'at least once in every three years you are called upon, before choosing your representatives to take a collected view of the position in the Commonwealth'.[13] Federal elections provide a unique opportunity to assess the national mood and weigh societal attitudes on a variety of issues. However far removed Australian citizens may feel from the political system, the battle for power affects the electorate in both direct and subtle ways. Elections can determine far more than a tax here or there; they can set the national agenda and even, in some instances, influence national identity. They can be messy, funny, confusing, and hostile. They are always fiercely contested and they invariably matter. Presented here are the stories behind ten elections that shaped modern Australia.

---

13   Alfred Deakin, *Prime Minister at Ballarat* (Ballarat: Berry, Anderson and Co., 1910), p.2.

Chapter 1

1901

GETTING THE JOB DONE[1]

Marian Simms[2]

The 1901 election is significant because it was the 'first' federal election, and importantly it produced a 'workable' national parliament. It got the job done in a pragmatic sense. Glitches and imperfections could be ironed out by future electoral legislation. The election was held over two days in March 1901 and was based on colonial lower house franchises and electoral laws with a minimal national constitutional overlay guaranteeing single (as opposed to plural) voting. The election is fascinating because of its hybridity, comprising modern 'moments' alongside traditional colonial elements. Those former 'moments' are particularly displayed through the importance of political leadership and media interest in those leaders, especially through the process of election campaigning. The proof of the leadership pudding was in the eating with Edmund Barton's 'Ministerialist' team achieving a plurality of seats in the lower house, if not in the Senate. On the other hand, the traditional elements were many, mainly relating to loose party structures and porous political boundaries. In keeping with the traditions of colonial parliaments, and their experiences of minority and coalition governments, the emergence of a minority federal government was not yet a cause for concern. In international terms it was a progressive election, with (loose) teams of Labor Party candidates in Queensland and New South Wales and women voting in two states, although in contrast with New Zealand the constitutional and political rights of Aboriginal peoples were highly circumscribed and would remain so for many years.

---

1 With apologies to Geoffrey Bolton, *Edmund Barton: The One Man for the Job* (Sydney: Allen & Unwin, 2000).
2 The author acknowledges the financial support of the National Council for the Centenary of Federation for enabling much of the research for this chapter.

ELECTIONS MATTER

Australia's first federal election was held on 29 and 30 March 1901. This chapter will outline its novel, innovative, and distinctive features from both contemporary and current perspectives. We should avoid seeing only the modern, or the roots of the modern, in the 1901 election, and equally the tendency to ignore or sideline debates over immigration restriction and indentured labour in Queensland as if they were peripheral to the federal democracy established in 1901. Such issues – which contemporaries and historians have marshalled under the banner of the 'White Australia Policy' – were at the heart of early Commonwealth politics.

The 1901 election was not a 'conventional election'.[3] As a 'one off' event, however, it was largely and deliberately ignored by students of colonial/state elections, although not by Labor historians for federation's role in the establishment of federal structures. The results and policies of the election could not contribute to debates such as those on relative party strengths and state-by-state trends. According to Peter Loveday, it was a 'pre party' election, making proper classification of candidates difficult – in his mind this could best be resolved by the analysis of voting behaviour of successful candidates once elected to the Commonwealth parliament.[4] With the digitisation of contemporary newspapers, periodicals, and government documents, the details of campaigning and voting provide additional insights into this important election. In this way, the 1901 election has become a case study of one, with all the methodological challenges of such case studies. It can also be viewed as an example of

---

3   J.A. La Nauze, *Alfred Deakin: A Biography* (Melbourne: Melbourne University Press, 1965), p.220.
4   Peter Loveday, 'Grouping MPs: The Use of Cluster Analysis', *Politics*, 5:2, 1970, pp.180-194.

Australian inventiveness, a widely-recognised quality of the colonial democratic experiment.

Uniformity and Diversity

While historians have tended to draw attention to differences, there was a basic level of uniformity across the states in how the federal election was conducted, as guaranteed by the Commonwealth constitution. For instance, plural voting (the practice of allowing an elector to vote in any constituency where they held property) was not permitted in the 1901 federal election. Plural voting had already been abolished in most colonies, but was retained in Queensland at a state level until after Federation. Hence Queensland voters were told not to 'vote more than ONCE; that is, they shall not vote more than once in the same Division, nor shall they vote in two Divisions'.[5] There was also uniformity in less significant matters: for the House blue ballots papers were used and for the Senate, yellow.[6] Apart from South Australia, which had pioneered boxes beside candidates' names, voters were required to strike through the names of candidates they did not want – for both the houses. This led to complaints – especially in New South Wales – with 50 candidates for the Senate and blunt blue pencils!

As the nature of the South Australian ballot papers would suggest, some electoral laws and processes varied among the colonies. There were differences in the suffrage laws. Women voted in South Australia and Western Australia but elsewhere could only attend political meetings or 'demonstrations'. The suffrage became an issue in the Victorian campaign, where the Legislative Council had recently

---

5   Election Notice, Qld, 1901.
6   Commonwealth of Australia, *Election Notice* 1901, as published in metropolitan newspapers in March 1901.

rejected a women's suffrage bill, with Deakin supporting and conservatives opposing.[7] In New South Wales, where key women's movement leaders, such as Rose Scott, had opposed federation, and there were signs that state suffrage legislation would soon be passed, it was not a major issue in the campaign.[8] As in this instance, policy issues were articulated differently between states, or even regions within states. Here was one of the tests of the first election: could the states with their different histories, industrial bases, and economic successes and failures be 'democratically' united in such a geographically vast nation? A thriving provincial press emphasised regional differences, including the popularity of land tax ideas in rural New South Wales, and the issue of indentured labour for the sugar industry of northern Queensland, which was also supported by the metropolitan newspapers of that state.[9]

The numbers game had dominated the federation debates – states' rights views were reflected in the equal number (six) of senators allocated to each founding 'original' state, another instance of uniformity. Each state was allocated a minimum of five House seats and a nexus was established between the two Houses (see Table 1); that is, the size of the House of Representatives should be roughly double that of the Senate. While there was to be a quota for calculating the number of lower house seats per state, it was a population-based formula that excluded 'races' ineligible to vote. The issue of race was prominent in contemporary discussion of federation, and tended to focus on the 'problem' of 'coloured' immigration and on migrant

---

7 See *Age*, 6 February 1901 and *Argus*, 9 March 1901.

8 Judith Allen 'Rose Scott (1847-1925)', *Australian Dictionary of Biography*, vol. 11 (Melbourne: Melbourne University Press 1988). Accessed online 20 March 2017.

9 Rod Kirkpatrick, 'The provincial press and politics: NSW, 1841-1930', *Australian Studies in Journalism*, 8, 1999, pp.96-117.

(so-called Kanaka) labour in Queensland, rather than on the status or future of Aboriginal people and Torres Strait Islanders. In fact, the constitution (section 51, xxvi) then excluded them from the law-making gaze of the Commonwealth.[10]

The federation debates produced a consensus that 'uniform' franchise laws should be enacted as soon as practical after the election of the new parliament, which the delegates agreed should have exclusive power to legislate electoral laws for the Commonwealth Parliament, including for an elected upper house. (This was followed in quick succession by restrictive immigration legislation and the new tariff.) The decade of formal discussion and deliberation over the federal compact had given colonial political leaders a national stage, the chance to form collegial (and not-so-collegial) relationships, and provided the opportunity for emerging groups, such as the Labor Party, to develop broader campaigning skills.[11] This is not inconsistent with L.F. Crisp's view that the 'founding fathers', the drafters of the constitution, were men of the establishment. There was only one trade union leader, William Trenwith, who then led the Labor Party in the Victorian parliament, at the Australasian Federation Convention of 1897-98.[12]

The move towards federation, as well as harnessing older interests and organisations, generated new ones. The role of the Australian Natives Association (ANA) is well known, and its forces were marshalled by Bendigo's Dr John Quick, notably in the Victorian gold

---

10 This was amended by the Constitution Alteration (Aboriginals) Act 1967, which also repealed section 127 excluding Aboriginal persons from the census.
11 Kathleen Dermody, 'The 1897 Federal Convention Election: A Success or Failure?', *Papers on Parliament* No.30, November 1997.
12 L.F. Crisp, *Australian National Government* (Melbourne: Longman Cheshire, 1983), p.14.

towns where it was strong.[13] Partly as a result of Edmund Barton's 'missionary' work, Federation Leagues (sometimes called Australasian Federation Leagues) were established in the Murray Valley district on the NSW/Victorian border.[14] These Leagues – sometimes called Commonwealth Leagues in Western Australia – were designed to be non-political, and to encompass both liberals and conservatives, as well as local luminaries. They had a spasmodic existence, waxing and waning, during the next decade, emerging in the campaigns for the election of delegates to the Federation Conventions (1897-98) in 1897, then for the referendum voting on the draft Constitution itself. Usually fuelled by Barton's visit to a region, the Leagues were to become important campaigning vehicles in some regions, such as in Queensland. Important factors for the northern colony were its latecomer status to the federation process and its own 'peculiar' institution of indentured labour.

The variation between state approaches to the 1901 election provided laboratory conditions for testing how best to conduct an election. The lessons learned were well-documented in the post-election review undertaken by state returning officers.[15] On balance, the South Australian system of electoral administration was given the biggest tick. Its successful elements were simple enrolment qualifications – residential qualification and being over twenty-one; voters enrolling for their locality; voters able to tick a box for their preferred candidate(s); and women's suffrage. Importantly, the right of South Australian women to stand for office was soon adopted by the

---

13   See *Official Report of the Federation Conference 1893* – Corowa 2001. See also Barton's correspondence with other political figures in NSW urging them to join the League. Sir Edmund Barton Papers, MS 51, series 1.
14   Edward Wilson, *Preface to Federation Conference Report*, no page numbers.
15   Commonwealth of Australia, *Report of Conference Re: Election Bills* 1901-02.

1901

Table 1: Voting and Franchise

State	Seats	Divided (into constituencies)	Voting system	Other	Franchise
NSW	26	Yes	First past the post – strike out names not voting for, leaving preferred candidate	Voter's rights	Manhood suffrage – residential qualification Restrictions on Chinese men
VIC	23	Yes	First past the post – Strike out names not voting for, leaving preferred candidate	Voter's rights	Manhood suffrage – residential qualification Restrictions on Chinese men
QLD	9	Yes	First past the post – with provision for contingent vote if no candidate gained a majority	Contingent vote – in multiple candidacies (more than two) write 1 and 2 next to your most preferred candidates, in order of preference	Manhood suffrage, based on property or residential. Restrictions on Aboriginal, Chinese and 'coloured' men
SA	7	No	First past the post – mark box of preferred candidates	Voter registration Allowed for plumping	Adult suffrage – residential qualification
WA	5	Yes	First past the post – Strike out names not voting for, leaving preferred candidate uncrossed	Voter registration	Adult suffrage – residential qualification Restrictions on Aboriginal, Chinese and 'coloured' people
TAS	5	No	Hare-Clark	Voter registration	Manhood suffrage – residential qualification

Commonwealth, producing greater uniformity in the 1903 federal election. Most of the other states had unfair and discriminatory voting qualifications, messy enrolment systems and, as we have seen, except for Western Australia, voting for males only. No state prohibited Indigenous Australians from enrolling and voting, but Queensland and Western Australia had convoluted property requirements for Aboriginal residents and 'natives' of 'Asia and Africa'. Some states had restrictive provisions on 'Chinese' (Victoria) and 'Indian immigrants' (Northern Territory – then governed from Adelaide). Aboriginal people, however, voted in South Australia and there was a discussion in the New South Wales parliament about whether they would be voting in the 1901 (federal) election. There were press reports of Aboriginal voting in New South Wales – and a sad tale of the police arresting an Aboriginal man in Collarenebri, allegedly for voting fraud. It was reported that 'Tinker, an Aboriginal, was committed for trial by the police magistrate on a charge of double voting at the recent election'.[16]

The new states were too busy with other matters to attend to the details of electoral systems for the upcoming federal election and there was a general air of uncertainty.[17] Would Western Australia join the federation? Would women's suffrage be enacted in Queensland, New South Wales and Victoria, joining South Australia and Western Australia on this matter? Most states stuck with the tried and true, due to a mix of inertia and strongly held preferences. The latter was true for Tasmania where the pioneering 'Hare-Clark' (or Spence) system – used at the colonial and local levels – was in turn

---

16   *Bathurst Free Press and Mining Journal*, 4 April 1901.
17   Joan Rydon, 'Electoral Methods', in Marian Simms (ed.), *1901: The Forgotten Election* (Brisbane: University of Queensland Press, 2001), pp.23-4

Table 2: Federation Conventions

Conference	Date	Place	Delegates	Selection
Australasian Federation Conference	February 1890	Melb.	Two per colony, including New Zealand	Appointed by colonial parliaments
National Australasian Convention	March–April 1891	Syd.	Seven per colony, including New Zealand	Elected by colonial parliaments
Australasian Federation Conference	July-August 1893	Corowa, NSW	From organisations such as the Australian Natives Association, Federation Leagues etc	Appointed by the organisations
People's Federal Convention*	Nov. 1896	Bathurst, NSW	From organisations such as the Federation Leagues, Australian Natives Association etc	Appointed by the organisations
Australasian Federal Convention	1897/1898	Adelaide; Sydney; Melbourne	10 delegates per colony – QLD did not attend	Elected in four/five colonies. WA appointed

Source: Drawn from Table 1, Chris Aulich and Rebecca Pietsch, 'Left on the Shelf: Local Government and the Australian Constitution', *Australian Journal of Public Administration*, 61, 2002, pp.14-23.

*See <http://purl.library.usyd.edu.au/setis/id/fed0058>

also utilised for both houses of the Commonwealth parliament. There was a similar pattern in Queensland where the 'Contingent Vote', a form of preferential voting introduced in 1892 for the Assembly elections, was used for the House of Representatives election in 1901. Voters were reminded of its operation: 'When there are three or more Candidates' for a seat in the more numerous House, and if there was no outright majority, then preferences are distributed to the two candidates with the most initial votes. It was not permitted for the Senate.[18]

New South Wales, Victoria, Queensland, and Western Australia divided their states into single member constituencies for the House

---

18   Commonwealth of Australia, *Election Notice* 1901, as published in Qld metropolitan newspapers in March 1901.

of Representatives, at a time when some colonies retained multi-member constituencies for their lower houses. Colonial parliaments also managed the drawing of their electoral maps, and the naming of electorates. Surprisingly, South Australia chose not to divide, leading to controversy. Along with Tasmania, it went to the election with the state as a single, large constituency for both houses. South Australia, however, allowed voters to 'plump' (a form of optional preferential system where voters could support fewer candidates than there were vacancies).

Campaign

The 1901 election had an unusual initiation, with the prime minister commissioned beforehand by a newly-arrived governor-general, who was severely unwell on the voyage out to Australia. It was expected that he would approach Barton, as the leading federationist from the premier colony, for this important role. Some, however, argued that one of the experienced colonial/state premiers should be approached. In this vein, Sir William Lyne, the New South Wales premier, was offered the commission. As Lyne was not able to convince the leading men of the day to serve under him, Barton was subsequently offered the prime ministership, and Lyne accepted a ministry under Barton.[19] The incumbent prime minister – sometimes called premier – and an executive council, in all consisting of seven ministers and an additional two, without portfolio – was sworn in on 1 January 1901. As I have argued elsewhere, it was to become the first national example of incumbency advantage. Ministers campaigned while going about their duties and local governments and organisations such as the

---

19   See La Nauze, *Alfred Deakin*, pp.205-08. The ministers were Barton, Deakin, Lyne, Turner, Kingston, Dickson and Forrest, with O'Connor, and the Tasmanian premier, Neil Lewis, as ministers without portfolio.

Australian Natives' Association (ANA) provided lavish receptions. There were claims and counter claims that some state members were using their railway passes to assist with their federal campaigns.[20]

A related issue was that the prime minister and some ministers and other federation leaders were unopposed in their constituencies, leaving Barton, Forrest, Turner, and Quick free to campaign nationally. But on 10 January, James Dickson, Queensland chief secretary and Barton's defence minister, died. He was replaced in the ministry by (future Senator) James Drake, another Queenslander and former minister as well as an ardent supporter of federation. Forrest was reshuffled into defence, and Drake took on the postmaster-general role. Alfred Deakin (Ballaarat) and William Lyne (Hume) were facing local electoral contests, and Charles Kingston (division of South Australia) was campaigning at large, as was Richard O'Connor (NSW, Senate). Lyne had access to a car as part of his state premier's role; he took quite some time to resign. Kingston, who had served as premier of South Australia for several years in the 1890s, was assured of the popular vote in his home state, and toured nationally on behalf of 'Mr Barton's Policy' – that is, Protectionism – while undertaking his work as Customs Minister.[21]

Barton's launch speech was broad enough to appeal to diverse interests. His policy planks included tariff protection, a transcontinental railway (for the West), abolition of 'coloured labour' (but some time in the future, for Queensland), and the introduction of old age pensions (for workers and those who supported 'fiscalism').[22]

---

20 Marian Simms, 'Election Days', in Simms (ed.), *1901*, p.5.
21 *Argus*, 28 February 1901.
22 According to his biographer David Day, the Labor stalwart and future prime minister, Andrew Fisher, believed Barton had 'snatched' Labor's policies and made them his own. David Day, *Andrew Fisher: Prime Minister of Australia* (Sydney: Harper Collins, 2008), pp.102-03.

His Cabinet colleagues, Lyne, Deakin, and Kingston, were present also, according to press reports. In Victorian circles, Deakin was seen as the *eminence grise*, although he had never been colonial premier.[23] In contrast George Reid, the unofficial opposition leader, was somewhat tied to Sydney in order to retain his seat against a strong, independent Protectionist campaign.

He was annoyed that Barton had taken over the liberal mantle, by calling his party in New South Wales the Australian Liberal Association (ALA) – although the Ministerialists campaigned under the Australian Liberal and Protectionist Organisation (ALPO) in some other states. Reid, who had been Free Trade premier of New South Wales between 1894 and 1899, chose the Australian Free Trade and Liberal Association (AFTLA) as the title of his party instead. It was usually shortened to FT in the NSW press. Reid had been a highly successful New South Wales premier, but had received much negative press for his apparent prevarication over the Constitution Bill, earning him the epithet 'Yes-No Reid'.

Reid did not make an official policy launch for the opposition, which did not exist as such in 1901, and there were expectations that he and his colleagues might eventually be included in government. Reid was generally seen as a rambling, if popular speaker. He responded by way of critique, not onslaught, to Barton's launch in Sydney and focussed on the iniquity of the tariff, accusing Barton of proposing a revenue tariff, not a protectionist policy that would encourage industry. Nationally, Reid suffered for not having time to distance himself from the defeat of the first Constitution Bill in New South Wales in 1898, and to create a new and positive national agenda. The *Bulletin* 'ridiculed him as "Dry Dog Reid"', an

---

23   See, for example, H.B. Higgins cited in the *Argus*, 12 March 1901.

unflattering distillation of Reid's infamous justification for Free Trade: 'Industries, like puppy dogs, should be thrown into the water in order that they might learn to swim.'[24]

Many accounts of the 1901 election tend to present a neat picture of the 'three elevens', Protection, Free Trade and Labor, a cricketing metaphor deployed by Deakin rather later – in 1904 – to depict the dilemma of early Commonwealth parliamentary politics.[25] This interpretation has underpinned narratives of the politics of the 'Australian Settlement', and the subsequent development of the party system,[26] and accorded with Deakin's understanding of Victorian colonial politics as divided between Liberals, Conservatives and Laborites.[27] Crisp, however, noted that the boundaries among Labor's opponents were not so 'tightly drawn', and he referred to 1901 as a contest between Labo(u)r and anti-Labo(u)r.[28] Tables 3 and 4 present a four-way grouping: Ministerialist, Free Trade, Labor and Independent/Other. The Ministerialist group includes protectionist supporters of Barton who received endorsement from a major Liberal Protectionist party such as the Australian Liberal Association or the Australian Liberal and Protection Organisation; candidates supporting the Barton platform, who were silent on the tariff question; candidates who supported Barton but were not endorsed by the Barton Party

---

24 Clem Lloyd and Jolyon Sykes, 'George Houston Reid: 'Dry Dog Days' in Simms (ed), *1901*, p.63.
25 See C.A. Hughes and B.D. Graham, *Voting for the Australian House of Representatives 1901-1964* (Canberra: Australian National University Press, 1964).
26 Paul Strangio and Nick Dyrenfurth (eds), *Confusion: The Making of the Australian Two-Party System* (Melbourne: Melbourne University Press, 2009).
27 See Stuart Macintyre, 'Alfred Deakin: "His Sacred Service"', in Simms (ed), *1901*, p.48.
28 L.F. Crisp, *The Australian Federal Labour Party, 1901-1951* (London: Longmans Green, 1955), pp.154ff and Loveday, 'Grouping MPs'.

(or parties); and/or candidates who were supportive of a moderate or revenue tariff only but backed Barton.

This approach to defining the 'Ministerialists' reflects the messy picture in the contemporary press of party endorsement, personal loyalty, policy orientation and ideological temper. High-profile candidates who were aligned with the incumbent Prime Minister Barton, without endorsing an orthodox protectionism on the tariff question, include free traders (such as B.R. Wise, who unsuccessfully contested the New South Wales seat of Canobolas) and 'Revenue-Tariffists' (such as J.C. Manifold, who was successful in Corangamite in western Victoria). They were called 'Ministerialists', or 'Bartonites', or 'Deakinites' if in Victoria.

Some Labor candidates supported free trade. Notable examples were Tom Brown (Canobolas – NSW) and W.M. (Billy) Hughes (West Sydney – NSW). Free trade was sometimes a short-hand for support for direct taxation (usually on land) rather than import duties, and it included remnants of the Henry George single tax movement. Henry George had undertaken a whirlwind speaking tour of Australia in 1890. He had defined free trade strictly, as was the way with dyed-in-the-wool single taxers: 'Why can't you have real FreeTrade … Abolish the custom houses and put a tax on land'.[29] At other times both free traders and protectionists embraced the designation 'Revenue-Tariffist'. These were often pragmatists, who accepted the need for customs revenue to support government activity, but might also include classical liberals of a conservative bent who favoured *laissez-faire* government.

---

29   Henry George, 'Tamworth Lecture', reproduced in M.L. Treadgold and J.M. Pullen, 'Henry George in Northern New South Wales: Newspaper accounts of two lectures', *History of Economics Review*, 23:1, 1978, pp.83-94.

1901

Table 3: House of Representative Results

Affiliation	Candidates	Seats contested	Unopposed	Elected
Ministerialist-Barton (incl. low or 'Revenue-Tariffist')	86	57	6	31 (3 others joined the M-B team after the election)
Free Trade – Reid	59	51	0	28 (2 left after the election)
Labor+	27	26	0	14
Independent	9	7	0	2
Total	151		6	75

+ In NSW – Two Labor candidates were also endorsed by Free Trade

In QLD – Two Labor candidates contested Maranoa

Table 4: Senate Results

Affiliation	Candidates	Elected	State trends
Ministerialist-Barton (incl. low or 'Revenue-Tariffist')	44	11	4 from Vic.; 1 from NSW; 0 from WA
Free Trade – Reid	54	17	5 from NSW; 3 from SA; 4 from WA
Labor	14	8	3 from QLD; 2 from WA
Independent/Other	14	0	
Total	126	36	

Note: Includes endorsed and non-endorsed candidates

ELECTIONS MATTER

On the protectionist side official party lines were also loose. In New South Wales eight of the twenty-six seats had two competing 'Protectionist' candidates in a wider field. This was a hangover from the colonial era when both multiple candidacies and multi-member seats were common. Candidate nomination, endorsement and selection processes included public meetings, private meetings, and internal party ballots followed by endorsement. Broadly speaking, Bartonites followed the first-named approach, Free Traders the second and the Labor Party the third method. As a direct consequence, there were rare instances of Labor candidates competing with one another. In one case, that of Maranoa in Queensland, a non-endorsed 'Labor' candidate, G.E. Bunning, declared at Longreach Town Hall that there were no federal parties, only groupings under two leaders: he declared himself for 'free trade' and whoever the eventual leader was, it would be determined on the floor of the house.[30] There were also state-by-state variations. The Reid forces in New South Wales allowed double endorsement in some cases. Reid explained that while Tom Brown was endorsed by Labor for Canobolas he had promised to vote for free trade measures in the new parliament.[31]

Barton's opening campaign speech was delivered on 17 January in West Maitland and attracted considerable press coverage. No copy remains, only his speaker's notes and newspaper reports.[32] The key elements were 'revenue without destruction', uniform railway gauge, transcontinental railway, uniform suffrage, 'White Australia' and guarding the Constitution. Versions of this speech were given by 'Bartonite' candidates in Queensland and Western Australia (called

---

30   *Morning Bulletin*, 28 February 1901.
31   *Sydney Morning Herald*, 6 February 1901.
32   *Argus*, 12 March 1901. See also Election Speeches 1901 Edmund Barton, Museum of Australian Democracy, Old Parliament House, Canberra.

the National Liberal and Protectionist League). In cases of multiple Protectionist candidacies, the favoured one on the day would be called 'the true Liberal and Protectionist candidate', as was P.J. O'Connor, one of three Protectionist candidates defeated by Labor stalwart Frank Tudor in the Melbourne seat of Yarra. Candidates and campaigns divided over other matters, including in Queensland so-called black labour, with Labor generally opposed and other candidates (and much of the press) more supportive.[33] The *Courier* judged that 'our own Labour members ... would rather see the sugar industry perish rather than keep the Kanaka'.[34]

Labor was for 'White Australia' and in favour of the immediate end to the indentured labour scheme. Western Australian Labor candidates opposed 'coloured' labour on ships and 'coloured' residents receiving pensions.[35] Labor was divided over the South African war, which was still raging in 1901, and it had been divided over federation. Under its leader J.C. (Chris) Watson, a printer (compositor) and union official and formerly a Labor member for Young in the New South Wales Legislative Assembly, Labor would support the Barton (1901–03) and Deakin (1903–04) minority governments and thereby implement White Australia as well as moderate protectionist policies.[36] By way of contrast, in New South Wales colonial politics, Labor had generally supported the government of George Reid from 1894 through to 1899. In response to Labor's growing numbers after 1895, Reid's social liberalism became more progressive, and

---

33   *Courier*, 8 March 1901.
34   *Courier*, 2 May 1901.
35   Brian De Garis, 'De Largie, Hugh' in Ann Millar (ed.), *The Biographical Dictionary of the Australian Senate*, vol.1, 1901-1929, (Melbourne: Melbourne University Press, 2000), pp.333-36.
36   H.S. Broadhead, 'JC Watson and the Caucus Crisis of 1905', *Australian Journal of Politics and History*, 8, 1962, pp.93-7.

friendships were formed that carried over into the federal sphere. Labor's federal platform, formulated in 1900, allowed a 'free vote' on the tariff, reflecting the diverse views within the party. Watson, himself a protectionist, but tolerant of free traders, received the support of Barton's Australian Liberal Association (ALA) in 1901. J.S.T. (James) McGowen, later to become New South Wales premier, was the only other Labor candidate to do so, but he narrowly lost to the endorsed Free Trade candidate. In 1901 Watson polled well in his country seat of Bland (which included much of his state seat), whereas McGowen polled second in a tight city contest in South Sydney (which included some of his old colonial seat of Redfern). With the exception of industrialising Newcastle, and Hughes in West Sydney, Labor's New South Wales electoral successes were in the bush, where the party appealed successfully to mining, railway and agricultural workers as well as small farmers. There were significant strengths in the Queensland bush, too, with Labor winning or polling very strongly in five of the six non-metropolitan seats. Labor's strong showing in New South Wales and Queensland was built upon successes at a colonial level, which the other colonies/states generally lacked. The Liberal-Labor connection of the 1890s, in Victoria and South Australia, and the existence of radical liberals such as Isaac Isaacs and Henry Bournes Higgins,[37] in Victoria, and Kingston in South Australia,[38] delayed the emergence of a strong Labor presence at the national level. Western Australia's Labor strongholds were the

---

37   Higgins, a Protectionist, accepted the Attorney-General's portfolio in the Watson-led first Labor (minority) federal government of 1904, which Crisp termed a 'happy and successful appointment ... never repeated'. Crisp, *Australian Federal Labour*, p.143 Apparently, Lyne had also wanted Isaac Isaacs in his putative cabinet. C.J. Lloyd, *The Parliament and the Press: The Federal Parliamentary Press Gallery 1901-88* (Melbourne: Melbourne University Press, 1988), p.39.

38   It is notable that Kingston was offered a place but for various reasons did not accept. Crisp, *Australian Federal Labour*, p.143.

mining and urban industrial areas, and Labor polled well for the Senate. In Tasmania Labor was in its infancy but it returned the former South Australian colonial politician, the flamboyant King O'Malley, as a member. O'Malley, who was almost certainly born in the United States, always claimed he was born in Canada, and the Chilean-born Watson was presented as a 'native' of New Zealand in 1901, when under section 34 of the Constitution 'subjects of the Queen' were *inter alia* qualified to run as candidates. [39]

Three contemporary features of Labor are striking. In the first instance, there was a 'free vote' on the fiscal question, which acknowledged the different colonial experiences of Labor, including its close ties in New South Wales with the radical liberalism that was an element of free trade politics there. (The term 'conscience vote' was not used at the time and was a much later development.) An illustration of the consequences of this flexibility and pragmatism on the 'fiscal question', as it was called, is Labor's vote splitting over Reid's want of confidence motion in the Barton Government's 'Financial and Trade Proposals' in October 1901.[40] Reid's motion failed by 25 votes to 39,[41] with three Labor members – Tom Brown, Billy Hughes and the fiery Hugh Mahon – supporting Reid, and a fourth, Josiah Thomas, abstaining. Thomas had also sought to add a 'land tax' clause to Reid's motion, which he subsequently withdrew.[42] When Brown and Hughes had campaigned as Labor candidates who

---

39   See *The Wyalong Star and Temora and Barmedan Advertiser* (reprinted from the *Launceston Examiner* – 'By One Who Knows Him'), 21 June 1901.
40   Commonwealth of Australia, *Votes and Proceedings of the House of Representatives*, 31 October 1901, no. 89.
41   W.G. McMinn, *George Reid* (Melbourne: Melbourne University Press, 1989), pp.190-92. Mahon was later expelled from the parliament for sedition.
42   Reid had applied land tax as a concession to NSW Labor in the mid-1890s. See Bede Nairn, 'McGowen, James Sinclair (1855-1922)' in *Australian Dictionary of Biography*, Accessed online 7 July 2016.

supported Free Trade in 1901, no endorsed Free Trade candidates opposed them. Mahon, an Irishman representing the Western Australian goldfield seat of Kalgoorlie, did not emphasise the fiscal issue in his campaign, but was thought to have a friendship with Reid and Western Australia was a free trade state.[43]

Secondly, the Labor team elected in 1901 was predominantly Protestant, of a somewhat evangelical type, with a minority of Catholics. They were more likely to be of Scottish than of Irish background. Labor would become more Catholic over the decade that followed, but the sea change really came after the conscription debate of World War I. Consequently, the Scullin Government of 1929–32 (See Millmow chapter) was 'Catholic' in a way that would have been unanticipated from the perspective of 1901.

Third, and despite its subsequent reputation as the party of Australian nationalism, the Labor Party was neither a whole-hearted supporter of federation, nor of the form of Australian federation eventually embodied in the constitution. There was unhappiness within the party about the manner in which states' rights had trumped the weight of numbers in the six seats allocated to each state for the Senate, not two as in the United States, and the subsequent decision to use a double dissolution as a deadlock provision, rather than a referendum, as proposed by some liberals in the various conventions of the 1890s.[44] Labor would also soon become frustrated at the apparent restrictions on the power of the federal government embodied in the constitution, culminating in its unsuccessful efforts to expand Commonwealth power in 1911 and 1913.

---

43 McMinn, *George Reid*, p.190.
44 See Crisp, *Australian Federal Labour*, pp.207ff. See also Jack Richardson, *Resolving Deadlocks in the Australian Parliament*, Research Paper 9, 2000-01, Department of the Parliamentary Library, Australian Parliament House, Canberra.

It is sometimes claimed that the Senate, which was meant to be a states' house, took on a national character very quickly due to the emergence of national parties soon after federation.[45] Yet there are important caveats to this generalisation if we take 1901 as our vantage point, even though it was to prove correct in the longer term. In the first instance, Reid's Free Traders performed better in the Senate than the House; the reverse was true for the Bartonites. (See Tables 3 and 4.) Labor polled better in the Senate than the House. More significantly, the three groups had strongholds in different states, especially as reflected in the Senate vote: Bartonites in Victoria and Tasmania; Reidites in New South Wales and Western Australia; and Labor in Queensland. South Australia was the most balanced of all, and each of the three principal groupings was well represented there. The Senate was directly elected, and therefore at least in that sense progressive as compared with other Westminster systems, such as the United Kingdom and Canada, with inherited and appointed members respectively. It also remained true to Westminster convention by providing a prime minister who was from the lower house, although ministers with important portfolios were from the Senate, and non-finance Bills could originate there.

Conclusion

The 1901 election was remarkable for its time, with a relatively democratic franchise, and especially so in those two states that had enfranchised women. Like colonial elections, it was largely well-administered and although conducted on two different if adjacent days, it proceeded in an orderly fashion. It reflected 'incrementalism',

---

45   Crisp, *Australian National Government*, pp.20-21; Rydon, 'Electoral Methods', pp.26-27.

and was built very much on the political experiences and styles of the 1890s and on a (sometimes aspirational) culture of deliberation and participation. To the extent that there were lapses in involvement, this was called out as 'apathy'.[46] The failure to provide for Aboriginal participation stands out, when compared for example with New Zealand's Māori seats.

The 1901 election can be best understood as the culmination of a long federation process, as the winners and many of the leaders had participated in those campaigns. Labor's failure in its own eyes during that earlier process had been in allowing the emergence of a 'states' rights' constitution, without a referendum to break deadlocks, which also frustrated some radical liberals, but the 1901 election had revealed that the Commonwealth would provide new opportunities for that party. For all its quirks, the 1901 election was ultimately about 'getting the job done'. To that extent, it did form a new nation.

---

46 According to John Forrest, the low turn-out in the West was regretted and 'The interest in the elections was not equal to that of the Perth Mayoral elections'. Interview in the *Sydney Morning Herald*, 2 April 1901.

INTERIM 1901–1910

Australia's first federal election produced a political landscape with three major players, the Ministerialists/Protectionists, Free Traders, and Labor. While Labor was the smallest of the three, it effectively held the balance of power in both houses. With a general preference for protectionism, the Labor MPs threw their support behind Barton who was able to lead the government effectively for a full term. Barton chose to retire from government and take a seat on the newly-formed High Court less than three months out from the next scheduled election. The attorney-general, Alfred Deakin, succeeded him as leader of the Protectionists and prime minister.

The federal election of 13 December 1903 was the first to allow women to vote and stand for parliament nationally following the *Commonwealth Franchise Act* 1902. Despite the big increase in voter turnout, the result was similar to the first election. The Protectionists were still the largest party, with 26 seats in the 75 seat lower house, but the other parties were closing in. Twenty-five Free Trade, 23 Labor, and one Independent were returned. The three major groupings were now so close that Deakin famously referred to Australian politics as a cricket match with 'three elevens'.

Australia's second federal parliament managed to see out a full term despite an extraordinary three changes in government. Initially, Labor was willing to support the Protectionists, as in the previous parliament, leaving Deakin to continue as prime minister. The two parties, however, were unable to find common ground over the contentious effort to legislate for a federal system of industrial arbitration and in

April 1904 Deakin resigned as prime minister. Chris Watson, who had led the federal Labor Party since 1901, was sworn in as prime minister on 27 April 1904. He became not only Australia's first Labor prime minister, but the first in the world. At just 37 years old he was, and remains, Australia's youngest prime minister. Born in Valparaíso, Chile, he also remains the only Australian prime minister not to be born in either Australia or the United Kingdom.

Watson's prime ministership was historic for many reasons but also brief. Frustrated by an inability to pass legislation, he followed Deakin's lead and stepped down after just four months. George Reid, leader of the Free Trade Party and a former premier of New South Wales, became the nation's fourth prime minister and held the post for nearly a year. The Protectionists and Labor were able to settle some of their differences in this time and used their combined majority to oust Reid in July 1905. Deakin now returned for his second and most successful stint as prime minister.

Australia's third election was held on 12 December 1906. In an effort to break the 'three elevens' impasse, Reid attempted to reframe Australian politics along Labor and non-Labor lines. The Free Traders rebranded as the Anti-Socialists and were the most successful party with 27 seats to Labor's 26. Internal division in the Protectionist Party saw it become the smallest of the parties with just 16 official seats and a further four considering themselves Independent Protectionists. Despite the poor result, Deakin's personal popularity across party lines helped him retain the prime ministership. With support from Labor, he would lead for two more years, passing a raft of important policies that gave shape to the Commonwealth. Labor eventually withdrew its support in November 1908, forcing Deakin to resign as prime minister. The Scottish immigrant and former miner, Andrew Fisher, formed Labor's second minority government.

In opposition, Deakin sought to find common cause with the Anti-Socialists, led now by Joseph Cook, and build something similar to the two-party system in Britain. The non-Labor parties merged to form the Commonwealth Liberal Party. While some in the progressive wing of the old Protectionists preferred to support Labor or sit as Independents, the merger produced the first lower house majority. After turning out the minority Labor government, Deakin was able to return as prime minister for the third time in June 1909 with Cook as his deputy. Having finally achieved a parliamentary majority, the Commonwealth Liberals were in no hurry to return to the polls. For the first and only time in Australian federal politics, the effluxion of time was required to force an election for the following year.

Chapter 2

1910

FISHER LEADS LABOR TO VICTORY

John Uhr[1]

The 1910 election was Australia's first contest between two competing political parties, with Deakin's Liberal Party in government facing Fisher's Labor Party in opposition. The 1909 'fusion' of the non-Labor parties meant that the former battle between 'the three elevens' had turned into a contest of 'two elevens'. The 1910 election was the first opportunity for the national electorate to determine whether the Liberals or Labor should govern. The leaders of both competing parties had already served as prime minister through internal parliamentary procedures: Deakin in 1903-04, 1905-08, and 1909-10; and Fisher in 1908-09. Now for the first time, power was passing to the electorate which could return Deakin or replace him with Fisher. This was the first national election dominated by competition between two very prominent party leaders. Serving prime minister Deakin significantly expanded the election period to eleven weeks, knowing he needed time to defeat well-organised Labor. Unlike Deakin, Fisher campaigned nationally, contrasting Labor's progressive policies with Deakin's cautious negativism.

Of course, voters in their electorates were voting for local candidates of political parties rather than party leaders: and they gave Labor a huge majority in both the House of Representatives and in the Senate. Fisher's national speaking tour during the long campaign helped increase voter turnout to an historical highpoint of 60%. Fisher was Labor's first truly effective national campaigner – a role often

---

1 My thanks to ANU PhD researcher in politics John Hawkins for his very important research on Andrew Fisher included in his doctoral study; and to another ANU PhD political science researcher James Frost for his professional editorial assistance.

neglected by those who focus on his significance as an innovative prime minister. Fisher became Labor's first popularly elected head of government in what was the world's first instance of an elected Labor or socialist government. Deakin became leader of the opposition before later retiring from politics. Fisher as a progressive social democrat might well have known that 'his election clearly changed forever the way Australians would think about the social aspirations of their democracy'.[2]

The federal election of 1910 was full of firsts. Although Labor had formed a brief minority government in 1904 with Chis Watson as prime minister, it was Andrew Fisher who became Labor's first popularly elected head of government. Fisher's government, rather than Watson's, marked the first time, anywhere in the world, that a Labor government was specifically elected. Taking place just after the 'fusion' of non-labor parties in 1909, the 1910 election can be seen as the birth of the two-party system in Australia (and the end of the 'three elevens'). Given a choice between Alfred Deakin's Liberals and Fisher-led Labor, this was also the first national election where two prominent party leaders took centre-stage. The new political reality was underlined by the longer-than-usual campaign period. Deakin and Fisher were the first to compete in a truly national campaign under the two-party system we are so familiar with today. It was certainly a nation-shaping election.

The 1910-1913 Fisher government used its considerable legislative power to pass more bills than any earlier government. Yet Labor lost the 1913 election by one seat to the Liberal Party, led by Joseph Cook. Fisher's persistence as leader of the opposition was productive: Labor regained office at the 1914 election when Cook called Australia's first double-dissolution election, with Labor again winning both houses. Labor had been represented in the national parliament since

---

2   Peter Bastian, *Andrew Fisher: An Underestimated Man* (Sydney: University of New South Wales Press, 2009), p.157.

the beginning of the Commonwealth in 1901. It had enjoyed two brief terms of minority government under prime ministers Watson in 1904 and Fisher in 1908-09. But something important happened in the lead up to the 1910 election that gave Labor the public confidence to finally win office on its own terms. What was that something? Put simply, it was the fall of three-time prime minister Alfred Deakin and the emergence of Andrew Fisher as the nation's leading election campaigner.

The Fisher Effect

A standard interpretation is that 'Fisher followed through' after Deakin. Something of a follower rather than innovator, he shared many political and policy programs with Deakin and simply 'took protectionism further'.[3] A strong case can be made, however, that Fisher was his own political man and his victory in 1910 was nation forming. His political education began in the Scottish mines, broadened in the mining industry of Queensland, and began to mature when he was elected to the Queensland parliament before Federation. Fisher was a minister in this world's first Labor government, led by Anderson Dawson, if only for one week, in 1899. In 1901, he represented the Queensland seat of Wide Bay in the new Commonwealth House of Representatives. His second term as minister was in the Watson Labor government, which held office for four months in 1904. His third term was as prime minister leading his own minority government for six months in 1908-09. His fourth term was again as prime minister in 1910, with a fifth term in 1914.

---

3 Alan Atkinson, *The Europeans in Australia: A History*, vol. 3, Nation (Sydney: University of New South Wales Press, 2014), p.365.

Fisher was the first prime minister to come from Queensland: the four who preceded him came from New South Wales (Barton, Watson, Reid) or Victoria (Deakin). Fisher's victory in 1910 represents the emergence of political power outside of Sydney and Melbourne; but it also represents in part the arrival of a national voice in Australian politics, with Fisher articulating a theme of political nationality more prominently than his political competitors. Perhaps more surprisingly, Fisher brought a higher theme of internationalism to Australian politics, conscious as he was of leading the world's first elected Labor government, which he, as an immigrant from Scotland, knew was a progressive movement emerging around the British parliamentary world.[4] The internationalism includes Fisher's well-studied commitment of Australian troops for the imperial cause in World War I but it also means Fisher's often-unnoticed pursuit of international policies relating to the promotion of labourism – including an early version of closer relations between Australia and New Zealand.[5] A Labor party can make its own contribution to the international cause of labourism but a Labor government can speak with national authority and public support.

With this election Labor had – compared to its earlier periods in minority government in 1904 and 1908-09 – won *power* as well as *office*. This was Australia's first national form of majority government. Cook, who earlier had been a Labor member in the New South Wales parliament, has been described as an 'irascible, untiring, humourless little man', which might go some way to explain

---

4 Ian Tregenza, 'Are We "All Socialists Now"? New Liberalism, State Socialism and the Australian Settlement', *Labour History*, 102, 2012, pp.87–98.

5 ALP, *Official Report of the 5th Commonwealth Conference of the Australian Labor Party* (Hobart, January 1912), pp.35–36.

Fisher's 1914 victory.[6] Fisher's leadership of federal Labor from 1907 until his retirement from parliament in 1915 gave the party four and a half years in government, with the 1910 victory marking its first effective opportunity to use its full parliamentary power to stamp its authority on Commonwealth policy and practice.

Yet Fisher knew that his role as leader was a delegation from his party colleagues. After his electoral victory at the 1910 elections, Fisher quietly advised the governor-general not to move to swear him in as prime minister until he had met with his newly-elected party colleagues and secured their permission to accept office as prime minister.[7] As Deakin so plainly saw, Fisher changed the rules of Australian politics through his commitment to new forms of *party* government quite distinct from earlier norms of *parliamentary* government. Fisher's preferred power-base was a party with strong caucus control over the ministry and indeed the chief minister – a system he had introduced when following Watson as party leader.[8]

Fisher's role as a leading election campaigner dates from October 1907, when he replaced Watson as leader of the federal parliamentary party. Election campaigns are very much constituency-based contests, but party leaders can energise and motivate supporters to campaign with increased effort. Scholars recognise that Fisher was undistinguished as a public speaker but they have also noticed that he was a dedicated servant of his party who saw the importance of

---

6   J.A. La Nauze, *Alfred Deakin, a Biography* (Sydney: Angus and Robertson, 1965), p.536.

7   L.F. Crisp, *The Australian Federal Labour Party, 1901-1951* (London: Longmans, 1955), p.146; Paul Strangio, Paul 't Hart, and James Walter, *Settling the Office: The Australian Prime Ministership from Federation to Reconstruction*, vol. 1 (Melbourne: Miegunyah Press, 2016), pp.70–71.

8   Crisp, *Australian Federal Labour*, pp.116–20, 126; Kim Beazley, 'A Warm-Hearted Prime Minister', *Canberra Times*, 25 January 1966.

active public representation involving speech after speech (perhaps indeed the same speech) personally delivered across Australia. A keen photographer, Fisher seemed to know the value of being seen and noted as the leader of the Labor Party. According to his biographer Peter Bastian: 'Fisher could claim to have seen more of the nation than any other prime minister or party leader,' allowing him to hope that as a consequence many more voters would see, hear and potentially support Fisher's party.[9] A secret of Fisher's campaigning was his preference for a rhetoric of record in contrast to his opponents' rhetoric of discord. His speeches recorded in weighty detail the state of the nation and the promise of his party to 'correct the record' through solid, sound public investment in national development. Reformers appeal to the sense of hope in a community which Fisher managed through several national tours between 1907 and 1910, which 'sometimes became marathons'.[10] Where the leader led, the party campaigners followed, harvesting the hope for an elected Labor government.

The 1910 Election

Earlier national elections, in 1901, 1903, and 1906, were contests with a larger number of parties and interests, many quite regionalised, with voters choosing their parliamentary representatives on the assumption that the elected parliament would then be responsible for determining which parties or party coalitions would form government and which would form opposition. Governments sometimes changed between elections as the national parliament experimented with transitions in government from one party to another.

---

9 Bastian, *Andrew Fisher*, pp.127, 168–70.
10 Ibid., p.127.

Labor's Chris Watson and Free Trade's George Reid served as prime ministers in 1904 and 1905 yet neither ever led their party to victory at a national election. Other prime ministers such as Barton and Deakin led minority governments whenever they could win parliamentary confidence. The electorate deferred greatly to parliament to determine which party or coalition held executive office. Voters in these early elections were relying on traditional nineteenth-century assumptions about elections and voting. Voters understood their role as 'selecting local representatives': before 1910, voters were not bothering about 'throwing this governing party out of government' or 'giving this opposition party a chance to govern'.

The twentieth-century practice of two-party contests was initiated in 1910. Voters were called on to determine which of two national parties (Labor and Liberal) should form government.[11] Something important happened during the third parliament elected in 1906 that changed the shape of Australian parliamentary politics. Central to this story of political development is the rise of Andrew Fisher as the leader of the Labor Party, upon the resignation of Watson in October 1907, and Fisher's refusal to continue supporting Alfred Deakin and his governing Protectionist party. Fisher broke Labor's effective coalition with Deakin (indeed, Fisher had first attempted such a separation when he moved against Deakin to help initiate the brief Watson ministry in 1904), preferring to promote Labor's independence as a party ready to govern in its own name. Fisher's confidence as party leader was justified when Deakin resigned office in November 1908. Fisher was prime minister of an (unelected) minority Labor government for six months, which was the time it took for Deakin to arrange 'the fusion' (or 'confusion' as Labor called it) of

---

11   La Nauze, *Alfred Deakin*, p.599.

anti-socialist parties under the new name of the Liberal Party, which won parliamentary support for a return to office.[12]

The 1910 election is noted for the prominent role of the press in highlighting the differences between the two competing parties – with the Sydney *Bulletin* and Melbourne's *Age* siding with Labor.[13] Fisher resigned from office in October 1915, possibly growing weary of extra-parliamentary pressure on the legislative process, taking up a new non-parliamentary role as High Commissioner in London.[14]

The Rise of Labor

The 1910 election saw Labor win a majority in both houses of the national parliament. The party had won parliamentary seats from the very first national election: of the 75 lower house seats, Labor won 14 in 1901, 23 in 1903, 26 in 1906 and eventually a majority of 43 in 1910, when voter turnout rose from just above 50% to above 60%. The striking feature is the steady rise (from 36.6% to 50% of votes) from the third to the fourth parliament which coincides with the start of Fisher's period as party leader in November 1907. Labor also won eight Senate seats in 1901, ten in 1903, five in 1906 but then 18 (of 36) in 1910: with a rise of percentage votes from around 30% in 1906 to over 50% in 1910. The developing character of the Labor Party is easily read through the reports of the Commonwealth Labor

---

12   Alfred Deakin, *Federated Australia: Selections from Letters to the Morning Post 1900-1910*, J.A. La Nauze (ed), *Studies in Australian Federation* (Melbourne: Cambridge University Press, 1968), pp.248–50, 257–59.
13   H.V. Evatt, *Australian Labour Leader* (Sydney: Angus and Robertson, 1940), p.244; Sawer, *Australian Federal Politics*, p.97.
14   Gavin Souter, *Acts of Parliament* (Melbourne: Melbourne University Press, 1988), pp.142–43.

conferences of 1902, 1905, 1908 – as well as the conference held in 1912 during the term of the Fisher government.[15]

One theme arising from the series of Labor conferences is the federated character of political Labor. Conferences comprised representatives from each state party and from the Commonwealth parliament, with slowly rising acceptance of the national importance of the federal Labor representatives. Yet much of the hard work of party development and electoral campaigning rested with the state party organisations. The conference reports contain many instances of rivalry across Labor ranks, including rivalry between one or more states and the federal representatives who tended to push for greater uniformity and cohesion, including some versions of 'unification' as an alternative to federalism.[16] The dilemma for the federal representatives is that they all were the products of their own state party cultures and were dependent on the campaign strength cultivated on a state by state basis. The evidence in the parliament leading up to the 1910 election is that Labor was feared by its parliamentary opponents as a remarkably successful mass political organisation, with a comparative advantage in skilful organisers active in the union movement. Hence, industrial labour provided political Labor with a resourceful network of organisers committed to growing the support base for state and indeed federal Labor campaigns.[17]

Deakin was among the first of Labor's opponents to note the growing popularity of the Labor Party, and Billy Hughes was, in

---

15 ALP, *Official Report of the Commonwealth Political Labour Conference* (Melbourne, July 1905); ALP, *Official Report of the Fourth Commonwealth Political Labour Conference* (Brisbane, July 1908); ALP, *Official Report of the 5th Commonwealth Conference of the Australian Labor Party*; ALP, *Official Report of the Australian Labor Conference* (Sydney, 1 December 1912).

16 Ibid.

17 Tregenza, 'Are We All Socialists Now'.

1910, the most prominent within Labor in publicising *The Case for Labor*.[18] Hughes also used all of his parliamentary flair to cast Deakin as a traitor to 'new protection' – the idea that protection for industry should be contingent on fair wages and conditions for workers – which was the doctrine favoured by Fisher.[19] Labor's sense was that Deakin's conservative forces were 'fusing' in order to make the case against Labor through a scare campaign against 'socialism'.[20] Deakin rightly feared that Fisher would be 'more dogmatic' than his predecessor Watson, but his 'dogmatism' really reflected his party's deep commitment to the policy of 'new protection' once so ably championed by Deakin.[21] During the period 1908-1910, Labor's leading policy advocates, including Fisher, campaigned very publicly against the 'negativism' dominating Deakin's desperate campaign of anti-socialism.[22] International critics like James Bryce (who had visited Australia in 1912) later judged Deakin's anti-socialism as 'very negatively weak', even claiming that Deakin's newly-fused Liberal Party was 'in effect a party of resistance or caution' unlikely to persuade voters away from Labor's initiatives.[23]

What is important is the strength of Labor's extra-parliamentary machine: the organisers and publicists who could be marshalled into a small army of combatants used to mobilise voters in this era before

---

18   William Morris Hughes, *The Case for Labor* (Sydney: Sydney University Press, 1970).
19   La Nauze, *Alfred Deakin*, pp.568–69.
20   Paul Strangio and Nick Dyrenfurth, (eds), *Confusion: The Making of the Australian Two Party System* (Melbourne: Melbourne University Press, 2009), pp.10–11.
21   Hughes, *The Case for Labor*, p.44.
22   La Nauze, *Alfred Deakin*, p.600; Nick Dyrenfurth, '"Vote Down the Conspiracy": Labor's View of Fusion', in Strangio and Dyrenfurth (eds), *Confusion*, pp.95, 98, 101.
23   James Bryce, *Modern Democracies*, 2 vols (London: Macmillan and Co., 1921), pp.231–32, 238.

compulsory voting. Deakin explained his loss at the 1910 election as an 'electoral cyclone' driven by the organisational superiority of Labor as a campaign machine.[24] He wrote extensively in the period 1908-10 about Labor's 'potent outside Leagues' of unionised supporters.[25] Deakin could see that while Fisher was scarcely socialistic, Labor's expanding 'caucus platform' generated by the series of party conferences in 1905 and 1908 was alarmingly less moderate.[26] During the 1910 election campaign Deakin noted the 'fierceness' of party competition had become 'most vigorous' and out of keeping with former patterns of political competition.[27]

Labor's strength posed its own problems for Fisher's pursuit of effective national government. Fisher's leadership of the federal party saw him nudge Labor towards greater central policy co-ordination, with frequent protests from state leaders. His management of the federal party before 1910 involved a steady modification of state resistance to central ambition. After the 1910 election, state Labor resistance arose most prominently in response to Fisher's agenda of constitutional referendums to confer greater power on the national parliament to regulate capitalism. Fisher held two sets of referendum questions: with two questions in 1911 and another six in 1913, all being defeated in part through the cagey opposition of state Labor leaders like Holman. State Labor parties made life harder for Fisher's federal Labor Party through protracted conflict over feared unification and centralisation.[28]

---

24 La Nauze, *Alfred Deakin*, p.603.
25 Deakin, *Federated Australia*, pp.144–45, 257, 262, 280–81.
26 Ibid., pp.247–48.
27 Ibid., pp.265, 280.
28 Crisp, *Australian Federal Labour*, pp.31–34, 50–51, 132–35, 232–33, 238.

Fisher's Strategy

The election victory for Labor reflected the capacity for campaigning developed by the Labor Party; but it also reflected the contribution Fisher made through his unusual strategy as public advocate, after becoming parliamentary leader in November 1907. Three examples highlight the innovative use of party power used by Fisher. The first is his clever use of the party's fourth conference held in Brisbane in July 1908 as his first national platform to identify the policy agenda he was developing. The second is his use of office when accepting his role as head of a minority government from November 1908 to May 1909. The third is his remarkable use of a prime ministerial speech in March 1909, two months before losing office, when parliamentary confidence swung back to Deakin's fusion government. This 'policy for Australia' address given in the Queensland city of Gympie broke the traditional mould of Australian politics by launching a national campaign of extensive public speaking a year or so ahead of the next likely election.

Fisher is rarely noted as a gifted public speaker.[29] He lacked many of the valuable charms of rhetorical excellence used by his rivals, especially Deakin. Yet Fisher saw his role as an advocate for policy reform: sometimes to lock in Deakin against conservatives wanting to wind back 'new protection', and at other times to roll out the extensive policy program which he helped Labor devise. Many party leaders in Australian politics have followed Fisher's lead in travelling across Australia as an advocate for their cause. Fisher appreciated that his real gift as an advocate was his sense of publicity, which was his most valued strategy. As party leader, Fisher was unrelenting in

---

29   Strangio, 't Hart and Walter, *Settling the Office*, p.77.

his public speaking schedule, always quick to identify Labor's plans for national development. Never theatrical, Fisher acted as a public informant rather than a party persuader, giving himself as much time as required to fill in the details of his party's program. This strategy worked deliberately against the kind of misinformation circulated by Deakin's negativism: voters had a chance to see and hear or read the Labor leader patiently and thoroughly outline his policies.[30]

Fisher's address at the Brisbane conference is a good example of how a party leader can mobilise his or her own resources.[31] Speaking to his party supporters, Fisher called for an 'authentic history' of the party, a progressive 'movement' with a practical 'march' worth celebrating. Another call was for 'searching statistics' to explain the 'facts and figures' of the social conditions of the people of Australia. Fisher then outlined the importance of 'the wisdom of women' to the labour movement, including the presence of women in the conferences of the Labor Party and as candidates for parliamentary election.[32] Fisher was also ahead of Labor on Indigenous policy although this is one of his more modest initiatives.[33] On policy substance, Fisher defended 'new protection' by reference to the role of Justice Higgins (and not Deakin) in meeting the needs of 'a human being living in a civilized community' – quoting from Higgins' famous Harvester Judgment of 1907. Finally, Fisher turned to 'this one great question' of socialism. 'We are all socialists now', stated Fisher, who then described the complementary work of politicians and propagandists – and the not so complementary strategies of parliamentary rule of law and

---

30 Tregenza, 'Are We All Socialists Now', pp.76–77.
31 ALP, *Official Report of the Fourth*, pp.13–14; Bastian, *Andrew Fisher*, pp.133–35.
32 Marian Sawer, 'Andrew Fisher and the Era of Liberal Reform', *Labour History*, 102, 2012, pp.71–86.
33 Atkinson, *Europeans in Australia*, p.335.

universal strike. Fisher drew attention away from any expectation that he as leader would be a propagandist or teacher, both useful roles but of less use in securing 'just remuneration' than the work of members of parliament.[34]

Fisher's 1909 Gympie 'policy speech' is available in a lengthy 22-page document.[35] This document illustrates the leader's publicity strategy with around thirty-two subsections of concise policy detail. The 34,000 word speech might have been an ordeal for the audience of 2000 present for its original delivery, given that it covered so many 'facts and figures'. But this somewhat dry account of national development is exactly what Fisher wanted to publicise: soberly advocating the need for social reform through an elected Labor government. Fisher's intention was to portray the social condition of Australia, showing what 'is new to and outside the ordinary sphere of politics in any other country in the world'. Quoting Higgins, Fisher identified 'an absolutely new charter of rights of the toilers of Australia' associated with 'the new protection principle'. Noting the reluctance of other political parties to stand by this principle, Fisher emphasised 'every act that this Government can do' to defend social justice – especially the initiatives of old age and invalid pensions attracting opposition criticism. The 'leader of the Opposition' earns Fisher's rebuke for his lack of support for Australian-based naval defence. Doing what he can 'to try and awaken the patriotism of Australians', Fisher spoke extensively about 'national defence policy' in the region of Australia as a core component of Labor's contribution to the defence of the British Empire. In fact, 'nationalisation' is declared

---

34   ALP, *Official Report of the Fourth*, pp.13–14.
35   Andrew Fisher, *A Policy for Australia* (Gympie, 1909); Deakin, *Federated Australia*, pp.262–65; Dyrenfurth, "'Vote Down the Conspiracy'", p.90; Bastian, *Andrew Fisher*, pp.140–43.

to be 'the policy of the Labor Party' – especially when it holds power in 'the national Parliament of Australia'. Fisher explained that some of his policy proposals might not be popular even though they were 'sound policy'. His government decided to submit policies to the people, knowing that some were 'slightly in advance of their ideas': 'proposals vilified, then accepted' is the formula he presents.[36]

In the twilight of the Deakin government in late 1909, Fisher spoke publicly about Labor's need to 'have a decided majority to carry out their principles' – and without such a majority, Labor 'had no right to be on the Government benches'.[37] As the time for the election drew near, Fisher used his media ability to increase this demand for a Labor majority and to diminish public regard for Deakin, even in Deakin's Ballaarat electorate, as a national statesman.[38] This theme of 'nationhood and citizenship' became central to Fisher's 1910 campaign.[39] Now a seasoned leader, he spent around five months campaigning across Australia to bolster Labor's claim to be a party ready for government. It was a message safeguarded by his own 'reassuring image'.[40]

The Defeat of Deakin

'What can you do with a man like that?', said Fisher repeatedly of Deakin in late 1909 and early 1910.[41] Fisher used this time for a last surge of national touring, with speeches across the country intended

---

36 Fisher, *A Policy for Australia*, pp.1–4, 8, 10, 19, 21.
37 Ibid.
38 'Speeches of Mr. A. Fisher M.P., and Senator Pearce', *Ballarat Star*, 12 October 1909.
39 'Mr. Fisher at Narandera', *Jerilderie Herald and Urana Advertiser*, 27 May 1910.
40 David Day, *Andrew Fisher: Prime Minister of Australia* (Sydney: Fourth Estate, 2008), pp.176–77, 191.
41 Ibid., p.190.

to rally voters for Labor. Fisher's formal campaign speech survives only in a press report, where he is identified as leader of the opposition which is an unusual indication of important public office for a party leader. The first sentence of this speech is a criticism of Deakin 'for his depreciation of the Labour Party, with its policy of progress'. Paragraph after paragraph hit out at Deakin.[42]

Bastian's biography of Fisher examines the long 1910 election campaign in terms of two competing leaders: Deakin versus Fisher.[43] Deakin competed fiercely, knowing that voters were being attracted to Labor by the twin effects of a capable party leader and a capacious army of party organisers. Fisher was confident that his extensive national campaigning over the previous twelve months had prepared voters to take the extra step to elect – rather than expect – a Labor government. Deakin misread electoral sentiment and nearly lost his own parliamentary seat. Fisher knew that the time had changed and that the first decade of parliamentary government was nearing its limits, to be replaced by a new form of party rather than parliamentary government.

Deakin's own electoral speech made light fun of the Labor Party and its 'Ishmaelitish methods': Labor members 'are all obliged to wear the same suits of the same material, the same pattern, the same size, and the same cut'. Deakin's theme of 'the Labour Opposition' elevated the importance of his main competitors, even while trying to ridicule their 'constant knee drill in caucus' and to paint Labor as confined to 'mere projects in the air'. In contrast to Labor, Deakin stressed the possibilities of shared action between the Commonwealth and

---

42   Andrew Fisher, Election Speech, Maryborough, Queensland, 1910, *Museum of Australian Democracy*, Accessed online. <http://electionspeeches.moadoph.gov.au/speeches/1910-andrew-fisher>

43   Bastian, *Andrew Fisher*, pp.154–57.

the states. Deakin's formulation of national unity contrasted strongly with that of Labor which he feared was threatening to override the states through a program of centralisation.[44]

Some of the most colourful detail of the 1910 election is to be found in Deakin's reports anonymously prepared for the British press.[45] These published articles provide a loser's view of Labor's election strategy. Deakin contrasted his own government's pragmatic federalism with what he described as Labor's pursuit of a 'unitary' form of government. Fisher would have described things differently, putting national unity ahead of unitary government. But this division of types of government was soon overtaken by Deakin's real fear, which was Labor's 'visionary aims of a new social Paradise to be conjured out of ballot-boxes'. Labor's election manifesto was thought to be 'a document of portentous length' with 'a long catalogue of aims' which Deakin thought would dampen a potential Labor government. Deakin feared that Labor's radicalism as a political party was hidden from view by the moderation of its parliamentary leadership, which is one way of praising Fisher for his canny political prudence.

Deakin's lament over the loss of his own government does draw attention to Labor's real innovation.[46] Deakin contrasts his new role as head of 'a powerless Opposition' with Fisher's role as head of 'a new system of parliamentary government'. Was it really true that responsible government 'on the British model' had ceased to exist as Deakin claimed? The fear was that caucus would now control everything, with the parliamentary process becoming 'the formal

---

44   Alfred Deakin, Election Speech, Ballarat, Victoria, 1910, *Museum of Australian Democracy*, Accessed online. <http://electionspeeches.moadoph.gov.au/speeches/1910-alfred-deakin>
45   Deakin, *Federated Australia*, pp.280–84.
46   Ibid., pp.284–88.

registration of Caucus decrees'. Noting that caucus had two earlier periods in 1904 and 1908-09 'of office without power', Deakin rued that for the first time Australia had a Labor government as 'ruler in its own right'.[47]

Conclusion

'The prime minister is thus the real ruler of the country; and, in a sense, it is he who makes the laws', claimed Deakin's friend and future biographer, Walter Murdoch.[48] This early appreciation of the power of heads of government was written in a civics book, requested by Deakin as a guide to Australian governance. When eventually published, the reference could refer equally to Deakin's rival and successor, Fisher. Yet the lesson in civics derived from Fisher's electoral success is that he went out of his way to let the community know that he was 'not of the demagogic type' likely to rule over and above his citizens, and that he welcomed being praised as the 'first Commoner in the Commonwealth'.[49]

There is something puzzling about Fisher's leadership of Labor as an election winner. He was an immigrant who spoke repeatedly about 'the nation' as an Australian civic order; yet he was also an internationalist who saw the need for civic powers larger than nation-states. He was a professed socialist but his public policies reflected more 'practical utilitarianism' than socialistic doctrine.[50] Australian voters learned to trust Labor under his leadership, even though he saw himself as a servant rather than the savant of that party. If

---

47 Ibid., p.287.
48 Walter Murdoch, *The Australian Citizen* (Melbourne: Whitcombe and Tombs, 1912), p.186.
49 'Andrew Fisher, Prime Minister', *Perth Truth*, 13 February 1909.
50 W.K. Hancock, *Australia* (Brisbane: Jacaranda Press, 1930), p.182; Sawer, *Australian Federal Politics*, pp.72–73.

Deakin was mournful at Labor's win in 1910, V.I. Lenin was surprisingly realistic about Labor's defeat three years later. He wrote a short article in *Pravda* noting the defeat of the Fisher government in 1913. Free of lament, Lenin described the Australian Labor Party as 'a liberal-bourgeois party' which is 'purely liberal' – with very limited ambitions to promote socialism.[51] Fisher's Labor Party had plenty of internal critics within Australia, including many state Labor leaders who shared some of Deakin's fears about excessive Commonwealth power possibly secured through the scheme of eight (unsuccessful) referendums attempted by Fisher. New South Wales Labor leader W.A. Holman provided a prime example of this type of internal Labor criticism.[52]

A century ago the Labor Party knew that it needed not only a political and industrial wing but administrative and propaganda experts also. Fisher was the classic expert administrator, trained in the industrial world of mining but never attracted to the cultural world of party propaganda. His parliamentary colleagues, like W. G. Spence, celebrated Labor as a 'propagandist Movement' with published works of political advocacy never attempted by Fisher.[53] Still, something very important remains with Fisher, whose 1909 Gympie address is described by Spence as 'the boldest and most National Australian policy ever enunciated': Labor won office in 1910 precisely because through that address, 'Anti-Labor was struck dumb'.[54] Could an election campaign for Labor have a better result?

---

51 V.I. Lenin, 'In Australia', *Pravda*, June 1913, 134 edition.
52 Evatt, *Australian Labour Leader*, pp.223, 243, 262–68; Raymond Markey, 'Postscript: The Significance of the Fisher Labor Government, 1910-13', *Labour History*, 102, 2012, p.122; Mark Hearn and Nick Dyrenfurth, 'Reinterpreting the Second Fisher Government', *Labor History*, 12, 2012, p.3.
53 William Guthrie Spence, *Australia's Awakening* (Sydney: The Worker Trustees, 1909), pp.377–78.
54 Ibid., 263.

INTERIM 1910–1929

Having served as prime minister on three occasions (a feat that would be matched only by his Labor rival, Andrew Fisher), 'affable' Alfred Deakin retired from politics in 1913. He was replaced as leader of the Liberal Party by Joseph Cook. The federal election on 31 May 1913 was closely fought. Despite a national vote of only 48.9%, the Liberals picked up seven seats and took precarious control of the lower house, 38 seats to Labor's 37. Labor still controlled the Senate and frustrated the Liberal policy agenda. As Europe descended into crisis, Cook asked the governor-general, Sir Ronald Munro Ferguson, to dissolve both houses and call the first ever double dissolution election.

The election of 5 September 1914 was a disaster for Cook and the Liberals. Fisher and his team stormed back to the government benches with a national vote of 50.9%. Labor secured 42 of 75 seats in the House of Representatives and 31 of 36 Senate spots. Fisher's third spell as prime minister was dominated by the war in Europe. As the full horrors of the Gallipoli campaign were made public in 1915, he chose to resign. For the remainder of the war he served as Australia's High Commissioner to the United Kingdom. Billy Hughes was elected unopposed as Labor leader, becoming Australia's seventh prime minister.

The Labor Party was deeply split on the issue of military conscription, as was the nation which narrowly rejected the measure in two referendum votes on the issue in 1916 and 1917. Hughes was a passionate advocate of conscription and, despite being leader, would be expelled from the party for having broken ranks on the issue. Hughes took many pro-conscription defectors with him and merged with the

Liberals to create a new Nationalist Party. The war still dominated politics when Australians went to the polls again on 5 May 1917. Hughes' Nationalists trounced Labor, led by Frank Tudor. Winning 53 seats in the lower house and 24 in the Senate, it was the first time a non-Labor government controlled both houses.

Peace came in 1918 and the next federal election was held the following year. It saw the introduction of preferential voting and the emergence of the Country Party as a political force. The Nationalists retained government. Tudor died in early 1922 and was replaced by Matthew Charlton. In the election of 16 December 1922, Labor emerged as the most popular single party with 30 lower house seats to the Nationalists' 26, 14 Country, and 5 Independent. In the negotiations that followed, Hughes was replaced by Stanley Melbourne Bruce as leader of the Nationalists. A non-Labor coalition was formed between Bruce's Nationalists and the Country Party led by Earle Page. Charlton retained leadership of the ALP.

Less than 60% of eligible voters took part in the 1922 election, prompting the introduction of compulsory voting laws. As a result, the federal election of 14 November 1925 saw a participation rate of 91.4% (bearing in mind that only a limited number of Aboriginal Australians had the right to vote at this stage and even those who legally could were not generally encouraged to do so). The coalition campaigned together and agreed to trade preferences, exploiting the issue of communism and union militancy effectively. The Bruce-Page government was comprehensively returned with a clear majority in both houses. Plagued by ill-health, Charlton retired in 1928 and was replaced by James Scullin. Labor performed better at the election on 17 November 1928. Although the Bruce-Page government was returned, the opposition was finally within striking distance.

Chapter 3

1929

THE PATRICIAN AND THE ORATOR

Alex Millmow[1]

The 1929 federal election campaign bore an uncanny resemblance to the 2007 election campaign in that both elections were fought on the matter of industrial relations, which the prime minister, more than anyone else, held to be a vital economic reform. In both cases it cost the prime minister not just office but also his seat in the House. There is arguably a lesson there for those who wish to meddle with Australian wages and conditions. Both election campaigns were also fought on the cusp of a major economic shock, namely, the Great Depression, and, in 2007, the Global Financial Crisis. On both occasions the Labor Party stormed to victory. In the case of James Scullin in 1929 the win would quickly become a poisoned chalice with the Wall Street Crash setting off an economic catastrophe that would engulf governments around the globe. In that sense Scullin's electoral victory over the headstrong Stanley Melbourne Bruce in a short and sweet election campaign in October 1929 was his finest hour. While his administration was much maligned and indeed cut short from its full term, it was probably only a Labor government that could have gathered sufficient support, especially from the trade unions, to pass the harsh economic stabilisation measures which ultimately saved Australia from defaulting on its foreign loans.

---

1   I would like to acknowledge the assistance of Philip D. O'Brien and my research student, Cameron Kent. Cameron was undertaking a master's thesis unearthing material on the pre-political life of Scullin that focused around Ballarat. Unfortunately, Cameron died before his research was written up. I dedicate this chapter to his memory.

ELECTIONS MATTER

The most striking outcome of the 2007 federal election was that Prime Minister John Howard not only lost government but his own seat of Bennelong. Howard learnt his ignominious fate on the evening of the election; he wore the rejection by the electorate with nonchalance such that not long after he became that most hallowed of political identities, a statesman. The story of that November night in 2007 has its precursor in the 1929 election, when another conservative prime minister, Stanley Melbourne Bruce, also lost his seat as the Labor Party stormed to victory. For Bruce, too, the defeat would prove a temporary eclipse, for he would go on to serve his country in other capacities. A Fox Movietone newsreel captured the moment Bruce left parliament, stepping into his car and driving off. He was the last prime minister never to have had any of his speeches as leader recorded by the movie newsreel. It would have been good for the 'talkies' to have captured that 'patrician hauteur' which Gough Whitlam felt characterised him.[2]

The 1929 election is noteworthy because it was mainly fought on one issue, industrial relations. Equally, in 2007, the key issue was Howard's industrial relations reform known as *WorkChoices*. In both cases industrial relations had become an obsession with the prime minister; both men, though, were blind to how the proposed legislation was seen by voters as a direct threat to their livelihoods. Many workers felt that wages and conditions of employment would be tampered with if the proposed legislation became reality.

The other thing that many recall about the 1929 election was just how unfortunate the Labor Party was to achieve office just two weeks

---

2   Julian Fitzgerald, *On Message: Political Communications of Australian Prime Ministers 1901-2014* (Canberra: Clareville Press, 2014), p.126.

before Wall Street crashed, throwing the global economy into a tailspin. James Scullin is arguably the most unfortunate Labor prime minister in Australian political history but it did not help things that his administration was dogged by feuds, rivalries and scandal.

This chapter discusses the 1929 federal election campaign, the main issues involved and, to set the scene, the circumstances by which those matters come to prominence. As always, economic management and the state of the economy were front and centre in this election campaign. Indeed, as we shall see, the whole election was triggered by concerns about the likely future of the economy. Bruce had antagonised the electorate by bringing in the odious-sounding amusement tax; it, too, would play a part in his political demise.

Before addressing the campaign, the chapter discusses the two leading protagonists who were compelling figures in their own right. It was the first federal election campaign with a Canberra focus, since the new national parliament had just opened in May 1927 with Bruce, in his element, dominating the proceedings. Bruce and his wife Ethel were the first occupants of the Lodge, the baronial-style prime ministerial residence in Canberra. This invited comment as yet another case of Bruce being removed from the mainstream of everyday Australian life.

The 1929 election campaign was waged in the press and increasingly on radio.[3] The deputy prime minister Earle Page recognised the power of the new medium: 'It has brought all sections of the community into closer touch. It destroys the sense of remoteness and loneliness'.[4] It was the first time, as we shall see, when political advertising really played out on the silver screen since the federal government

---

3   Ibid., p.120.
4   Ibid., p.121.

had, in puritan mode, introduced an amusement tax on the gross receipts received by theatre and entertainment venues. This was the outcome of a Royal Commission on the Moving Picture Industry in Australia which Bruce had authorised in 1927. It inquired into the importation, production and employment implications of the industry. Bruce had been astonished at the boom in the construction of cinemas and picture palaces and, moreover, at what was being shown within them. Bruce felt that the local cinema chains, dominated by overseas interests, were an ideal tax opportunity. However, he did not consult with the industry over the proposed tax, resulting in a forceful response by those affected.[5]

The Patrician

Australia had never seen a prime minister like Bruce. Elevated to high office at the age of just 39, Bruce had a face that spoke a thousand words. Serene and aloof, he had a fixed and compelling gaze giving little clue to his true feelings. Described by Labor politician Frank Anstey as 'an English gentleman born in Australia', Bruce, after an early education in Melbourne, went off to Cambridge University where his rough edges were smoothed out. Bruce had fought at Gallipoli and Flanders as an officer in the British Army. He was invalided out after incurring two wounds and returned to Melbourne to take charge of his father's importing company. Kosmas Tsokhas judges that Bruce had:

> the demeanour and style to never feel embarrassed in the presence of the British upper class or business elite. He was at home in their world. He did not have an Australian accent ... He had

---

5   Ibid., p.125.

an aura of relaxed superiority. He was not one to panic or to give off signs of insecurity or vulnerability.[6]

After just one year back in Melbourne, a political opportunity arose and Bruce was quickly parachuted into a safe seat for the Nationalists. One of the most meteoric careers in Australian politics followed; first, as treasurer appointed by William (Billy) Hughes and then as prime minister in December 1922 because the Country Party, led by Earle Page and having the balance of power, refused to serve in any coalition government led by Hughes. Bruce, the embodiment of 'Brains, breeding and business', took the reins.[7] Always elegant in appearance, the lordly Bruce had the good sense to close down parliament when he went off to London for an imperial conference. Apparently that highhandedness did not irritate as much as the habit of calling people by their surname and using phrases such as 'fellah' and 'old boy'. In turn, he liked to be addressed as 'S.M.', never Stanley. It was that patrician hauteur and conceit, coupled with economics, that would undo him.[8]

The fat years of expansion, of 'Men, Money and Markets', were being replaced by concerns about the alarming rise in Australia's external indebtedness. The country's exuberance even worried British economist John Maynard Keynes, who advised against further investing in Australian securities on the London capital market. Economically literate, Bruce asked a panel of Australian economists to report on the Australian tariff and, specifically, to inquire whether protectionism had gone too far. They answered in the affirmative but

---

6 Kosmas Tsokhas, 'Tradition, Fantasy and Britishness: Four Australian Prime Ministers', *Journal of Contemporary Asia*, 31:1, 2001, p.11.
7 Cecil Edwards, *Bruce of Melbourne* (London: Heinemann, 1965), p.191.
8 See David Lee, *Stanley Melbourne Bruce: Australian Internationalist* (London: Continuum, 2010).

justified the existing tariff as having been necessary for Australia's overall development. When the Commonwealth incurred its first budget deficit in 1928, it indicated an economy turning sour. His treasurer, the energetic Page, was described by a government backbencher as 'The most tragic treasurer Australia has ever known'. The mud stuck as the economy slowed. In August 1929 Page had brought down a budget with tax imposts designed to contain the deficit. There was an amusement tax of 5% imposed on the gross receipts of all theatre and entertainment, with even a surcharge on American films, that irritated Hollywood moguls as well as cinema-goers.

If it was designed to avert economic disaster it was all too late. The official Actuary of the South Australian government, Leslie Melville, noted as early as 1927 that the prices of Australian wool and wheat exports were slipping but not, alas, the interest rates on Australia's overseas debt. The country was heading into national bankruptcy or what economists call a sovereign debt crisis.[9] Little wonder that Bruce turned to industrial relations reform as the escape option for Australia.

The Populist

Born in 1876 near Ballarat of Irish-Catholic lineage, James Henry Scullin's world was as proletarian and rustic as Bruce's background was privileged. In his earlier life Scullin had been a fencer, drover, miner, grocer, journalist, editor and union organiser. An interest in studying law, which he never consummated, enticed him to take to public debating. A small, slight man with auburn hair, Scullin had

---

9   Selwyn Cornish, 'Sir Leslie Melville: An Interview', *Economic Record*, 69:207, 1993, pp. 437–57.

the gift of the gab but he was not one to wield the knife in the political sense. Politics was his overriding interest with many nights spent engaging and networking within the labour movement.

He had the audacity to challenge Prime Minister Alfred Deakin for the seat of Ballaarat in the 1906 Federal Election. He lost but still attracted one-third of votes cast. During that campaign, Scullin was once accompanied by another impressive orator, Ramsay MacDonald from Britain's Independent Labour Party. They would meet up again in London as respective prime ministers in the dark days of 1930. Scullin had some early success as the federal member for Corangamite (1910-13). Apart from being an Australian nationalist, Scullin fought hard for the party to retain its commitment to the socialisation clause in its platform, having been instrumental in its adoption in 1931. He re-entered federal parliament as the Federal Member for the safe seat of Yarra in 1922, defeating 26 other aspirants. Like Bruce, he enjoyed a stellar rise, becoming opposition leader just six years later when the ineffective Matthew Charlton stood down.

It was Bruce's misfortune that the new opposition leader's greatest strength, as a speaker and communicator, was in eloquently championing the case for the preservation of the federal arbitration system simply because it underpinned Australian wages and conditions; indeed it would prove to be Scullin's finest hour as opposition leader.[10] While contemptuous of the new art of economics, Scullin was literate enough to warn that Australia had incurred an excessive level of foreign debt to fund low-yielding infrastructure projects at a time when export prices were slipping. He would capitalise on this argument during the election campaign. His warnings had an air of Greek tragedy about them. As his biographer, John Robertson, later

---

10   Kim Beazley, 'Labour unluckiest leader', *Canberra Times*, 22 February 1966.

remarked, 'It is often the fate of prophets to be ignored; but it does not always follow that the prophet is destroyed by the calamity he has foreseen'.[11]

The Background

Bruce had only just been re-elected in late 1928 with a comfortable majority of 12 when an act of treachery, coupled with his own impulsiveness, combined to force him to the polls again. Australia would go to a House of Representatives election over the same issue that had dominated the 1928 contest. Deteriorating economic conditions and the closure of the London market to further Australian capital raising formed the backdrop. There was also an intractable industrial dispute in the coal mines of the northern districts of New South Wales, with miners refusing a wage cut followed by an employer lock-out of some 12,000 of them. Bruce withdrew the prosecution against the powerful mine owner, John Brown, ostensibly to bring the dispute to some form of resolution. Unionists, however, felt that Bruce was blatantly on the side of the employers.

It stuck in Bruce's craw that Australia had an overlapping system of arbitration operating at both state and federal levels. Moreover, unions could get the best for their members by playing state and Commonwealth authorities off each other. This confusing and inefficient system allowed wages to escalate faster than productivity although workers were actually trying to restore their real wages to what they once were. Bruce always argued that his campaign for industrial relations reform was not about pursuing a reduction in wages. Earlier he had failed in a referendum to have the Commonwealth take over

---

[11] John Robertson, *J. H. Scullin: A Political Biography* (Perth: University of Western Australia Press, 1974), p.3.

the arbitration powers from the states. But in 1929, without consulting cabinet, Bruce did an about-face, introducing the Maritime Industries Bill which proposed to strip the Commonwealth of its arbitration powers and pass them on to the states. Only the shipping industry and the Commonwealth public service would still be subject to federal arbitration.

Bruce had decided, as he put it, 'to go over the top', a reference to the trench warfare with which he was so familiar.[12] This might today be called a 'captain's call', and Bruce expected his party to follow. Nationalist party officials tried in vain to change the prime minister's mind. His biographer, Cecil Edwards, suggests that Bruce had no reason to take a backward step since everything had gone his way over the past six years, but now his inexperience was to be damaging. Bruce underestimated just how sacrosanct federal arbitration was to Australian workers. Labor parliamentarians warned him about signing his own death warrant, crying 'Wait till the people get hold of you'. What brought that judgement to bear, though, was a cabal within Bruce's own party. When the bill entered the committee stage, Hughes moved an amendment stating that the bill should not be proclaimed until it had been put to the people.

After delivering a scathing speech, rich in nautical metaphor, about Bruce behaving like an erratic, headstrong captain, Hughes crossed the floor with three other members in tow.[13] The amendment had the vote of the opposition as well as the four Nationalist Party defectors and two Independents. Since Bruce took it upon himself to regard the amendment as a vote of no confidence in his government

---

12   Ina M. Cumpston, *Lord Bruce of Melbourne* (Melbourne: Longman Cheshire, 1989), p.92.
13   Norman Abjorensen, *The Manner of their Going: Prime Ministerial Exits from Lyne to Abbott* (Melbourne: Australian Scholarly Publishing, 2015), pp.86-7.

when it passed – by a solitary vote – he asked the governor-general to dissolve the House of Representatives. After informing members of this, Bruce crossed the chamber and shook Scullin's hand, telling him 'We are going into the ring'.

It was the first time in federal politics that a government had been defeated on the floor of the House so early in the life of the parliament, leading to its dissolution. Again Bruce could have deferred going to the polls by putting aside Hughes' amendment. He told his biographer:

> We couldn't have wriggled out of it that way. We would have taken our time to sort out the industrial problem if we had not been so obsessed by this impending financial and economic cataclysm that we believed it was imperative to put our own industrial house in order, and at once.[14]

It was not a fresh insight. Bruce had expressed the same sentiments publicly during the 1928 campaign and had told a Premiers Conference in May 1929 that the industrial relations system was 'the most important question' bearing upon Australian production costs.[15] The parliamentary contretemps was Hughes' sweet revenge for being dumped as prime minister in 1922 but, more importantly, for being overlooked when it came to appointing the Australian High Commissioner in London in 1927.[16] It would be a short campaign, with the election falling on 12 October.

---

14   Edwards, *Bruce of Melbourne*, p.187.
15   Paul Strangio, Paul 't Hart and James Walter, *Settling the Office: The Australian Prime Ministership from Federation to Reconstruction* (Melbourne: Miegunyah Press, 2016), pp.145-6.
16   Transcript of interview with Joseph Alexander, p.30, ORAL TRC 121/10 (transcript), National Library of Australia (NLA).

The Campaign

Electioneering only really lasted three weeks. Those pitching for office had to travel through their electorates by rail, sea and road; the leaders of the main political parties could not visit Western Australia because of logistics and time. Scullin largely confined his campaign to Victoria while his campaign director, the impressive former Queensland premier E.G. Theodore, handled electioneering engagements in New South Wales, where he now held a seat. In contrast Bruce covered five states and some 2500 miles.[17] In one instance he flew from Sydney to Queensland, the first time an Australian politician had undertaken electioneering by plane.[18] It was a campaign of large and, at times, heated meetings. There was an instance of a voter suffering a fatal coronary in Footscray after an affray at an electioneering function. Both policy speeches by the main party leaders were dreadfully long. Bruce spoke for two hours. The numbers listening, too, were gargantuan. In one address at the Exhibition Hall in Adelaide, 4000 turned out to hear Bruce speak, while at Glenelg Town Hall, another 1000 were present. Scullin's election policy speech at Richmond Town Hall had, naturally enough, an overflow audience with a crowd of 1000 inside.

Despite the prime minister's rosy optimism the odds were against him from the outset. For the first two weeks of the campaign Bruce had to contend with negative advertising appearing on the silver screen. American film companies and local cinema owners launched a campaign to overturn the recently introduced amusement tax. Cinema-goers were asked to sign petitions and telegrams of protest were sent to every member of parliament. Page felt the campaign

---

17   'Mr Bruce tour; pleased with prospects', *Argus*, 27 September 1929.
18   'By Plane', *Sydney Morning Herald*, 23 September 1929.

was so effective because the cinemas had almost free access to the community; it was stopped midway through the campaign.[19] Bruce was particularly angered at the misrepresentation of his industrial relations reform as well as of his policy on pensions. In one speech he thundered about Theodore's claims:

> He is one of the most lusty individuals you could imagine, yet what did he do in the war? He almost preached disloyalty ... he conducted a peace-by negotiation campaign, which did a great deal to hearten our enemies.[20]

Behind the scenes Bruce had his colleague, the Attorney-General John Latham, establish contact with the Queensland Premier to see if Theodore had committed any improprieties when he held that office.[21] That inquiry would bear fruit in July 1930. The Mungana affair revolved around the sale of mines at inflated prices to the Queensland Labor government after World War I. After it was disclosed that Ted Theodore had held shares in some of these mining companies which had been sold to the Queensland government, he was forced to stand down.

Scullin's first shots in the campaign were to seek to capitalise on the inconvenience for voters of having another general election thrust upon them just eleven months after the last one. He made reference to the cost of the election itself (£100,000). Scullin said the Bruce-Page government had 'disobeyed its mandate'.[22] Voting had been made compulsory in 1924 and many, no doubt, would have resented

---

19 Robert Murray, *The Confident Years: Australia in the Twenties*, (Melbourne: Allen Lane, 1978), p.243.
20 'The federal election campaign', *Mercury*, 10 October 1929.
21 Ross Fitzgerald, *Red Ted: The Life of E.G. Theodore*, (Brisbane: University of Queensland Press, 1994), p.253.
22 Robertson, *J.H. Scullin*, p.162.

being compelled to vote again so soon and, more importantly, on a proposal that they had also stridently opposed in the 1926 referendum on the Commonwealth industrial powers.

Bruce opened his campaign in his constituency at the Boomerang Theatre, Dandenong, on 18 September. Apologising for the inevitable dullness of a policy speech, Bruce promised his supporters 'plenty of fun when he came again'. He was prepared to confine the election contest to one issue, industrial relations, encapsulated in the slogan 'One arbitration or two'. It did not seem to dampen the enthusiasm of his audience. He emphasised that while the reforms would lower the cost of production, they would not lower the standard of living. He also said that labour was jeopardising the White Australia policy because the executive of the Australasian Council of Trade Unions had affiliated itself with the Pan Pacific Trade Union secretariat. That organisation had spoken out against the discriminatory immigration laws practiced by Australia.

During the campaign Bruce took heart from the release of the report of the Royal Commission appointed on the Constitution and its view that industrial legislation should be the province of the states. He was in high spirits after touring through Victoria. Bruce claimed that in every state he visited there was support for his position. In one meeting at Prahran City Hall, a day before the election, some 3000 turned out to hear Bruce support the local candidate, Sir Arthur Robinson. Bruce was heckled by shouts of 'importer of blackfellows and dagoes'. A part of the crowd started provocatively singing 'John Brown's body', a reference to a hated mining magnate.[23] Seemingly unfazed, Bruce left the venue with an enigmatic smile on his face. It was his last public appearance as prime minister.

---

23 'The federal election campaign; Prime Minister's Tour', *Mercury*, 10 October 1929.

ELECTIONS MATTER

Scullin also opened his campaign in his own electorate, on 19 September. He was warmly welcomed to the podium. One account recorded that he gave the most stirring speech of his life.[24] There was some truth in his claim, too, that this was 'probably the most momentous campaign' in Australia's history, since the federal arbitration system was at stake. Knowing he was in the box seat, Scullin did not have to cover all the party platform. He also had the luxury of not having to contest his own seat.[25] After ridiculing the Bruce-Page government for attempting to 'turn back the clock 25 years' and revert to the old position of leaving all industrial legislation to the states, he asked how the reforms could arrest the budget deficit or put the 180,000 unemployed back to work. Scullin pointed to the 'reckless finance' of the Bruce-Page Government, which 'had emptied the Federal Treasury and accumulated a huge deficit' since it took office. There had been wasteful expenditure on Commissions and Boards. He also attacked the 'slander on workers' in Bruce's claim that there had been some indication of a slowdown on production and in his insistence that wages be based more on productivity. Scullin interpreted this as a formula to both speed-up and lengthen the hours of the working day while reducing wages.

In attacking the amusement tax, Scullin pointed out in his address how some forms of entertainment bore no tax. Land tax, for instance, had recently been lifted from golf courses (and it was widely known that Bruce enjoyed the game). Theodore could not resist describing the tax as a 'paltry and inglorious attempt to extract money from the children's entertainment'.[26] Scullin already knew that he was likely to

---

24 'Labour launches its campaign', *Worker*, 25 September 1929.
25 Nine members – 6 Labor and 3 Country Party – were elected unopposed.
26 L.L. Robson, *Australian Commentaries: Selected Articles from the Roundtable*, (Melbourne: Melbourne University Press, 1975), p.147.

inherit an ailing economy, perhaps even a day of reckoning, but he was prepared to accept the poisoned chalice. 'Return us to power', he intoned,

> and we shall have a return to sane finance. Is Labor fit to govern? The one thing certain is that it could not possibly make a worse mess of it than the Bruce-Page ministry. It will not be pleasant to take charge and clean up the mess which the Ministry has left, but somebody has to do it, and the sooner it is taken in hand the better for the country. The first thing to be done is to save Australia. Return the Labor party to power and you will have saved that. The rest will follow.

He wanted the challenge of economic re-adjustment and was prepared to face the risks.

Earle Page gave his policy speech, on behalf of the Country Party, at Grafton. He called upon the great body of opinion in the primary industries to support the Bruce initiative and mocked Labor's view that the federal arbitration system was the 'the temple of industry'.[27] Journalists Joe Alexander, the head of Keith Murdoch's press bureau in Canberra, and Warren Denning, were assigned to accompany Bruce during the campaign. Alexander had already noted that Bruce, despite his great urbanity, seemed unable to make friends who would be helpful to him in politics. According to Alexander it was not just industrial relations that was Bruce's undoing; it was Page's stewardship of the economy. Everywhere he went Bruce was assailed by his connection with Page. Alexander recalled an anecdote from a meeting on the campaign trail in rural Queensland. A farmer called out 'Mr Bruce, is it a fact that you have a very powerful sleeping

---

27   'Dr Page's speech', *Sydney Morning Herald*, 24 September 1929.

partner?" then looking at Mrs Bruce: 'I don't mean Mrs Bruce'. The farmer was right about Bruce's dependence on Page and the Country Party.[28]

The Outcome

In those days there was not the modern pre-election polling that we have now, but by the end of the first week in October, Scullin was confidently predicting that Labor would increase its number of seats. He was proved more right than he imagined. Scullin was at his home as the election results came in. Before the evening was out he knew he would become Australia's ninth prime minister. Scullin not only became the first Australian-born Labor prime minister but the magnitude of the victory, a gain of 15 seats at the expense of the nationalists on a swing of 4.2 percent, was the largest in the party's history at that time. A minder told Scullin that a large majority might spell trouble in terms of party loyalty.[29] Bruce was shocked. Denning imagined how he would have reacted as the election results filtered in:

> The Bruce façade cracked just once or twice to reveal behind it an angry, human, perhaps a suffering, man; but the cracks came only once or twice, and on election night it was the same sphinx-like figure which watched seat after seat, minister after minister, crash into the dust and inglory of defeat.[30]

A further indignity for Bruce was losing his own seat by 305 votes to Jack Holloway, secretary of the Melbourne Trades Hall.[31] It was the

---

28   Alexander, Interview Transcript, p.24.
29   Robertson, *J.H. Scullin*, p.167.
30   Warren Denning Papers, NLA MS MS 5129.
31   Murray, *The Confident Years*, p.247.

second time Holloway had challenged the prime minister for the seat of Flinders, having fallen foul of Bruce over an earlier timber strike. There was a real degree of animus directed towards Bruce in this election: some 5000 voters who favoured him in 1928 changed their vote and his share of the vote fell from 60% to 49%. Abjorensen reports that the backlash against him was 11% as against a nationwide swing against the government of 4.5%.[32] Bruce admitted to 'a real feeling of disappointment … the people have said that they do not want my services, and I am going into the banishment to which they have sent me'.[33] Alexander recalls visiting a 'very depressed' Bruce days after the election: 'even his unflappable urbanity seemed to be shaken'.[34] At the declaration of the poll for Flinders on 25 October, Bruce stated that he had done what he considered the best for the country. In a note to a party colleague, Bruce attributed his defeat to 'the apprehension that was created in the minds of the people by lying propaganda that the standard of living was to be destroyed, and wages to be reduced'.[35]

Two interesting seats changed hands in this election, one of which would quickly produce a prime minister and the other an aspirant to that lofty position. In the seat of Wilmot, in Tasmania, the former Labor premier, Joseph Lyons, was elected. In the South Australian division of Wakefield, Charles Hawker, Cambridge-educated and decorated war hero, won the seat for the Nationals.

Afterwards and away from it all in London, Bruce was philosophical, telling a former cabinet colleague:

---

32   Abjorensen, *The Manner of their Going*, p.88.
33   *Sydney Morning Herald*, 26 October 1929.
34   Abjorensen, *The Manner of their Going*, p.88. Alexander, Interview Transcript, p.33.
35   Cumpston, *Lord Bruce of Melbourne*, p.95.

> We did our best while in office to educate the people to the need to get down the costs of production ... last year the slump in wheat and wool prices forced us to take action before public opinion was sufficiently educated ... I gather, however, that our successors are having a fairly troublesome time, and, as far as I am concerned, they are welcome to the job.[36]

The Great Depression hit Australia particularly hard and early. While he later told colleagues he was happy not to be in government, some felt Bruce might have deliberately lost office because he could see what was coming.[37] Bruce dismissed this interpretation as making him out to be more Machiavellian than he ever was.[38] If anything, Australia was a beneficiary of the turn of events. For, as Bruce freely admitted, had he won the 1929 election his government would have been swept from office by the time the next election was due to be held. In that case he felt that he would have retired from public life and never become Australia's high commissioner in London, since the Labor government, perhaps under Theodore, would hardly have recommended his appointment.[39] In that case Australia would not have had the forceful negotiator that Bruce became, with his city connections being particularly successful in converting Australia's debt to lower interest rates.

The hypotheticals and 'what ifs' can be extended further. It was argued, even by an authority such as Keynes, that the mostly deflationary 1931 Premiers' Plan of austerity, along with reductions in costs,

---

36 S.M. Bruce to George Pearce, 27 May 1930, Pearce Papers, NLA, manuscript no. 1927.
37 Edwards, *Bruce of Melbourne*, p.199.
38 H. Mishael, 'Bruce: Eminent Australian', *West Australian*, 15 March 1966.
39 Edwards, *Bruce of Melbourne*, pp.189-90.

including a 10% wage cut, could only have been engineered and implemented by a Labor government. Had Bruce faced the same challenge of austerity and wage cuts there would, given his record, perhaps have been blood in the streets. In a sense then, James Scullin was far from the tragic figure he is so often characterised as.

INTERIM 1929–1940

Unlucky or not, Labor's landslide victory in 1929 was followed by a demoralising defeat in 1931. Like Cook's Liberals, who were victorious in 1913 only to be shown the door in 1914, Scullin and Labor were turfed out after a single, foreshortened term. Once again, the Labor Party was deeply divided. Scullin's response to the Great Depression was bitterly opposed by renegade New South Wales premier Jack Lang. Lang and his supporters were expelled from the party but others at federal level, including the popular Tasmanian postmaster-general, Joseph Lyons, left of their own accord. With so many defections Scullin was obliged to seek a fresh election. Former Labor members and various Independents merged with the remaining Nationalists to form the United Australia Party (UAP). The choice of name was no accident, and compared to the UAP, Labor looked hopelessly divided. The election result on 19 December 1931 saw the UAP, led by Lyons, win an overwhelming majority. Scullin retained leadership of the ALP.

Labor performed slightly better at the next federal election on 15 September 1934 but the relative positions of the UAP, ALP, and Country Party (CP) remained. Labor was still thwarted in New South Wales where Lang successfully ran rebel candidates. The UAP and CP entered a formal coalition arrangement, while Scullin was replaced by John Curtin as Labor leader in 1935. The election of 23 October 1937 was another victory for the Lyons government, which again controlled both houses. It was a success of sorts for Labor as well, however. The ALP was able to regain several of the key New

South Wales seats it had lost to Lang Labor. As the Labor Party finally moved towards greater stability, on the other side of the world the dark clouds of war were again building in Europe.

Chapter 4

1940

WHAT TO DO IN AN ELECTORAL DRAW

Benjamin T. Jones

Even in committed democracies, it is not unusual for elections to be suspended in times of war. In the grim war year of 1940 there were certainly some calls for the scheduled federal election to be delayed and for the formation of an emergency government with special powers. The decision was made to conduct the election as normal and the result was nation-shaping. Although Robert Menzies and his United Australia Party-Country Party coalition retained power, the ultimate victor was the Australian Labor Party and John Curtin, who would rise to the task of wartime leader just over a year later. The hung parliament of 1940 was an unlikely outcome and reveals the ever-present role of fortune in politics. Were it not for the tragic deaths of several frontbenchers, the UAP failing to run a candidate in a key division, Curtin defying the odds to retain his own seat, and the slowly revealed impact of postal votes, Menzies would almost certainly have secured an absolute majority in the House of Representatives and served as prime minister for the remainder of the war. The 1940 result exemplifies the flexibility of Australia's Westminster system and its ability to function without a clear majority winner. It also highlights the sometimes crucial function of Independent MPs. At a philosophic level, Australia was still negotiating and constructing its national identity in 1940. Menzies and Curtin were not the polar opposites sometimes presented but they were different leaders with different visions of Australia and its place in the world. The hung parliament meant that both men would serve as prime minister during the turbulent war years, securing two very different legacies. The direction of Australia's war effort and the agenda of the early post-war years were dramatically shaped by the election of 1940.

1940

Australia had three different prime ministers in 2013. The year began with Julia Gillard in the top job before a party coup in June replaced her with Kevin Rudd and a general election in September replaced him with Tony Abbott. While the quick turnaround of leaders was extraordinary, it was not unprecedented. In the ominous war year of 1941, Australia also saw three different prime ministers. This case was even more remarkable than 2013 as all three served in the same parliament. The prime ministerships of Robert Menzies, Arthur Fadden, and John Curtin were all predicated on the inconclusive result of the 1940 federal election. The electors of the now defunct Melbourne seat of Henty were not to know that their votes for Arthur Coles would dramatically alter the course of Australia's sixteenth parliament. Never before or since has an Independent MP so radically influenced Australia's leadership and history.

In a 2004 *Age* poll of historians and political scientists, John Curtin was voted Australia's greatest prime minister.[1] His wartime leadership saw him narrowly beat Australia's longest serving prime minister, Robert Menzies, for the title. Despite claims that his true 'gift' was in economic policy, Curtin's legacy is necessarily tied to World War II.[2] His iconic, if often misunderstood, 'look to America' newspaper article provided evidence to some of a new independence.[3] His bold defiance of Winston Churchill in demanding Australian troops return home furthered his legend among the radical-nationalist

---

1 'Curtin: our greatest PM', *Age*, 18 December 2004.
2 John Edwards has suggested that the excessive focus on Curtin's wartime leadership has obscured his economic achievements. See John Edwards, *Curtin's Gift: Reinterpreting Australia's Greatest Prime Minister* (Sydney: Allen and Unwin, 2005).
3 Manning Clark led this polarising interpretation of Curtin and Menzies. As Paul Kelly has noted, 'In Clark's fantasy, Menzies was the old dead tree … Curtin, by contrast, was the young green tree'. Paul Kelly, *The March of Patriots: The Struggle for Modern Australia* (Melbourne: Melbourne University Press, 2010), p.74.

school of historians. And yet, Curtin's prime ministership, and the mythology that has grown from it, were the result of 'outrageous fortune' and a huge political gamble. He repeatedly refused Menzies' offers of an emergency unity government, and insisted the Australian Labor Party (ALP) would only govern in its own right. He may never have had the chance but for the 1940 election producing a very unlikely hung parliament that allowed two Independents to become kingmakers. This political contest highlights both the crucial role Independent members of parliament have played at two junctures in Australian political history – 1941 and 2010 – and the flexibility of the political system. Philosophically, the campaign reveals the tensions in Australia's dual identity as both independent nation and loyal dominion. It was an election that undoubtedly shaped the nation. Were it not for a series of unforeseeable events and a handful of votes, the national story might have been vastly different.

A National Disaster

Australia's Westminster parliamentary system provides a distinct advantage to the incumbent government by offering an election window rather than a set date. Normally, the government has the luxury of calling either an early or late election depending on its prospects. Nevertheless, external factors can force the government's hand and this was certainly the case in 1940. The Canberra Air Disaster of 13 August saw 10 people lose their lives as a flight from Melbourne attempted to land in the national capital. Three of Menzies' trusted cabinet ministers perished along with Chief of the General Staff, Sir Cyril Brudenell Bingham White, and six officers. The tragedy robbed Menzies of three of his most experienced and able frontbenchers: the

Minister for the Army, Geoffrey Austin Street, Minister for Scientific and Industrial Research, Sir Henry Somer Gullett, and Minister for Air and Civil Aviation, James Valentine Fairbairn, who might have been at the controls when the RAAF Hudson Bomber nose-dived into a hill.[4]

It is difficult to overstate the significance of this disaster for the 1940 election and Australian political history more generally. The *Sydney Morning Herald* bleakly proclaimed:

> The loss is the heavier in that it has come at a time when the whole Empire is bracing itself to meet an onslaught unmatched in history for power and ferocity, and when Australia herself needs all the ability and experience she can find to direct the part that she must play in freedom's fight for survival.[5]

In power for nearly a decade, infighting and instability were becoming an unwanted feature of United Australia Party (UAP) rule. The loss of stabilising figures in Street, Gullett, and Fairbairn weighed heavily on Menzies. In his memoirs he would write: 'this was a dreadful calamity, for my three colleagues were my close and loyal friends; each of them had a place not only in my Cabinet, but in my heart'.[6] Only a twist of fate spared the government from an even greater loss. Assistant treasurer and future prime minister, Arthur Fadden,

---

4   Andrew Tink has argued that it was in fact Fairbairn rather than listed pilot Robert Hitchcock who was at the controls. This theory, however, which has been persistent from 1940 till present day, is rejected by Cameron Hazlehurst who concludes: 'it is scarcely conceivable that, with the lives of six important passengers in his hands, Hitchcock would have surrendered his seat to Fairbairn or that Fairbairn would have been foolhardy enough to displace him'. See Andrew Tink, *Air Disaster Canberra: The plane crash that destroyed a government* (Sydney: NewSouth Publishing, 2013), p.175, and Cameron Hazlehurst, *Ten Journeys to Cameron's Farm: An Australian Tragedy* (Canberra: ANU ePress, 2015), p.563.
5   'The Need of the Hour', *Sydney Morning Herald*, 16 August 1940.
6   Hazlehurst, *Ten Journeys*, p.625.

and Minister for Trade and Customs, George McLeay, were both invited on the ill-fated plane but chose to travel by rail instead. With an election due by the end of January 1941, Menzies was left with the unpalatable choice of calling three by-elections that would only stand for a matter of months, or bring the general election forward to September. Although personally shaken by the tragedy, he chose the latter course.

In Menzies' mind, only the temporary formation of a national all-party government, led by him, could legitimise delaying an election beyond January. Curtin and the ALP dismissed the suggestion, however, and were quick to point out that comparable dominions like Canada and New Zealand continued to function without such an arrangement.[7] The vitriol between Menzies and the Country Party's leader Earle Page had spilled onto the floor of the House of Representatives the previous year. On 20 April 1939, Page effectively accused the newly elected UAP leader of cowardice for not taking part in World War I.[8] In turn, Menzies refused to work with Page, forcing him to step down as leader. Labor dismissed the idea of an emergency union. If the conservative coalition could not govern in unity there was little hope of a functional all-party government.[9] In full campaign mode it argued that Menzies had been 'at odds with his present colleagues ever since they came together and the complete lack of cohesion ... makes talk of a national government a sheer absurdity'.[10]

---

7 'Mr Curtin in Sydney', *Age*, 14 September 1940.
8 Paul Davey, *The Nationals: The Progressive, Country, and National Party in New South Wales, 1919-2006* (Sydney: federation Press, 2006), pp.126-130.
9 'Curtin Pledges Party', *Daily News*, 30 August 1940.
10 Ibid.

The timing of the election does reveal Menzies' deep reverence for parliamentary democracy and the Westminster system. There were calls within his own ranks to delay the election beyond the January deadline.[11] Doing so would have required a special Act by the British parliament to suspend the Australian constitution. The notion was anathema to Menzies. Even in the throes of war, and despite his well-known affection for monarchy, he insisted that a government is only legitimate if democratically endorsed. When confirming the much speculated-on election date of 21 September he claimed that 'victory at the polls would give to me and to the Government an authority which nothing but a popular vote can give'.[12] He was curtly dismissive also of calls to appoint non-parliamentarians to cabinet as an emergency response to the Canberra Air Disaster, announcing:

> I cannot accept the view expressed in some quarters that I should appoint non-Parliamentary people to Cabinet, or that I should in some way endeavor to constrain or dictate the choice of the electors. Democracy is among the things we are fighting for.[13]

The early election did not augur well for the government, but with Curtin refusing to accept a unity government, Menzies saw no alternative than to contest an election in the normal way.

Menzies and Curtin

Like the timing of the election, the timing of Menzies' first prime ministership was determined by ill-fate. The conservative UAP was formed in 1931 by Labor dissidents and the remnants of the divided

---

11   'Federal Move. Postpone Election?', *Queensland Times*, 17 June 1940.
12   'Why an Election is to be Held', *Age*, 22 August 1940.
13   Ibid.

ELECTIONS MATTER

Nationalist Party. Led by the popular Joseph Lyons, the UAP won the 1931 election and was returned in 1934 and 1937, governing in coalition with the CP from 1934. As tensions built across Europe in 1939, they were building also in the UAP cabinet with deputy leader Menzies resigning to the backbench over a policy dispute. Lyons' sudden death from a coronary occlusion on 7 April 1939 prevented an almost certain leadership challenge. Leader of the CP, Sir Earle Page, served as caretaker prime minister until the UAP could elect a new leader. Menzies defeated former prime minister Billy Hughes and was sworn in on 26 April.

Problems surfaced immediately, with Page, a staunch ally of Lyons, refusing to serve under Menzies. Infighting and white-anting proved internecine but not fatal to the government. While the formal coalition was dissolved, a majority of CP MPs still preferred the UAP to Labor, allowing Menzies to continue governing in minority. The situation in Europe deteriorated and just five months after Menzies assumed the prime ministership, Germany invaded Poland, prompting a British declaration of war on 3 September. Menzies immediately performed his 'melancholy duty' and informed Australia that it too was at war.

The rhetoric of Menzies' speech is significant not only for its weighty substance but its pan-Britannic tenor. Menzies informed the nation that 'in consequence of the persistence by Germany in her invasion of Poland, Great Britain has declared war upon her, and that, *as a result*, Australia is also at war'.[14] So far as Menzies was concerned, there was no element of choice involved. Australia's status as a Dominion of the British Empire, and the sovereignty that

---

14   Emphasis added. 'Australia Stands Firm at Great Britain's Side', *Advertiser*, 4 September 1939.

implied, was a source of national pride, something Menzies regularly reminded Whitehall. Nevertheless, Menzies felt no need to distinguish between choice and duty in this dark moment. Australia's fight against Germany was a *fait accompli*, an automatic 'result' of Britain's decision. He noted: 'there can be no doubt that where Great Britain stands there stands the people of the entire British world'.[15] In contrast, Curtin's declaration of war on Japan just two years later was made on Australia's behalf, independently of Britain.

The crude binary that Curtin stood for Australian nationalism as opposed to Menzies' British race patriotism is unhelpful and bends the facts beyond reasonable interpretation. James Curran has highlighted just how committed Curtin was to imperial cooperation.[16] There was, however, a difference in tone and emphasis between the two leaders. Where Menzies was resolute in seeking a united British response, Curtin spoke of being first and foremost 'loyal to this soil'.[17] Explaining Labor's war policy to the House of Representatives he said the ALP 'is concerned primarily with the defence and safety of the people of *this* Commonwealth … it is also concerned with the safety and integrity of the *British* Commonwealth'.[18] Much of the 1940 election was a battle to define Australia's place as autonomous yet connected.

On the Campaign Trail

There was never a question of Australia's support for Britain, but the degree of that support and how it should be framed came to

---

15 Ibid.
16 James Curran: *Curtin's Empire* (Melbourne: Cambridge University Press, 2011).
17 'Federal Labor Leader States War Time Policy', *Daily Advertiser*, 11 September 1939.
18 Emphasis added.

dominate the election. The surrender of France on 22 June 1940, after only six weeks of fighting, terrified the entire British world. With the balance of power in Europe dramatically shifting in Hitler's favour, the motherland's peril was keenly felt in Australia. Menzies launched his campaign at Camberwell Town Hall in Melbourne on 2 September. He insisted that he and his party would fully support the 'brave and inspiring leadership of Winston Churchill'.[19] The speech had little in the way of policy but emphasised the priority of winning the war at all costs. Menzies cast himself as the peacemaker and the man looking beyond petty political squabbles to the larger, imperial picture. He repeated his call for a unity government and confirmed the offer would still stand if the UAP was returned:

> If returned to power, I shall continue to do all that in me lies to induce Labour to share on a full and fair basis the responsibilities of Government, and to present to our common enemies a united national front.[20]

Menzies drew no distinction between the needs of Australia and the broader Empire. He insisted that Australia was 'not only politically but morally, spiritually and materially, an integral part of the great British family of nations'.[21] Declaring this the most fateful election in Australian history, he closed by quoting Churchill: 'Let us go forward together in all parts of the Empire'.[22]

Churchill's resolute leadership in the face of Nazi aggression made him a revered figure throughout the Empire. His defiant 'finest hour'

---

19 'The Men for the Task', *Argus*, 3 September, 1940.
20 Ibid.
21 'Most Fateful Election in Australia's History, Declares Mr. Menzies', *Advertiser*, 3 September 1940.
22 Ibid.

speech was well reported in Australia.[23] By the time the 1940 election campaign officially began, the Battle of Britain had been raging for two months. The UAP were quick to paint themselves as the party that truly supported Churchill and Britain. One campaign poster drew particular ire from Curtin and Labor. It depicted Churchill and Menzies side by side, with the former apparently endorsing the latter. Campaigning in Hobart, Curtin vented his frustration, calling it 'a monstrous perversion … to regard Mr Churchill as a partisan in an Australian election'.[24] Contesting the Sydney seat of Barton, Labor's new star recruit, former High Court justice H.V. 'Doc' Evatt, accused Menzies of hypocrisy, reminding voters that he and most of the government had supported Neville Chamberlain's appeasement policy. He claimed:

> Today every bomb that falls on London proves that Mr Churchill was right and that Mr Chamberlain and the appeasers were wrong. How in these circumstances, Mr Menzies dares to make political capital out of Mr Churchill is hard to understand.[25]

The UAP was unfazed by Labor's protestations and continued to suggest that they were the party who truly supported Churchill and the Empire.

Curtin launched his campaign in Perth on 28 August, declaring that Labor was 'inflexible in support of the British cause'.[26] While

---

23 For example, 'France's Treaty Obligations', *Sydney Morning Herald*, 19 June 1940; 'Churchill Rouses Commons', *Telegraph* (Brisbane), 19 June 1940; 'Britain Unshaken', *West Australian*, 19 June 1940; 'Calm Survey of Situation', *Advertiser*, 20 June 1940; 'A Battle for Life', *Mercury*, 19 June 1940.
24 UAP Election Poster, *Sydney Morning Herald*, 10 September 1940.
25 Ibid.
26 'Election Campaign Opened in Perth', *Canberra Times*, 29 August 1940.

making a few expected swipes at the UAP for their management of the war effort, Curtin essentially presented a unity ticket with the government insofar as total victory was concerned. Curtin did outline a number of key policies that differentiated himself from Menzies and the government. He argued that the UAP had broken a pledge on soldiers' pay and that Labor would increase the weekly salary. Curtin's policy included national control of banks and credit as well as government intervention in housing and the wheat board.

Like Menzies, Curtin was a committed democrat and went to lengths to insist that expanded government powers must be temporary and must be balanced with regular elections. He argued:

> In war, as well as in peace, we stand for the principle that, in matters of government, the consent of the people should be sought at regular intervals. While giving tremendous authority to the government, we have insisted that the authority of Parliament over the Government is authority derived from the people and which the people must determine. Just as the Government can be saved from blunders by having to consult Parliament, so also is it the regular obligation of Parliament to consult the people.[27]

Even at this early stage, Curtin was concerned with post-war reconstruction and the transition to a peacetime economy. He insisted that 'attention must be given to the planning of our future so that we shall be in a position to honour our promises to those who will bring us victory'.[28] The ultimate goal was a thriving peace where the voices of the working class held equal sway with all other quarters. This was

---

27   Ibid.
28   Ibid.

the essence of what he termed 'complete democracy'.[29] Leading up to the election, his posters would read 'save democracy, vote Labor'.[30]

Labor took part in the long-standing Australian political tradition of appropriating campaign slogans from the United States. In this case it was Franklin Delano Roosevelt's post-Depression policies known as the New Deal that took centre stage. Labor's 'New Deal' was 'for the soldier, for the soldier's wife, widows, the aged and infirm, the taxpayer, the working man, the primary producer'.[31] It was a slogan that prioritised the war while maintaining their ideological commitment to workers. Menzies retorted: 'We must remember all the time that we are fighting, not for the spoils of victory, but for a better world in which a fair deal will not need to be called a new deal'.[32] The UAP slogan further emphasised Menzies' belief in common cause with the whole British world. It urged loyal Australians to 'back the government that's backing Churchill'.[33]

Curtin's refusal to take part in a unity government became a sticking point of the campaign. Melbourne's *Argus* applauded Menzies' bipartisan gesture and considered him to possess a 'thoroughly nationalist spirit'. Unsurprisingly, the *Australian Worker*, mouthpiece of the powerful union of the same name, had a different view. It sarcastically found the offer akin to 'a man entering an old-established but bankrupt business … forced to accept responsibility for acts of folly that had been committed by the older partners'.[34] The decision

---

29 Ibid.
30 'Save Democracy Vote Labor', *Telegraph* (Brisbane), 10 September 1940.
31 'A New Deal', *Advocate*, 10 September 1940.
32 'Most Fateful Election in Australia's History, Declares Mr. Menzies', *Advertiser*, 3 September 1940.
33 'Australia Must Have a United Government', *Argus*, 13 September 1940.
34 'Federal Election Campaign in Full Swing Everywhere', *Australian Worker*, 4 September 1940.

allowed the UAP to portray Labor as petty partisans, unable to look past internal squabbles even in an emergency. Its advertisements told electors that 'Labour place their party before the country's security'.[35]

As the election date drew near, the advertisements and rhetoric became increasingly personal. With Queenslanders feeling more vulnerable to attack than the southern states, Labor bought space in Brisbane's *Courier Mail* and *Telegraph* to declare the troops were chronically undersupplied and underprepared.[36] Again Menzies was derided as 'Australia's Chamberlain'.[37] Meanwhile, the UAP and CP lampooned the conflicts within the labour movement. As noted in the previous chapter, the irascible New South Wales Labor premier, Jack Lang, had formed a breakaway state party in 1931 to protest Prime Minister Jim Scullin's economic policies during the Great Depression. In 1940, he led a second breakaway party to contest federal seats, the Australian Labor Party Non-Communist (ALPNC).[38] Lang's followers included Jack Beasley, who would lead the renegade party. The far-left formed their own splinter party, the State Labor Party (SLP), which only contested seats in New South Wales. The SLP was led by trade unionists Jack Hughes and Walter Evans, both of whom would prove to be Communists. Consequently, there were three separate Labor tickets. The UAP seized on this disunity and declared: 'Australia dare not take the risk of changing from the unified single purpose of the UAP and CP Government to the brawling, three faction Labour alternatives'.[39] The CP advertisements

---

35 'Labour place their party before the country's security', *Courier-Mail*, 20 September 1940.
36 'Mr. Menzies Elected', *Courier-Mail*, 20 September 1940. 'Mr. Menzies Elected', *Telegraph*, 20 September 1940.
37 'Mr. Menzies Elected', *Courier-Mail*, 20 September 1940.
38 'New Labor Party', *Tweed Daily*, 19 April 1940.
39 'This or This', *Mercury*, 17 September 1940.

Advocate, 20 September 1940.   *Advocate*, 10 September 1940.

asked the electors: 'If Labor cannot govern itself how can it govern Australia?' In contrast, the government would work together for the common good, 'the British way'.[40] The message was somewhat undermined by the government's rancorous infighting.

The Results Trickle in

Nazi bombs continued to fall over London as Australians went to the polls on Saturday, 21 September 1940. The results were slow to trickle in but it was soon apparent it would be an extremely tight race. The major dailies did not publish on the Sabbath, but even by Monday many seats still hung in the balance. In an effort to beat the pack, the *Canberra Times* announced that the government had been returned with a reduced majority and, sensationally, that John Curtin had lost his seat of Fremantle.[41] Both headlines would prove incorrect. The *Age* was more measured, noting that 'the new parliament will be very evenly matched' but it was likely the UAP would

---

40   'Labour Unity', *Forbes Advocate*, 17 September 1940.
41   'Government Returned', *Canberra Times*, 23 September 1940.

continue to govern with CP support.[42] Other papers simply reported seat-by-seat results without any grand narrative.

By Wednesday, the *Canberra Times* was still predicting a UAP majority of four as 'almost certain' with Curtin's position upgraded to 'precarious but not yet lost'.[43] Over the following weekend, predictions of a government majority dropped from four to two, prompting Fadden's misguided prophecy that 'the worst thing that can happen is that the government can have 38 seats' in a House of 75.[44] Boosted by strong support from the postal votes of soldiers, Curtin's fortunes improved and it became likely he would in fact retain Fremantle. The make-up of the lower house was to be determined by nail-biting results in the New South Wales seats of Robertson, Hume, and Riverina, the Victorian seat of Ballaarat, and Maranoa in south Queensland. While Robertson and Hume were retained by the UAP and CP respectively, Riverina was a surprise Labor gain with John Langtry overcoming a steep 7.2% margin to win the seat from Horace Nock.[45] The large rural seat of Maranoa was another unexpected gain for Labor, won by Frank Baker. Ballaarat looked likely to fall to the UAP's Edward Montgomery but was ultimately held by Labor's Reg Pollard. Labor's unexpected victory in these three cliffhanger seats made the situation for the government even more dire than Fadden's worst-case prediction.

All 75 lower house seats had been contested. When the final votes were tallied in early October, the government and opposition were

---

42 'The Elector's Verdict', *Age*, 23 September 1940.
43 'Government Position Improves', *Canberra Times*, 25 September 1940.
44 'Federal Election Surprises', *Sunday Mail*, 29 September 1940.
45 'Legislative Election 21 September 1940: New South Wales', *Australian Election Archive*. Accessed online. <http://psephos.adam-carr.net/countries/a/australia/1940/1940repsnsw.txt>

left with 36 seats each, with two Independents holding the balance of power. A third Independent, Adair Blair, won the seat of Northern Territory which did not carry full voting rights and thus could not be used to form government. While the official Australian Labor Party gained several seats from the UAP and CP, four sitting members had switched their allegiance to Jack Lang's Labor splinter, reducing the net gain to three. Led by Jack Beasley, who retained the seat of West Sydney, Tom Sheehan in Cook, Sol Rosevear in Dalley, and Dan Mulcahy in Lang, all defected to the ALPNC. Nonetheless, the rebels were willing to sit alongside the mainstream Labor MPs. Perhaps having learned from the Langites' role in the destruction of the Scullin Government in 1931, they did not contemplate giving Menzies a working majority. Possibly the two most significant gains for the ALP were the Sydney seats of Barton and Macquarie won by Evatt and Ben Chifley respectively. While both men were destined to become Labor leaders and revered figures in ALP folklore, neither was parachuted into a safe seat. Barton was held by the UAP's Albert Lane with a 1.8% margin, but Evatt's high profile, indefatigable campaigning, and dogged oratory resulted in a remarkable 16.4% increase of primary votes and a comfortable victory.[46] Macquarie, which at the time stretched from Penrith in western Sydney to Chifley's hometown of Bathurst, was and still is something of a bellwether seat. Chifley had won it in 1928 but lost to the UAP's John Lawson in 1931. Having failed to win it back during the 1930s, a double-digit swing after preferences to Labor (10.2%) was an unexpected achievement.[47]

---

46   Ibid.
47   Ibid.

Coles and Wilson

The UAP picked up four seats, three from the ALP and one due to Percy Spender, who won the Sydney seat of Warringah in 1937 as an Independent, later joining the government ranks. As a result of a strange set of circumstances, the UAP lost the conservative Melbourne seat of Henty. The seat had been safely held for the UAP by Gullett. Following his tragic death, the presumptive UAP candidate was Arthur Coles, co-founder of the eponymous supermarket chain and Melbourne's Lord Mayor. Despite endorsement as a UAP candidate, the headstrong Coles believed passionately in the cause of a national government. He claimed that the 'sincere popular wish' was that 'sectional differences should be shelved for unity of war effort'.[48] As a result, he insisted on running as a Nationalist Independent, leaving the UAP without a candidate. Running against Labor's Arthur Haywood and three other Independents, Coles won the seat easily with 54.6% of the vote before preferences.[49]

The other voting Independent to emerge victorious was Alexander Wilson who retained the Victorian seat of Wimmera in the north-western wheat belt. Wilson had won the seat from the CP's Hugh McClelland in 1937 and, buoyed by Labor preferences, beat him even more convincingly in 1940. Unlike Coles, who expressed support for the government, Wilson had often voted with Labor in the previous parliament. Such was the goodwill towards the Independent, the Ouyen branch of the ALP considered not running a candidate against him.[50] While the two Independents were dismissed by some as parliamentary amateurs, Christopher Hayman has

---

48   'Five Claimants for Henty', *Argus*, 11 September 1940.
49   Legislative Election 21 September 1940.
50   'Wimmera', *Age*, 31 August 1940.

argued that they were important, not only for their crucial votes but their political acumen also. He writes:

> far from being cranks, Coles and Wilson, between September 1940 and June/July 1941 built up an end-game bargaining potential by setting out on what grounds they would support any government.[51]

Unexpected Outcomes

The 1940 election was the closest thing Australian democracy has had to a perfect draw. After the government coalition and the Labor parties each secured 36 seats, of the two voting Independents, Coles was certainly inclined to support the government. Wilson, the former wheat farmer who had been a member of the Victorian United Country Party, was less predictable. With the lower house evenly split, the Senate remained narrowly under conservative control. Half the Senators were up for re-election in 1940. The UAP and CP ran on a joint ticket and won 50.4% of the national vote, a net increase of 5.6% on 1937.[52] When the new parliament sat, the coalition held a slender majority of 19 to 17 over Labor in the upper house.

With the ALPNC siphoning votes and four seats away from the official ALP, the 1940 election can appear to be a loss for all major parties. Despite its strong polling in the Senate, the ruling UAP suffered a 2.8% swing against it in the lower house, resulting in the loss of four seats. The CP fared little better with a negative swing of 2% costing them three seats. The ALP technically suffered a negative

---

51 Christopher Hayman, 'The Balance of Power in Second World War Australia: The Deliberative Role of Coles and Wilson in the House of Representatives from 1940' (PhD Thesis, University of New South Wales, 2005), p.217.
52 Senate Election 21 September 1940.

swing of 3% despite picking up three seats. The ALPNC, however, won over 200,000 votes or 5.2% and four seats. If added together, the Labor parties actually increased their national vote share by 2.2% and won seven extra seats. The labour movement saw its greatest success in New South Wales, where the two Labor factions enjoyed a combined 3.3% boost. If the votes cast for State Labor are factored in, the gains are even more emphatic. Despite this strong result, the Labor splits, the initial strong polling of the UAP, and Curtin's scare in Fremantle led to a general mood of defeat. This was reflected in the press, which consistently reported that Menzies had been returned. The pro-Labor scandal sheet *Truth* indignantly referred to the mainstream media's presentation of a 'great and glorious' victory for Menzies as the 'cheekiest' element of the election.[53] The paper did have some grounds for gloating. While the major dailies were initially confident of Menzies' return and Curtin's defeat, the *Truth*'s 22 September headline read, 'Labor Gains: Govt. May Go'.[54] It correctly predicted that Menzies was 'scarcely in a position to carry on the Government of the country for long without Labor's O.K.'.[55]

A Change of Leadership

The story of the sixteenth parliament of Australia is familiar. Sitting for the first time on 20 November 1940, Coles and Wilson initially agreed to support Menzies and provide the coalition government with a working majority. Curtin again refused all offers of a unity government but did agree to join the tripartisan Advisory War Council. Dedicated to the imperial cause, Menzies spent four crucial months in early 1941 in London. He returned to Australia in August

---

53 'Who Did Win the Election, Anyway?', *Truth* (Brisbane), 6 October 1940.
54 'Labor Gains: Govt. May Go', *Truth* (Brisbane), 22 September 1940.
55 Who Did Win the Election, Anyway?

to find he had lost his popularity in the electorate and support in his own cabinet. He was forced to resign in August with Treasurer and CP leader, Arthur Fadden, sworn in as the new prime minister.

The government could have survived the full term except, once again, a strange set of circumstances involving Arthur Coles cost the UAP a crucial seat. Despite winning Henty as an Independent, Coles became a passionate supporter of Menzies and announced in June that he had decided to formally join the UAP, giving the government a crucial 37-36 majority.[56] So disgusted was Coles with what he saw as a betrayal, he stormed out of the UAP meeting which chose 78 year old former prime minister Billy Hughes as its new leader, and declared he had quit the party.[57] Along with Wilson, he crossed the floor to declare no confidence in Fadden's first budget, effectively ending the government. Rather than forcing a new election, the two Independents promised the governor-general, Lord Gowrie, that they would support Labor for the remainder of the term. As a result, Curtin was sworn in as prime minister on 7 October. The unlikely war-time leadership of a man briefly imprisoned in 1916 for defying the call-up for military camp had begun.

Conclusion

The 1940 election took place under extraordinary circumstances. While it is common enough to have a single issue dominate an election, it is rare for the two major parties to agree on that issue. The war consumed everything and, despite some difference in defence policy, the UAP, CP and ALP were all committed to helping Britain and to victory. The fault lines of this debate were on how best to achieve

---

56   'Only One Independent Left', *West Australian*, 27 June 1941.
57   'Mr Menzies Resigns', *Sydney Morning Herald*, 29 August 1941.

a common goal. There was clearly a difference in emphasis and approach. While Menzies trumpeted his devotion to Churchill and the Empire, Curtin focused on pay and conditions for the troops, and how to make the transition most effectively to a post-war economy. Menzies' decision to spend those crucial early months of 1941 in Britain rather than Australia proved fatal to the government but not to the parliament, which managed to see a full term.

Australians in the first half-century of Federation still proudly identified as British. Following the defeat of Fadden's budget, the UAP's Sir George Ball jumped to his feet and accused the Labor Party of being 'anti-British'.[58] A more personal and insulting slur could barely be mustered. It caused an uproar in the House with both sides yelling until the comment was reluctantly withdrawn. Both sides of politics cherished the Deakinite mantle of 'Independent Australian Britons'.[59] The election represented a difference of degree rather than ideology. To what extent were Australians independent? Even if the policy of seeking assistance from the United States had been the same, Menzies never would have stated that Australia 'looks to America, free of any pangs as to our traditional links of kinship to the United Kingdom', as Curtin did in December 1941.[60] Indeed, he immediately criticised Curtin's choice of words as a 'great blunder'.[61] Yet, as Curran reminds us, this did not represent a great nationalist triumph. Two days later, Curtin clarified to the press that 'our loyalty to His Majesty the King goes to the very core of our national life'.[62]

---

58 'Labor Will Govern', *National Advocate* (Bathurst), 4 October 1941.
59 J.A. La Nauze, *Alfred Deakin: A Biography*, vol. 2 (Melbourne: Melbourne University Press, 1965), p.483.
60 'The Task Ahead', *Herald* (Melbourne), 27 December 1941.
61 Curran, *Curtin's Empire*, p.13.
62 Ibid., p.14.

Even in this damage control speech, however, he subtly reinforced Australia's independence by emphasising the nation was a Dominion rather than colony.

Although Churchill dramatically replaced Chamberlain as prime minister of the United Kingdom in 1940, as a general rule democracies are reluctant to switch leaders during a war or national crisis. The 1940 elections in the United States and Canada saw Roosevelt and William Lyon Mackenzie King safely returned. New Zealand postponed its scheduled election till 1943 but the incumbent Labour Party won convincingly. Despite internal tensions in the coalition and the UAP itself, every indicator was that Menzies would win and lead Australia for the entirety of World War II. Andrew Tink has suggested the Canberra Air Disaster was the 'plane crash that destroyed a government'.[63] While perhaps an exaggeration, his emphasis on the impact of that tragedy is understandable.

To the extent we can practice clairvoyance on an alternate history, had Gullett survived the doomed flight he almost certainly would have retained Henty and would have supported Menzies and the government. Curtin's wartime legacy is tied to his insistence that the 6th and 7th Divisions return to Australia despite strong pressure from Churchill to divert them to Burma. Would Menzies have done the same had he won the 1940 election with a majority? It is fair to presume with reasonable confidence that Menzies and the government, having campaigned in 1940 on how strongly they backed Churchill, would have followed the imperial policy and duly sent the troops to Burma. When he learned that Churchill had diverted the troops anyway, Curtin sent a defiant cable on 23 February 1942

---

63 Andrew Tink, 'Fatal Flight', *Sydney Morning Herald*, 23 March 2013 and *Air Disaster Canberra*.

and declared emphatically: 'We feel a primary obligation to save Australia'.[64] Geoffrey Serle has claimed: 'Never had the division between those backing supposed Imperial and Australian interests been so exposed; Curtin's decision was a landmark in Australian history'.[65]

Even if the nationalist school overplayed their hand, the mythology of Curtin is significant in and of itself. He died on 5 July 1945, just months before the Japanese surrender. Had the Canberra Air Disaster not claimed three key ministers, had the 1940 election not been pulled forward, had the UAP run a candidate in Henty, had 641 votes gone against him in Fremantle: Curtin's prime ministership might never have happened. The butterfly effect from this would have been enormous. The UAP would have been in power for over 13 years if Menzies had seen out the war as prime minister. Perhaps he would have retired satisfied rather than burning with ambition for a second term. Would it have been Labor that dominated Australian politics in the 1950s and 60s? Would the Liberal Party even exist? What we can say with certainty is that Australian political and cultural history would have been vastly different had the 1940 federal election not produced such a precarious result. It was most certainly an election that mattered.

---

64   Lloyd Ross, *John Curtin: A Biography* (Melbourne: Sun Books, 1977), p.262.
65   Geoffrey Serle, 'Curtin, John (1885–1945)', *Australian Dictionary of Biography*, vol. 13, (Melbourne: Melbourne University Press, 1993).

INTERIM 1940–1954

Following Curtin's dramatic and unlikely ascension to the prime ministership in 1941, Labor enjoyed its longest period in power. The conservative parties were in disarray after Wilson and Coles declared no confidence in Arthur Fadden's first budget and crossed the floor. By 1943 they were still seen as unstable and unready to rule. Despite being the senior partner in the coalition, the UAP's elderly leader, Billy Hughes, was considered an unsuitable wartime leader. As a result, Fadden, leader of the Country Party, was retained as opposition leader despite his short and unsuccessful tenure as prime minister. In contrast, John Curtin was a popular leader and, particularly after Japan entered the war in December 1941, Australians were not inclined to change horses.

The 1943 election was a Labor landslide. The two-party preferred margin of 58.2% remains the best result in ALP history. Labor also wrestled back control of the Senate for the first time in 22 years. The 1943 election was also significant for seeing the first women elected to federal parliament. Dorothy Tangney won a place in the Senate on the ALP's Western Australian ticket, and the UAP's Enid Lyons (widow of former prime minister Joseph Lyons) won the Tasmanian seat of Darwin in the House of Representatives. Just months before the Japanese surrender that concluded World War II, Curtin died in office in July 1945. He was temporarily replaced as prime minister by Frank Forde before Ben Chifley, the train driver from Bathurst, was elected leader of the Labor Party and prime minister.

ELECTIONS MATTER

Labor's long period in office continued under Chifley's leadership. Following the 1943 disaster Menzies regained control of the flailing UAP but it eventually dissolved with a new party emerging to unite the anti-Labor forces: the Liberal Party of Australia. Contesting the 1946 election, Menzies' new party performed reasonably well, securing a 12.6% increase in its primary vote compared to the UAP in 1943. Labor ceded ground but retained control of both houses. In a symbolic victory, the troublesome Coles lost his seat of Henty to the Liberals' Jo Gullett, whose father, Sir Henry, had held the seat before his death in the Canberra Air Disaster. The dyspeptic Jack Lang also entered the House, winning the seat of Reid from Labor's Charles Morgan. Chifley's post-war reconstruction schemes were generally popular but often ran into the obstacle of the constitution and his plan to nationalise the banks produced a strong anti-Labor mobilisation that greatly helped Menzies. Against a backdrop of Cold War politics and fear of communism, the Liberal Party won the election of 1949 though Labor retained control of the Senate.

1949 saw the beginning of Menzies' record breaking second term in office. The Liberals attempted to capitalise on a perception that Labor was soft on communism by introducing a bill to ban the Communist Party in 1950. If repeatedly blocked, it would have given Menzies a double dissolution trigger and an opportunity to win back the Senate while still enjoying general popularity. Labor anticipated this possibility and allowed the bill to pass, only for it to be struck down as unconstitutional by the High Court. Labor's resistance to Menzies' banking reform did provide a trigger for the second double dissolution election in Australian history (the first being in 1914). In 1951, it was certainly a gamble by the Liberals to go back to the polls just 16 months after winning government. But it was a gamble that paid off and the Liberals were comfortably returned, winning 69 of the now 121 seat House of Representatives, along with control of the Senate. Chifley suffered a heart attack and died less than two months later.

Former High Court Justice H.V. 'Doc' Evatt would take the leadership of the Labor Party. On 9 May 1953 there was a half-senate election which saw the ALP win ground despite the government retaining control. It served as a warm-up for the next federal election scheduled for the following year.

Chapter 5

1954

DID PETROV MATTER?

Bridget Brooklyn

Occurring well into the Cold War years, the 'Petrov' election of 1954 demonstrates, even more than most elections, the peril of hindsight. We tend to see its significance as arising out of the tumultuous circumstances surrounding the announcement of Prime Minister Menzies, on 13 April 1954 – just as Parliament was to rise for the election campaign – that the Third Secretary at the Soviet Embassy, Vladimir Petrov, had defected. But this Cold War script was not played to the gallery, due in part to Menzies' gag on Petrov talk during the campaign (albeit an order not universally observed). The greatest significance of the return of the Liberal-Country Party coalition on 29 May 1954 is not as an affirmation of repressive anti-communism, but as an example of the mundane expectations of Australians. Voters are revealed as wishing to tend the first green shoots of post-war recovery, rather than engage in an 'all-in' effort against the Red menace. In a year typified as quintessentially 'Cold War', the final result – a swing to the Australian Labor Party, but not sufficient to oust the coalition – illustrates the tendency of the electorate at this time to pull towards the centre, rather than decisively towards left or right. The 1954 election is a reminder of one of the things Australian voters commonly prize about their governments: the promise of stability in the midst of high drama.

When we consider the significance of certain elections in our political history, we must be wary of the dangers of applying that significance in retrospect. The 1954 federal election provides ample illustration: we tend to link it with the events that happened after it. The most explosive hearings of the Royal Commission on Espionage, and the disastrous ALP Split of 1955 – again over communism – have tended to overshadow the issues as they might have sat in the minds of voters at the time of the election on 29 May. There is also the fact that the Cold War ended, and the fact that 'we' won it – I use the scare quotes here because 'our' Cold War opened up bitter divisions in Australian society, as elsewhere. Many historians have analysed the ways in which the democratic freedoms prized by Menzies were sacrificed to red-under-the-bed hysteria during his long incumbency. For a long time some of these historians suspected that Menzies, demonstrating political malice aforethought *par excellence*, had engineered the Petrov defection. The declassification of key ASIO files in 1984, and a subsequent book by Robert Manne, saw the conspiracy theory off, but the circumstances surrounding the election still tends to point to 'our' victory against communism as nothing much to be proud of.

In May 1954, several factors prevented Petrov from becoming an election issue. First of all, it occurred too far into the election cycle for it to make a significant difference. The timing of Menzies' announcement, for so long shrouded in conspiracy theory, caught the leader of the opposition, Dr H.V. Evatt, off guard,[1] but it was not months in the making. Menzies sought not so much to implicate Evatt, but to generate heat at a time when the government's popularity was waning.[2] This was possibly due to the gloss having worn off the shiny new Liberal Party, whose coalition with the Country Party had unleashed a 'horror budget' in 1951 that raised taxes and duties in a number of key areas, including company tax, sales tax,

---

1   Robert Manne, *The Petrov Affair: Politics and Espionage* (Sydney: Pergamon, 1987), pp.73–76.
2   Ibid., p.93.

and alcohol and tobacco. However, the Labor Party, led by a man who was beginning to display the kind of intemperate behaviour and language that has hung over his legacy ever since, did not manage to convince the electorate to return to Labor, despite five less-than-perfect years under the coalition.

Petrov, the Coalition Victory and the Split: the Noes Have It

The customary issues of stability, certainty, and the hip pocket were more central to the election than communism. We must bear in mind that much surrounding the Petrov announcement, such as the appointment of a royal commission into espionage, had initial bipartisan support, and that the conflict that emerged around the commission hearings occurred some time after Menzies defeated Evatt. Did Menzies' Petrov revelations nevertheless significantly aid a coalition victory? Would Labor have been spared its Split if it had won that election? The answers are, to the first question, a firm 'no', and to the second, a more equivocal 'no'.

Let us examine the first 'no'. The Petrov revelations, and the subsequent allegations of conspiracy, made startling news, occupying headlines in Australia and around the world.[3] Hard on the heels of Menzies' announcement on 13 April, the Royal Commission on Espionage began sitting. Hearings opened on 17 May, well before the election. The most controversial hearings, however, occurred well after the election, when Evatt's sense of having had victory snatched from him by the Petrov revelations drove him to ever wilder accusations and constructions, leading him eventually to be excluded from

---

3   For example, 'Fears on Extent of Red Spying Here', *Adelaide Advertiser*, 15 April 1954; 'U.S. Keeps Watch on Australia's Atomic Security', *Courier-Mail* (Brisbane), 15 April 1954.

the hearings altogether. This was when the political damage to Evatt and his party was most comprehensively done. Any damage prior to the election was comparatively negligible, and outweighed by other, more mundane electoral concerns.

Conspiracy theories are their most enticing when they have a core of veracity. This could be said of the theory of Menzies engineering the timing of Petrov's impending defection. Even though he did not nurse his knowledge of the Petrov defection for as long as his enemies initially suspected, Menzies remains tainted with suspicion. The allegations of conspiracy have been disproved, but he was nevertheless capable of getting down into the gutter. But what was Menzies really capable of? Victory was important to him and to the Liberals, and the coalition's declining support since 1949 was a matter of concern. Although he did not orchestrate the defection, Menzies certainly orchestrated the announcement, delaying it until Evatt was away in Sydney – more, probably, to keep Evatt on the back foot than anything more insidious. This does not reveal Menzies in his best light.[4] But it could be argued that in the long game of politics, Menzies worked hard to present himself as a highly credible leader, and in this instance displayed the political *nous* that voters generally forgive when it is combined with the perception of strong leadership. The 1954 election, and the months leading up to the following one of 1955, stood him in good stead as a leader in contrast to Evatt's disordered, combative and often naive leadership style.[5]

In answer to the second question – whether the ALP would have warded off the Split if it had won the election – 'no' again because, as with the election loss itself, Petrov was a contributing complication

---

4   Manne, *The Petrov Affair*, p.73.
5   Ibid., p.264.

rather than a final blow to the party. While the ALP really began to fracture with the events of 1954, the cracks had begun to appear in the mid-1940s – and were then widened by Evatt's turbulent leadership. Much of this turbulence did surround the events of the Petrov defection and the following Royal Commission, but then Evatt already had a tendency to rush in where angels feared to tread. He would probably have opted for aggressive measures under any circumstances that involved disaffected members of the Catholic Right.

In the mid-1940s the ALP had endorsed the formation of Industrial Groups to combat Communist union leadership, but the increasingly strident interventions from 1949 by non-party-member B.A. Santamaria, and the influence of his Catholic Social Studies Movement on the Industrial Groups, strained the existing divisions between the left and right of the ALP.[6] Extreme polarities were forming, even without the Petrov element. Tensions within the party were compounded by the leadership of Evatt, whose unpopularity with the Catholic Right can be dated to 1951. In that year he appeared in the High Court to challenge legislation to ban the Communist Party – legislation that his own party had supported. The Catholic Right's hostility to Evatt, independent of the Petrov revelations, was manifest during the 1954 campaign when the ALP's W.M. Bourke broke party ranks to oppose Evatt's election promise to abolish the means test on the old age pension.[7] Despite all this, the vote could conceivably have gone to Labor, and therefore we must ask why it did not. The result was not one of the electorate singing loudly, and with one

---

6   Jenny Hocking, *Gough Whitlam, A Moment in History: The Biography*, vol.1 (Melbourne: Miegunyah Press, 2008), p.141.
7   Manne, *The Petrov Affair*, p.107.

voice, a paean to the coalition. Instead, endorsement of another coalition term could be described as comfortable but modest compared to 1949, when the coalition had won 50.26% of the vote, and 74 seats, against Labor's 45.98%, and 48 seats (effectively 47 as the Member for Northern Territory did not have full voting rights until 1968).

Hindsight has tended to harden the Menzies years into a solid block of conservative dominion, whereas the years immediately following 1949 were actually quite shaky for him. The 1951 double dissolution election, aimed at consolidating the coalition ascendancy, resulted in a curate's egg for the government: five seats lost in the lower house were to some degree offset by the securing of a 32:28 majority in the Senate.[8] Signs of discontent with the coalition were suggested in the Liberals' loss of government in Victoria and by-election losses in the seats of Flinders and Werriwa, all in 1952, and in the half-Senate election of 1953, which delivered 17 seats to the ALP and 15 to the coalition.[9] To cap it off, early 1953 had seen a big swing to Labor in the New South Wales state election, and a Labor victory in Western Australia.

The campaign was bitter. The result was close. The coalition won 49.3% of the two-party preferred vote against Labor's 50.7%, but achieved a workable majority of seven seats in the House of Representatives. In the aftermath, Evatt and his fellow travellers made much of this narrow margin, suggesting that Labor had been robbed.[10] This gripe cannot be sustained when the effect of the total

---

8 Ian Hancock, *National and Permanent? The Federal Organisation of the Liberal Party of Australia, 1944–1965* (Melbourne: Melbourne University Press, 2000), pp.132–33.

9 Colin A. Hughes and B.D. Graham, *A Handbook of Australian Government and Politics 1890–1964* (Canberra: ANU Press, 1968), pp.379-94, 492-3; Hancock, *National and Permanent?*, p.120.

10 See, for example, 'Aust. People Censured Government, Evatt Says', *Weekly Times* (Melbourne), 2 June 1954; 'Minority Menzies', *Tribune*, 2 June 1954; 'Labor in

of six uncontested coalition-held seats (Bradfield, Wentworth and Richmond in New South Wales, Mallee and Murray in Victoria, and Angas in South Australia) are calculated. Again, what is often represented now as an unbroken chain of successful Menzies victories, with 1949 ushering in an era of post-war conservatism, insularity and smugness, did not look that way to those turning up at their local polling place on 29 May 1954.

By the time of the coalition's low ebb in popularity in 1952, disaffected conservatives were naming economic issues, such as inflation, not communism, as a principal concern.[11] The fact that such potentially explosive material as the Petrov defection, followed by the dramatic, highly publicised defection of his wife Evdokia, did not immediately catch fire, is one indication that fear of communism was only one of a number of the electorate's anxieties. The austere years were still in recent memory; it is hard to imagine how they could not still play a part, as they had done in 1949. This was not so much an election that pitted the menace of the Soviet Union against 'the Australian way of life' as one that reflected the revived Liberals' consistent steering of a course between 'national planning' and the 'controlled economy' associated with Labor under Chifley.[12]

This is reflected in Menzies' conduct of the campaign. In terms of Cold War themes, the coalition campaign, at least for Menzies' part, avoided using Petrov to suggest any serious ALP-Soviet nexus. Menzies was astute enough to realise that over-egging the Petrov pudding would not be electorally successful. It was more persuasive

---

Majority says Evatt', *Worker,* 31 May 1954.

11   John Murphy, *Imagining the Fifties: Private Sentiment and Political Culture in Menzies' Australia* (Sydney: UNSW/Pluto Press, 2000), p.119.

12   Marian Simms, *A Liberal Nation: The Liberal Party & Australian Politics* (Sydney: Hale & Iremonger, 1982), p.24.

to emphasise the dead hand of socialist mediocrity, rather than any suggestion of Labor's supposed totalitarian intentions. To besmirch the opposition in this way might have alienated swinging voters who had chosen Labor at some point in the recent long and successful terms of two of Labor's – and indeed, the country's – heroes, John Curtin and Ben Chifley. It would also besmirch the memory of his own good relationships with these leaders.

The 1940s and 1950s were the decades of towering political personalities – Curtin, Chifley, now Menzies, and even Hughes and Evatt – though still with a sufficiently strong grounding in party politics not to be 'presidential.' But that was changing. By the time Evatt had become leader of the opposition in June 1951, the Liberal Party had become, in the words of Ian Hancock, 'a machine for re-electing the Menzies government.'[13] With Evatt at Labor's helm, the Liberal organisation thought that a battle over personalities, rather than implementing policy, might bring the electorate back. Of these two larger-than-life personalities it was Menzies who had more of the qualities suited to the Australian political scene. Although Evatt's real undoing lay ahead of him, his profligate campaign behaviour, discussed below, was already fitting him for classical tragedy.[14] Nevertheless, it was not a one-horse race. The support of the middle class, which has come to be identified so closely with Menzies' long incumbency, could not be counted on. Indeed, the period from 1952 to early 1954 was marked by disappointment among middle-class voters at the economic woes of the coalition – recession, the 'horror budget' and inflation.[15]

---

13 Hancock, *National and Permanent?*, p.120.
14 John Murphy, *Evatt: A Life* (Sydney: NewSouth Publishing, 2016), p.13; Allan Dalziel, *Evatt, the Enigma* (Melbourne: Lansdowne, 1967), p.16.
15 Ibid., pp.105, 121.

And for all his association with middle-class individualism, Menzies had to appeal to values that existed across the class divide. In post-Depression decades Liberal thinking embraced a modified form of Keynesianism rather than any *laissez-faire*-ism.[16] Even in his heartland of middle Australia, Menzies could not stand to gain by too savage an assault on 'consensus Keynesianism'. That said, the electorate was equally chary of governmental overreach, which had occurred with Chifley's failed attempt to nationalise the private banks. Apart from Labor's somewhat ambivalent 'socialisation objective', which had been part of its platform since 1921, there was Labor's patchy record in curbing the post-war militancy of the unions, some of which had Communist leadership.

A Matter of Degree

While Menzies was always careful not to accuse Evatt of actually *being* a Communist, the 'almost a fellow traveller' insinuations were put to greatest effect in tandem with the suggestion of too close an association with Communists. This could be combined with an attack on the Keynesianism of post-war Labor as creeping socialism, despite the fact that Menzies emphatically did not want to lead a party or a government that did not embrace Keynesianism, to some degree.[17]

Degree was all-important.[18] Some commitment to social spending was necessary, but had to remain consistent with the conservatives' belief in the effort of the individual. Hence, for instance, the modification – rather than abolition – of the means test for the pension, and a small increase in the level of income and the value

---

16 Simms, *A Liberal Nation*, pp.42-43.
17 Hancock, *National and Permanent?*, pp.61–3.
18 Simms, *A Liberal Nation*, p.49.

of property permissible to pension recipients.[19] By contrast, Evatt began his campaign by launching himself headlong into a series of extravagant and uncosted promises. The most notorious of these was his proposal to abolish the means test on the old age pension (to be renamed a 'retiring allowance' and increased, along with invalid pensions, from £3.10.0 to £4.0.0 a week). This was to be accompanied by an increase in permissible income from £2 a week to £6 a week, while removing property as a consideration in determining eligibility for the pension. He also pledged to increase widow and repatriation pensions (to be renamed 'war compensation'), while also lifting child endowment, putting universal health care insurance in place, raising the Commonwealth commitment to road building and instigating housing loans at 3%, repayable in 45 years. He offered cuts in the sales tax on household furniture and equipment.[20]

If social spending was a difference of degree rather than principle, the degree was very significant in this campaign. While Evatt laid the groundwork for his own defeat, Menzies could add another dimension by pointing to the ways Labor ran with the Communists in matters of industrial relations, jeopardising the 'industrial peace' delivered by the coalition:

> We ... brought down a Bill to provide effective Secret Ballots for union office, so that the rank and file of unionists could have a fair chance of throwing out Communist leaders.

---

19 Robert Menzies, 'Federal Election, 1954: Policy Speech of the Prime Minister (the Right Hon. R.G. Menzies, C.H., Q.C., M.P.,)' [abridged], delivered in the Canterbury Memorial Hall, Victoria, on May 4, 1954, *Museum of Australian Democracy*, Accessed online. <http://explore.moadoph.gov.au/trails/landmark-speeches#milestone=menzies-policy-speech-1954>

20 Herbert Evatt, '1954 Election Policy Speech', delivered at Hurstville, NSW, 6 May, 1954, *Museum of Australian Democracy*, Accessed online. <http://moadoph.gov.au/search?keywords=evatt+speech+1954>; Manne, *The Petrov Affair*, p.106–7.

The Labour Party fiercely opposed this democratic measure. So did the Communists.[21]

The rhetoric of individualism could also be used to foil the appeal of communism or socialism, which Menzies warned might be the result if Labor's planning became too zealous:

> We believe in the individual, in his freedom, in his ambition, in his dignity. If he becomes submerged in the mass, and loses his personal significance, we have tyranny. And because of this, we believe in free enterprise; not enterprise free of social obligation[.][22]

The appeals to individualism were restrained, not overplayed. Importantly, they were juxtaposed with frequent appeals to consensus values – democracy, social obligation. In this way, Menzies drew on the bipartisan legacy of values that found expression in two earlier signature political speeches: both his 'Forgotten People' radio broadcast and Chifley's 'Light on the Hill' conference speech have a point of similarity, despite their respective resonance with two different classes. They share an articulation of faith in the judgment and support of ordinary Australians.

'Kicking the Communist Can'

The election results do not suggest a country in the grip of Cold War panic. In 1950 Menzies had managed, with the eventual acquiescence of the Labor Party, to pass legislation to ban the Communist Party of Australia (CPA). This was overturned by the High Court, following

---

21 Menzies, 'Federal Election', pp.10–11.
22 Ibid., p.21.

a challenge mounted by a number of Communist-led unions. One of these, the Waterside Workers' Federation, was represented by Evatt – at that time sitting in opposition as the member for Barton. This move was regarded then, as now, as a serious error of political judgment that began (but by no means ended) with its suggestion of disloyalty to the ALP, which had supported the passage of the legislation. While Evatt may have opposed the ban, he was bound by the ALP pledge to support his party's position. Appearing in public in his alternative role as barrister muddied the political waters, creating further rancour that contributed to the ALP's 1955 Split.[23]

As well as taking part in the High Court challenge, Evatt was closely involved in Menzies' next big tilt at communism. In 1951 Menzies made another attempt at banning the CPA, this time by constitutional referendum. In a country where attempts to change the constitution in this way normally fail, this one went down only narrowly, in part due to Evatt's tireless campaign urging Australians to reject the proposal.

The result itself is odd – John Murphy refers to polling that demonstrates how the wish to ban the Communist Party showed a consistently high rate throughout the years 1947–52, that is, both before and after the referendum. So the result was anomalous; Australians' characteristic reluctance to vote 'Yes' in a referendum does not offer a complete explanation. Perhaps it was also the electorate's discomfort with the coalition's proposed policy of 'declaring' someone a Communist, thus putting the onus of proof of the opposite on the person so declared.[24] This complete reversal of the presumption of innocence aroused much opposition, even among Liberals, and may also have

---

23 Mark Aarons, *The Family File* (Melbourne: Black Inc., 2010), p.142.
24 Murphy, *Imagining the Fifties*, p.103.

stuck in the electorate's craw. Even so, Evatt's guilt by association with communists hung around him like a miasma in the nostrils of his party's Catholic Right faction.

For the coalition, 'bread and butter' issues, another source of anxiety during the economically unstable first half of the 1950s,[25] meant crafting a winning formula of new promises coupled with reminders to the electorate of its record on social services – just in case voters were in danger of thinking that Labor was the only party that could deliver on these things. Apart from liberalising the pension means test, a rise in the old age pension from £2/2/6 to £3/10/0 per week and a doubling of the unemployment benefit were among the achievements listed in Menzies' policy speech.[26] In a political atmosphere where acceptance of the need for a social safety net was held on both sides of politics, the use of rhetoric could provide a shorthand for making fine distinctions. Simms and Tsokhas note how, in the early 1950s, Menzies' use of the word 'socialism' could refer back to Chifley's attempt to nationalise the banks, and to 'cleaning up socialistic experiments'.[27] From this a distinction between Labor standing for too much government intervention on the one hand, and the promise of individual freedom on the other, could also be implied. The term 'socialism' did not have to be minutely parsed in order to pit governmental overreach against a 'commonsense' commitment to moderate Keynesian remedies on the other.

While Menzies tended to focus on Evatt's domestic policies as socialistic, rather than relying too heavily on 'kicking the communist can', he was not entirely successful in enjoining all of the coalition to

---

25   Ibid., p.105.
26   Menzies, 'Federal Election', p.17.
27   Marian Simms and Kosmas Tsokhas, 'Ideology, Rhetoric and Liberal Party Policies on Public Enterprises', *Politics*, 14:2, 1979, p.257.

refrain from mentioning Petrov during the campaign. The gag was ignored by Sir Eric Harrison when he spoke in support of a young and ambitious parliamentarian named Malcolm Fraser.[28] Menzies' coalition partner, Country Party leader Sir Arthur Fadden, was even less shy, repeatedly making Petrov a main theme and referring to Evatt's 'association with Communistic fellow travellers'.[29] But this did not necessarily do the coalition any favours, with the press on both sides of the political fence noting that it reflected poorly on Fadden.[30]

The idea of Cold War panic can seem rather quaint to us now: the times are routinely summed up by images of falling dominoes jostling with those of wasp-waisted housewives in ecstasy over their kitchen appliances. So it can be difficult to place ourselves in the position of those, like members of the Liberal Party, who saw combating the threat of socialism and communism as urgent.[31] Given what Murphy describes as the 'fragility' of Menzies' middle-class support, however, it was necessary for him to keep his appeal broad.[32] Fear of communism was found across the population, so its face could be drawn in a number of different ways. The decade of the 1950s is easily lampooned, but not so easily categorised. Historians of everything from sex to multiculturalism point to the importance of that decade as laying the groundwork for the perceived social revolutions of the 1960s and 1970s.[33] Even though vague ideas about the Australian

---

28 Manne, *The Petrov Affair*, p.102.
29 'Menzies; 'Evatt "A Risk" – Fadden. Action against Reds', *Courier-Mail* (Brisbane), 6 May 1954.
30 Manne, *The Petrov Affair*, p.102.
31 See, for example, Hancock, *National and Permanent?*, pp.37, 67, 112, 118.
32 Murphy, *Imagining the Fifties*, p.126.
33 For example, Frank Bongiorno, *The Sex Lives of Australians: A History* (Melbourne: Black Inc., 2012), pp.205; 221–2; Tim Rowse, 'The Post-War Social Science of Assimilation 1947–1966', in Tim Rowse (ed) *Contesting Assimilation*, (Perth: API Network, 2005), pp.151–68.

'way of life' were characteristic of Australian mid-century conservatism, the sense of threat to this way of life was generally vague and unspecific. As Richard White has shown, Australians were subject to a sense of threat from a number of quarters, not just communism.[34]

Kicking the Keynesian Can

Instead of communism, then, the principal fear generated was that in which Labor was presented as 'the horrible alternative' – horrible for a number of reasons other than communism. One plank of the campaign was to depict Evatt as willing to compromise with Communists, as we have seen. The second plank was a fear campaign about the economy.[35] The 'bogey' was not so much rampant communism as rampant Keynesianism. For all Menzies' tentative embrace of Keynesian principles, his campaign strategy was to target Evatt's proposed spending, describing it for example as 'the deadliest attack on the stability of Australia', accusing Evatt of buying votes with promises of irresponsible expenditure, and accusing him of not releasing his policy costs.[36] This was juxtaposed with the perennial hip-pocket enticements to be expected if the coalition were returned.

With the campaign showing signs of a 'presidential' race, voter perception of the leader was particularly important. As we have seen, Evatt's campaign promises did quite a bit of Menzies' work for him. The printed booklet of Menzies' policy speech, with his own promise,

---

34 Richard White, 'The Australian Way of Life', *[Australian] Historical Studies*, 18:73, October 1979, pp.536–38.
35 Hancock, *National and Permanent?*, pp.145-46.
36 'Menzies at Maitland: "'Deadly" Labor Policy', *Newcastle Sun*, 11 May 1954; 'Menzies Says Evatt's Policy "Peurile"', *Illawarra Daily Mercury*, 8 May 1954; 'P.M. Challenges Dr. Evatt Again: Asks Estimate of Cost of Labor Promises,' *Age*, 15 May 1954, p.3.

'Vote for the Menzies Government and Prosperity on May 29', offered both strong leadership and the promise of wealth in one succinct line.[37] The final result was not an overwhelming indictment of Evatt's perceived closeness to communism, or an indication of a general smug conservatism, but possibly a cautious embrace of the individualism that was one of Menzies' trademarks. It was all the more attractive for being wrapped in a reassuring blanket of modest Keynesian public spending, as distinct from the lavish promises made by Evatt.[38]

What If?

Sydney *Sun-Herald*, 16 May, 1954.

Given the swing to Labor, what could have happened if Labor had won? The two main questions around a possible Evatt prime ministership are, first, what the consequences would have been for the Petrov Royal Commission and, second, whether the party would have gone through its damaging Split of 1955. Without the Split, a key component of the long coalition ascendancy – the sundering of the anti-coalition vote between the ALP and the Democratic Labor Party (DLP) – may well have meant no Ming Dynasty, no conservative ascendancy, no protracted wilderness years for Labor.

But before we tumble too far down the rabbit-hole of hypotheticals, let us pull ourselves back to just one: our imaginary Labor

---

37 Menzies, 'Policy Speech'.
38 'Victorians Did Not Want Evatt', *Telegraph* (Brisbane), 5 June 1954; 'Menzies Reviews Election: "Sound Progress" Preferred', *Sydney Morning Herald*, 1 June 1954; 'Evatt Bids Fail', *Launceston Examiner*, 31 May 1954.

government elected in 1954, which would have inherited a Royal Commission on Espionage in full swing. Perhaps Evatt could have contained the damage by not making his other very bad political decision – to appear before the Commission on behalf of members of his staff implicated in the Petrov documents. Yet, it seems unlikely that prime ministerial office would have prevented him from doing what he strongly believed was the right thing to do. Of course, the sense of persecution would have been diminished if he had succeeded in becoming prime minister, but as we have seen, even a calmer series of Royal Commission hearings is unlikely to have poured sufficient oil over Labor's very troubled waters – a showdown between Evatt and his opponents on the Right seems to have been inevitable.

Division, namely the friction between the anti-Communist Catholic right wing and the rest of the party, was the 'sleeper' within the Labor Party that would have awoken regardless of the election outcome in 1954. In the case of both the real electoral defeat and the imaginary victory, Evatt's own tendency toward tackling his opponents head-on, without thought of the long-term political fallout, was an unfortunate aggravation of the long-simmering grievances within the party. The gauntlet thrown down to the Groupers in his 5 October 1954 statement alleging disloyalty, particularly in the Victorian Branch of the ALP, was one such gesture. While both his election defeat and the Petrov Royal Commission were key factors in Evatt's perception of a Movement plot against him in 1955,[39] there remains the fact that Catholic Right opposition to Evatt had been mounting since he had defended the Communist Party in the High Court in 1951. Bill Bourke's open disloyalty in the face of Evatt's

---

39   Robert Murray, *The Split: Australian Labor in the Fifties* (Melbourne: Cheshire, 1970), p.183.

1954 election plan to abolish the means test shows how far opposition to Evatt as leader could go.

This division within the Labor Party at the time can legitimately be described as a Cold War, and even a Petrov issue. But it is less of a Cold War matter than a more broadly ideological one. In the 1940s, the divide in the Labor Party between those who saw the battle against communism as the most pressing issue of the age – that is, a large proportion of its Catholic membership – and those who did not, made it unlikely that these factions would ever have resolved their differences. It was not just communism. Another sleeper was the long-standing wish of conservative Catholics, often alienated by the Liberals' overriding Protestantism, to have somewhere else to go.[40] With the Split leading to the formation of the DLP, now they did.

The 1954 election results suggest that Cold War fears loomed less overwhelmingly as an election issue to those living through the time than is often assumed. Our retrospective emphasis on Cold War anxieties invites the conclusion that the electorate was engaged in a trade-off of civil liberty for material wealth. It is unlikely, however, that voters of the time saw the choice so starkly, or that the Petrov revelations alone signified that Labor could not be trusted with national security. Fears of communism engaged some of the people some of the time; for the rest, the choice to stick with the coalition occurred at the level of everyday expectations and concerns. The close election result suggests instead that a general faith in what *either* side had to offer in terms of both prosperity and national security was fairly high, but that the coalition under Menzies offered more of what they wanted, and more realistically.

---

40   Hancock, *National and Permanent?*, pp.41-42.

Rather than a narrowly 'Cold War' or 'Petrov' election, the 1954 coalition victory represents the coming together of domestic concerns and increasing Labor disunity, combined with the ascendancy of a new political force. This election should be noted as one that separated the torrid drama of these Cold War events from the kitchen-sink drama of the Labor Party, which was to run for many years. As Manne has observed, it was 1955, not 1954, that sealed the ALP's fate and Menzies' ascendancy. In the face of, first, the beginnings of the Split in October 1954 and, second, Evatt's embarrassing revelation to parliament that he had written to the Soviet foreign minister, Vyacheslav Molotov, to ask whether the documents that Petrov had taken from the Soviet Embassy and given to Australian authorities were genuine, Menzies' 1955 election victory was the one that put the uncertainties of the early years behind him.[41]

Australian democracy – unique and far more vibrant than it is normally given credit for – nevertheless has a tendency toward conservatism in the literal meaning of the word. In 1954, this conservatism included the habit of opting for the *status quo* rather than for drastic measures when it came to weeding out Communists. What matters about the 1954 election is its demonstration that Australian political decisions are not made *in extremis*, but more with regard to the material comforts and sense of stability that consistently appeal to the Australian voter. These were things that Menzies – much more than the febrile Evatt and his increasingly troubled party – could offer.

---

41   Manne, *The Petrov Affair*, p.264.

INTERIM 1954–1969

Australians went to the polls again just eighteen months later, on 10 December 1955. Doubtless the early election was called, at least partly, to take advantage of the Labor Party Split that saw the emergence of a separate Anti-Communist Labor Party (ACL). ACL candidates ran against Labor in South Australia and Tasmania but were most damaging in Victoria where the ALP's House of Representatives vote dropped by 13.2%. The ACL's primary vote of 5.1% was enough to win a Senate spot in Victoria and to devastate the ALP's election prospects. At least in part, the Split helped secure the safe return of the Liberals with an increased majority of 75 to Labor's 47.

The impact of the ALP Split was arguably not felt in full until the election of 22 November 1958, where the Liberals again increased their dominance by claiming 77 of 122 lower house seats (a post-war record majority of 32). The ACL rebranded as the Democratic Labor Party (DLP) in 1957 and, despite Evatt offering to resign as leader if they returned to the ALP fold, they determined to contest seats in all states at the next federal election. The DLP increased its primary vote in the lower house to 9.4%, more than the Country Party (at 9.3%). In the Senate, they secured a second seat, this time from Tasmania. DLP preferences to the conservative coalition helped ensure the government was returned.

Evatt's long and tumultuous tenure as ALP leader came to an end in 1960 when he was appointed Chief Justice of the Supreme Court of New South Wales. He was replaced by Arthur Calwell, with Gough Whitlam serving as his deputy. The new team very nearly secured victory at their first attempt in December 1961. With widespread dissatisfaction with Menzies' deflationary economic policies and the backdrop of a credit squeeze, the ALP won the two-party preferred poll with 50.5% and equalled the coalition with 62 seats in the lower house. Unfortunately for Labor, the seats for the Northern Territory and Australian Capital Territory did not carry full voting rights, so the coalition maintained a threadbare two seat majority. Again, DLP preferences helped ensure the Liberals remained in power.

Calwell hoped to build on his gains but was frustrated at the 1963 House of Representatives election and 1964 Senate election. Despite the DLP steadily losing ground, the government was able to capitalise on a perception that Labor was secretly ruled by hidden factions. In 1962 Menzies announced that the United States would open a naval communications base in Western Australia at North West Cape. Labor was split on the issue, with its left faction committed to nuclear-free waters and opposed to any foreign military presence. Calwell took the issue to the party executive which in turn called for a conference. A photograph in Sydney's *Daily Telegraph* of Calwell and Whitlam apparently waiting for their orders from the Federal Labor Conference in Canberra led the political journalist, Alan Reid, to claim that the ALP was governed by 36 'virtually unknown men'. Menzies seized on this and claimed the party was ruled by 'faceless men', an accusation which has haunted federal Labor since.

Menzies called time on his record-breaking run as prime minister in January 1966 having served in the role for over 18 years in his two spells. It was perfect timing for the Liberal Party, as the new leader, Harold Holt, was younger and more informal and contemporary in his manner, better suiting the image of Australia in the mid-1960s. The Vietnam War came to dominate Australian politics. Calwell was a passionate opponent of Australia's involvement, especially the use of 'our voteless, conscripted 20 year olds'. Holt, by contrast, significantly increased Australia's role in the conflict before calling an election for 26 November 1966. With public support still largely behind the war effort, Holt secured a still-standing record two-party preferred vote of 56.9%. This translated to a new post-war record majority of 40 seats in the House of Representatives (82 of 124). Humiliated by the result, Calwell retired the following January. His younger deputy Gough Whitlam, defeated Jim Cairns and others to assume leadership of the ALP.

Chapter 6

1969

'OUR POLITICS ARE NO LONGER FROZEN'

Richard Reid

Gough Whitlam was the giant of Australian politics from the late 1960s to the mid-1970s. The Labor Party's 'It's Time' campaign in 1972 ended a coalition government which had held office since 1949. The change in Australian public policy his election wrought, and the circumstances of his dismissal, have cast a shadow over the period preceding the short-lived Whitlam ascendancy. But Whitlam's victory built on many years of hard work as opposition leader, and 1972 was not his first general election as Labor leader. In 1969 he first sought to take office from an ageing coalition government. It was not time in 1969 for Whitlam, but rather for John Gorton – if only just. Labor's failure to displace the coalition at this election, during a period when the long post-war boom continued and government revenues remained buoyant, had powerful consequences for the Labor government that did come to power at the end of 1972 facing a very different economic environment, one much less favourable to the achievement of its program.

Why the 1969 election? Surely a book on nation-shaping elections would be better served by looking at Whitlam's iconic 'It's Time' victory in 1972, or even the emphatic coalition win under Harold Holt in 1966. In comparison 1969 – although containing one of the largest swings against a government in Australian federal political history – seems rather less important as a defining Australian election. This chapter demonstrates that even an election that sees the return of a long-serving government can be an important moment in Australian history: elections which seem to stall history rather than make it can really matter.

The title of this chapter is taken from the political scientist Alan Hughes' assessment of Australian politics in the months following the 1969 election. He concluded not only that 'our politics are no longer frozen', but that, with Whitlam, 'the thaw has arrived'. His was an astute judgment: this is why the 1969 election is important. For some, of course, the thaw was less thorough than expected. David Williamson dramatised this disappointment in his 1971 play *Don's Party*, in which a group of friends and acquaintances come together at Don's suburban home for an election-night party. Williamson's work of this era captured a society undergoing a rapid, if sometimes troubled, transition, and *Don's Party* was no exception. The election and the disappointment of many of Don's circle, provide the backdrop to a party that degenerates into emotional carnage – a feeling no doubt shared by many a Labor supporter on 25 October 1969.

The 1969 election demonstrated that huge majorities can disappear in an instant and that change might not be as far away as it seems. Now, of course, it can be argued that 1969 was proof that change cannot always be delivered in one election when the government has a large buffer from its previous victory. But this conclusion underplays the enormity of what the ALP achieved in 1969. This was no ordinary governing majority that Labor faced. In 1966 – the so-called Vietnam election – the coalition had won two to every one ALP seat. Yet in 1969 Labor almost destroyed the coalition's governing majority, and in so doing fatally wounded John Gorton's prime ministership. His Liberal Party colleague, Malcolm Fraser, and the party room would deliver the final blow in 1971, replacing him with William McMahon. Whitlam and Labor reaped the rewards in 1972.

John Gorton had been elected leader of the Liberal Party following the presumed death by drowning of Harold Holt in December 1967, and was formally sworn in as prime minister on 10 January 1968. Gorton's background was a mixture of privilege and hardship as a student at Sydney Church of England Grammar, Geelong Grammar and Oxford University; a World War II pilot involved in serious crashes that permanently damaged his face; and an orchardist in country Victoria. He had been a member of the Country Party before being elected to the Senate in 1949 as a Liberal and, without ever becoming a star, he steadily increased his reputation as a competent minister in the governments of Robert Menzies and Harold Holt, holding a series of portfolios that included the navy, works, interior, and education and science. He eventually led the government in the Senate. His selection as prime minister was the result of intra-coalition conflict between the Country Party leader, John 'Black Jack' McEwen, and the Liberal Party deputy leader and federal treasurer, William McMahon. McEwen had refused to serve under McMahon if he were elected as leader; the veto was announced on 20 December 1967. Gorton's biographer, Ian Hancock, has downplayed the importance of the veto, arguing that '[i]t was almost inconceivable in early 1968 that the federal parliamentary Liberal Party would elect as leader someone who was despised and distrusted by so many of its members, especially when there were other very acceptable candidates on offer'.[1] Yet whether or not the veto was crucial in 1968,

---

1   Ian Hancock, *John Gorton: He Did it His Way* (Sydney: Hodder, 2002), p.145.

it certainly stopped McMahon from nominating for the position of leader and left Gorton to defeat Paul Hasluck, Billy Snedden and Les Bury. Following his victory Gorton gave up his seat in the Senate and was elected to the House of Representatives in Holt's former seat of Higgins.

The dramatic turn of events that occurred over Christmas 1967 provide one of those important 'what ifs' of Australian politics. Would Harold Holt, if he had not drowned, have been able to modernise the government and extend its almost two decades of power into the 1970s? Would McMahon have won the leadership after Holt's death if it were not for the McEwen veto and, if so, how would McMahon have fared in the 1969 election against Whitlam? McMahon might have been widely distrusted, but Gorton turned out an erratic and scandal-prone leader whose performance, in the face of a resurgent Labor opposition, did his government few favours.

A Rising Star

Gough Whitlam was elected as deputy leader of the ALP in 1960. Like Gorton, he had served in the RAAF in the Second World War – as a navigator – and he had been a Sydney barrister prior to entering the House of Representatives in 1952. He was a generation younger than the existing leadership of the party. By the mid-1960s Whitlam was seen to be undermining the leadership of the party by Arthur Calwell; conflict that degenerated into what two scholars have called 'open warfare'.[2] After Labor's devastating defeat in 1966, Calwell's leadership was unsalvageable: 'The 1966 election campaign brought to a head the bitterness developing between Calwell and his deputy

---

2 Fredrik Bynander and Paul 't Hart, 'The Politics of Party Leader Survival and Succession: Australia in Comparative Perspective', *Australian Journal of Political Science*, 42:1, 2007, p.63.

leader'.³ Although Calwell's subsequent resignation was 'voluntary', he knew that after a third consecutive defeat at the polls, his time was up.⁴

Whitlam was elected ALP leader on 8 February 1967, inheriting a party in 'shambles', 'particularly in Victoria'.⁵ It was in that state that the split of 1955 had carried with it the most far-reaching consequences. The Victorian Labor government of John Cain – the first majority Labor government in the state's history – had fallen and it would not have a Labor successor until his son, also John Cain, won the 1982 election. In federal politics after 1954, Victorian Labor candidates suffered from preference flows to the coalition from the breakaway anti-communist Democratic Labor Party which in Victoria was capable of gathering as much as 15% of the vote at elections, mainly from Catholic voters alienated from the ALP. The split had left in its wake much rancour but also a Victorian Labor Party branch dominated by a left-wing union oligarchy. Not only did the party branch consistently under-perform at federal elections, under the stewardship of party secretary Bill Hartley from the mid-1960s it became increasingly doctrinaire and authoritarian. While Whitlam had a small and beleaguered group of allies in the Victorian branch, that branch's ruling group hated this man whom 'many commentators heralded ... as a non-doctrinaire moderniser who would rein in left-wing extremists, and make the party once again electable'.⁶ At

---

3   Colm Kiernan, *Calwell: A Personal and Political Biography* (Melbourne: Thomas Nelson, 1978), p.260.
4   Bynander and 't Hart, 'The Politics of Party', p.63.
5   Race Mathews, 'Whitlam Re-visited: A Personal Memoir', in Hugh Emy, Owen Hughes and Race Mathews (eds), *Whitlam Re-Visited: Policy Development, Policies and Outcomes* (Sydney: Pluto Press, 1993), p.11.
6   Ashley Lavelle, 'Labor and Vietnam: A Reappraisal', *Labour History*, 90, 2006, p.122.

the June 1967 Victorian State ALP conference, amid some booing and jeering, Whitlam had taunted the Victorian comrades for reveling in their ideological purity: 'Certainly, the impotent are pure'.[7]

Whitlam led the ALP in the half-Senate election on 25 November 1967. The election, while not yielding any gains, saw Whitlam prevent any further losses in the wake of the disastrous 1966 House of Representatives election. Whitlam's relationship with his party was tense from the beginning, with the issue of state aid (government funding) to non-government schools – which Whitlam favoured – proving especially contentious. The conflict came to a head in April 1968. At a federal executive meeting Whitlam was repeatedly defeated, leaving him, as the *Canberra Times* reported, 'humiliated'. In an attempt to reassert his position as leader, Whitlam announced that he would resign and seek re-election. On 30 April, he narrowly defeated the Victorian left-wing MP Jim Cairns by 38 votes to 32.[8]

The government had its own problems. The Freeth statement was one of several pre-election trials for the government. Gordon Freeth, who had taken over from Paul Hasluck as minister for external affairs when the latter was appointed governor-general, had made a statement in the House of Representatives playing down the dangers of a Soviet presence in the Indian Ocean.[9] The *Canberra Times* judged correctly that Freeth's 'relaxed response to the growing Russian interest in South-east Asia and his moderate statement on the problem of Communist China were a departure from the traditional approach

---

7   Gough Whitlam, in Troy Bramston (ed.), *For the True Believers: Great Labor Speeches that Shaped History* (Sydney: Federation Press, 2012), pp.226-7.
8   See Mike Powell, 'The Whitlam Labor Government: Barnard and Whitlam: A Significant Historical Dyad', *Australian Journal of Politics and History*, 43:2, 1997, pp.183-199.
9   Alan Hughes, 'Political Review', *Australian Quarterly*, 41:4, 1969, pp.15-25, 20.

of his predecessors'.[10] But the statement aroused Cold War passions: Freeth later conceded that he had put it 'in too normal and diplomatic terms'.[11] The DLP was particularly upset about the government's apparent departure from anti-Communist foreign policy orthodoxy, in an area seen as the coalition's greatest strength over Labor.[12] Freeth went on to lose his seat to the ALP in the 1969 election, a seat he had held since 1949. His defeat was widely understood to have resulted from the dose of realism he had bravely – or foolishly – offered on the new realities of international politics, as the United States faltered in Vietnam.

The 1969 Campaign

The four party leaders, Whitlam, Gorton, McEwen (Country Party) and Vince Gair (DLP), each made policy speeches for their parties that began the 'official' campaign. But in practice the 1969 election campaign was a very long one since, as the political scientist Don Aitkin remarked, they had all 'begun to campaign during the parliamentary recess before the Budget, and that session was more a continuation of the campaign than a break in it'.[13] He continued:

> In terms of their contribution to the total outcome, the style of the policy speeches may have been as important as their content. Mr. Whitlam's speech was delivered to an enthusiastic public audience in Sydney's Town Hall, and was one of the Leader of the Opposition's best performances, confident, well timed, and even witty. The prime minister's campaign opening, on the other hand, was almost a caricature of what such an occasion

---

10 'Govt warms to Russian moves', *Canberra Times*, 15 August 1969.
11 Ibid.
12 See Hughes, 'Political Review', pp.19-20.
13 Don Aitkin, 'The 1969 Federal Election', *Politics*, 5:1, 1970, pp.45-53, 47.

should be. He spoke slowly and seriously to a small hand-picked audience which included in its front row his wife, Mr. McEwen and Mr. McMahon.[14]

When Gorton made his policy speech on Wednesday 8 October 1969 he recalled Australia's turn to the coalition nearly 20 years before, a choice, he argued, which was a reaction against the controlling socialist (and Communist-influenced) Labor governments. It was perhaps not the best way to position his party for the 1970s. But Gorton went on to speak of his record as prime minister over the previous 20 months, saying that he was 'proud that we have achieved what we have'.[15] He then outlined his plans for government, covering the areas of defence, Vietnam, Malaysia-Singapore, taxation reform, national development, education, social welfare, health, housing, immigration, the arts, trade, primary industry and shipping and transport. Very revealing was the absence of any discussion of Indigenous policy from the speech, considering that this was the first House of Representatives election since the Commonwealth gained more power over Aboriginal policy as the result of the 1967 referendum, and Gorton was himself Aboriginal affairs minister.[16]

Gorton was an Australian nationalist, but he also made clear the coalition's continued support of the United States' position on Vietnam:

---

14 Aitkin, 'The 1969 Federal Election', p.47.
15 John Gorton, *Federal Election Policy Speech*, 8 October 1969, p.4.
16 Indigenous policy was included in the printed pamphlet. Whilst this speaks to the increasing role for the federal government in Indigenous policy following the 1967 referendum, it demonstrates the still peripheral treatment it received. For more on this history see Will Sanders, 'Changing Agendas in Australian Indigenous Policy: Federalism, Competing Principles and Generational Dynamics', *Australian Journal of Public Administration*, 72:2, 2013, pp.156-170.

> Should there be developments which result in plans for continuing reduction of United States forces over a period then we would expect to be phased in to that programme and would see that we are. But we will not unilaterally withdraw. To do so would be to abandon an objective, to betray our allies, and, I believe, to imperil our future security.[17]

In contrast, the ALP pledged to end conscription and withdraw Australian forces. But the shadow of the 1966 humiliation loomed: Whitlam pointedly focused his campaign on issues other than Vietnam.[18] Hughes argued that the Labor Party won 'hands down' on domestic issues but that foreign policy remained 'the sticking point for many a marginal voter, and probably cost Mr. Whitlam the office of Prime Minister. Mr. Gorton discovered in himself and his party an almost complete kit of D.L.P. attitudes'.[19] The real importance of Vietnam in the 1969 election was its likely effect on DLP preferences, especially in the wake of the controversy over the Freeth statement which, as Hughes suggested, induced additional caution on the part of the coalition. These preferences were decisive in the final result, especially in Victoria, the DLP's heartland and a continuing source of ALP difficulty and disappointment.

Results

The Liberal Party won 46 seats and the Country Party 20, giving the government 66 seats out of 125 in the House of Representatives. The

---

17　Gorton, *Federal Election Policy Speech*, p.8.
18　Keith Moore, 'The Vietnam War and Youthful Protest during the 1960s – Challenging the Myth', in Chanel Hopkinson and Carly Hall (eds), *Social Change in the 21st Century Conference*, 2006, p.7.
19　Hughes, 'Political Review', p.23.

Labor Party won 59 seats, 4 short of victory, leaving the government with a majority of 7. There were two Independents in the parliament prior to the election. Sam Benson was a Labor renegade who was expelled from the party over its Vietnam policy. He retained the Melbourne seat of Batman as an Independent in 1966 but retired before the 1969 election. Horrie Garrick regained the seat for the ALP. Edward St John had won the Sydney seat of Warringah as a Liberal in 1966 but quit the party towards the end of his term to sit as an Independent. Michael MacKellar comfortably regained the seat for the Liberals in 1969.

The Whitlam-led Labor Party made tremendous gains in the 1969 election. It increased its primary vote by seven percentage points, whereas the coalition primary vote fell by 6.5. The ALP's gain of 18 seats saw it achieve the largest proportion of the seats held by the Labor Party in the House of Representatives since the 1961 election. More than reversing its losses in 1966, the Labor Party was now reconfirmed as a viable contender for government, and a rejuvenated opposition. The swing was not the result of the youth vote, although at a time when the voting age was still twenty-one, 1969 was really the first general election at which a significant number of post-war baby-boomers voted. But contemporary commentary pointed out that 'all age groups swung equally to Labor'.[20]

In large part, the Labor defeat was the result of DLP preferences. The political scientist L.F. Crisp concluded that there could be 'no doubt that D.L.P. preferences alone clinched sufficient majorities for government candidates in 1969 to keep the Liberal-Country Party coalition alive', a view endorsed by the psephologist Malcolm Mack-

---

20   Ibid., p.17.

erras and senior coalition MP David Fairbairn.[21] Political scientists had already begun to question the future viability of the DLP. Crisp, after the 1969 election but prior to the 1970 half-Senate election, argued that the 1969 results 'should be read against the apparent evidence that the D.L.P. is running out of issues'. Crisp nominated the resolution of state aid of non-government schools – and especially the Catholic system, dear to DLP hearts – as one of these issues, as well as the declining domestic salience of the Vietnam War.[22] But Crisp under-estimated the DLP, which went on to pick up an extra seat in the 1970 half-Senate election, taking its total to five senators, and he also paid too little attention to the Victorian Labor Party, which continued to bicker over state aid, to its cost in the 1970 state election. But in the longer term, his comments about the DLP 'running out of issues' were vindicated, with that party losing all of its seats at the 1974 double dissolution election.

All that, however, was well into the future. The 1969 election was for the House of Representatives only, but there were two casual vacancies filled for the Senate. In these, the Liberal Party successfully defended its seat in Victoria, but the Labor Party won a seat from the Liberals in South Australia.[23] This gain in South Australia gave the ALP more senators than the coalition, with 28 to 27, but the DLP still held the balance of power with four seats (and there was one Independent senator – Reg Turnbull).

---

21 L.F. Crisp, 'The D.L.P. Vote 1958-1969 – And After', *Politics*, 5:1, 1970, pp.62-66, 62; Malcolm Mackerras, 'Another Second Preference Government', *Australian Quarterly*, 41:4, 1969, pp.26-32; David Fairbairn, quoted in B.A. Santamaria, 'Struggle on Two Fronts: The D.L.P. and the 1969 Election', *Australian Quarterly*, 41:4, 1969, p.33.
22 Crisp, 'The D.L.P. Vote', p.66.
23 Hughes, 'Political Review', p.16.

Most subsequent commentary assumes that Whitlam's dynamic leadership was critical to the revival of the Labor Party's fortunes in the late 1960s, but his role in the gains made by the ALP in 1969 has been under-examined. It is of course difficult, in the absence of survey data, to know with any certainty the factors that produced the swing. Most attention has been focused on the government losing seats rather than Labor gaining them. This lack of attention is in contrast to Whitlam's dominant personal presence in 1972, but it seems clear that Whitlam's growing political authority and public presence also played a role in the 1969 swing that put Labor within touching distance of the government benches they had vacated two decades earlier.

Still, there were more complex reasons for the large swing to Labor in 1969 than Whitlam's formidable campaigning skills. On the basis of opinion polling, Hughes concluded that the 'Labor position was established *before* the campaign, and merely *sustained* in its duration'.[24] He saw four factors at play: 'the steep decline in the popular estimation of the prime minister; the damage done to the Government's reputation by its ill-advised statement on the growth of Russian power in the Indian Ocean area [the Freeth statement]; the long-standing popularity of Labor's domestic policies, and the new mood on the Vietnamese war; and the early preparation of the public for the Labor campaign'.[25] Mackerras boiled it down to three contributors, two in common with Hughes: the personal performance of John Gorton, and the 'deterioration in public support for the Vietnam commitment'.[26] His third explanatory factor was state aid,

---

24   Emphasis in original, ibid., p.18.
25   Ibid.
26   Mackerras, 'Another Second Preference', p.30.

with Mackerras arguing that it had become 'a liability to the Government. The compromise of 1963, whereby non-Catholic independent schools got a good slice of State aid[,] is now seen by most parents with children at State schools as being little more than a system of gifts to the schools of the rich'.[27] But this opinion seems idiosyncratic; both major parties now formally accepted government financial support to non-government schools and doing so was probably essential if Labor was to win back the support of at least some Catholics lost in the turbulence of the 1950s and 1960s, or to win over new Catholic voters who supported 'justice' for their school system.

The election of Gorton as Liberal leader in 1968, however, had proved more problematic, a point made at the time in a growing chorus of critical political commentary – most famously in Alan Reid's excoriating *The Gorton Experiment* (1971) – as well as by recent commentators who argue that after his brief honeymoon, Gorton's 'idiosyncratic style soon put off colleagues and had voters wondering'.[28] There was controversy over the influence supposedly exerted over Gorton by his 22-year old female principal private secretary, Ainsley Gotto, as there was over a late-night visit to the US Embassy in the company of a 19-year old female journalist, Geraldine Willesee. These matters contributed to the impression of Gorton as unpredictable at best.[29]

Short-Term Implications

Following the election, David Fairbairn, a very proper Cambridge-educated grazier and establishment figure – and, like Gorton, ex-Geelong Grammar and RAAF – refused to serve any longer in

---

27 Ibid.
28 Bynander and 't Hart, 'The Politics of Party', p.66.
29 Hancock, *John Gorton*, pp.162, 214-16.

Cabinet under Gorton.[30] Fairbairn told Gorton in a telegram that he did not believe the prime minister was willing to learn lessons from the election defeat, and he said that 'some people' had approached him asking him to stand for the leadership.[31] A ballot for the leadership was held on 7 November: that there was a crisis within weeks of an election that delivered victory to the coalition seems evidence of the deep-seated disappointment within the government's ranks. The seriousness of the situation only seemed to have dawned late on Gorton, as Alan Reid argues:

> Gorton, who had taken an almost offhand attitude since the election, suddenly seemed to realise that with the McMahon-Fairbairn combination ranged against him, and McEwen moving from a position of support into neutrality at best and possibly hostility, he needed to adopt a more positive and conciliatory attitude.[32]

Gorton defeated Fairbairn, who came last in the poll, and McMahon, who had nominated after McEwen's veto was relaxed.[33] Although he had managed to hold on, Gorton's perceived personal responsibility for the loss of seats wounded him, and he would never fully recover from the blow.

The narrow defeat of the ALP in the 1969 election, and the particularly poor, but unsurprising, showing in Victoria, aided Whitlam's quest for internal party reforms. In 1970 the result was the 'Intervention'. The federal ALP executive authorised a take-over and reconstruction of both the Victorian and New South Wales branches

---

30 Ibid., p.23.
31 Ibid., p.244.
32 Alan Reid, *The Gorton Experiment* (Sydney: Shakespeare Head Press, 1971), p.372.
33 Hughes, 'Political Review', p.23.

of the party, but the Victorian Central Executive (VCE) was the prime target in this manoeuvre, which was engineered by Whitlam, Clyde Cameron and the South Australian powerbroker Mick Young. Branch rules were reformed to enforce proportional representation and power-sharing between contending factions, and the absolute dominance of the Left within Victoria was mitigated. Whitlam's then principal private secretary Race Mathews, who had himself been among the VCE's opponents, would later judge that 'the way ahead for the party's return to government was at long last cleared'[34]. Clearly the results of 1969 had important implications for the governance of the Labor Party, and they paved the way for significant, and necessary, party reform – necessary, that is, if Labor was to secure a sufficient number of seats in Victoria to form a national government.

What If?

Had the ALP won the 1969 election, the repercussions would have been significant. Although the opinion polls had, on balance, predicted a coalition victory, there was an expectation among some Labor supporters that government might yet be possible.[35] In any case, the near victory of the ALP arguably magnified the impatience of Whitlam when he was eventually able to take government in 1972. Perhaps, had the ALP won office in 1969, the government led by Whitlam might have been more measured in its approach. Arguably, however, any government led by Whitlam after such a long span of conservative administration was going to seek quick and decisive policy change.

---

34 Mathews, 'Whitlam Re-visited', p.12.
35 See Aitkin, 'The 1969 Federal Election', pp.45-53.

The changed economic circumstances by the time the ALP came to office in 1972 – and especially from 1973 – were a challenge for the new government.[36] During the 1969 election the Australian economy was still enjoying the effects of the long boom and in this climate Labor's policies for increased intervention in the economy and greatly expanded public spending were entrenched. But by 1972 the problems of the local and international economy – notably inflation – were becoming more visible. By the mid-1970s, 'stagflation' – a combination of inflation, low growth and unemployment – was in effect.[37] In other words, Whitlam seems to have missed his window of economic opportunity by losing the 1969 election. Worse still, the economic woes of the 1970s were to some extent attributed to Whitlam's government, even as the wider international economy entered more difficult times, with the decision of a cartel of oil-producing countries to increase prices late in 1973 having acted as a powerful trigger.[38] Had Labor been elected in 1969, with the economy stronger, its economic interventionism and social spending might have been better placed, and its popularity more resilient. We would perhaps have had no Whitlam dismissal of 1975, with all the turmoil and bitterness that that crisis brought, and all the consequences it had for politics into the 1980s and beyond.

The challenge to Gorton from McMahon and Fairbairn following the election might also be seen as a turning point in Australian politics. Mackerras has argued persuasively that this challenge set a new precedent: 'This is a phenomenon ... [that] really began with the

---

36 See also Greg Whitwell, 'Economic Affairs', in H. Emy, O. Hughes and R. Mathews (eds) *Whitlam Re-Visited*, pp. 32-62.
37 See Ashley Lavelle, 'Social Democrats and Neo-Liberalism: A Case Study of the Australian Labor Party', *Political Studies*, 53:4, 2005, pp.753-771.
38 Whitwell, 'Economic Affairs', p.59.

McMahon-Gorton rivalry. Prior to that you had a dominant leader. You did not have anything like this'.[39] Whether the 1969 challenge set a new precedent for internal challenge to the prime minister is debatable, but its long-term implications for Australian politics are worthy of consideration. McMahon would later succeed in ousting Gorton in 1971 following a leadership contest triggered by the resignation of Malcolm Fraser from Gorton's cabinet.

Conclusion

The 1969 election strengthened the position of Gough Whitlam both in the Labor Party and in the electorate as a whole. It built him a strong platform from which to launch his victorious 1972 election campaign. By demolishing much of the coalition majority, won in 1966, the ALP was finally back in striking distance of the treasury benches. The 1969 election also spelt the death knell for the long-surviving coalition government. It indicated that the Menzies era was well and truly over. The result immediately brought blame and a leadership challenge to the door of the prime minister, a position from which Gorton was never able to recover. As Reid argues, 'The Gorton experiment might not have succeeded completely ... it was certainly not a failure. Gorton was back in office which was the main purpose of the exercise'.[40] This being said, the 1969 election entrenched instability in the government, and the successful challenge from McMahon in 1971 did nothing to revive the coalition's fortunes.[41]

---

39 Malcolm Mackerras, Quoted in Mark Metherell, 'Eerie echoes of Labor blasts from past', *Sydney Morning Herald*, 25 February 2012.
40 Reid, *The Gorton Experiment*, p.348.
41 Bynander and 't Hart, 'The Politics of Party', p.66.

The parallels between the 1969 House of Representatives election and the 2016 double dissolution election are notable. Both governments were seen to 'lose' the election but retain government. In the case of 1969 the coalition still held a respectable governing majority of seven, compared to one in 2016. Both prime ministers, John Gorton and Malcolm Turnbull, were the target of heavy criticism and blame for the result, from their parties and backbenchers.[42] In both instances this was arguably compounded by the fact that each was also seen not to have delivered on expectations for their mid-term ascendency to the prime ministership – in the case of Gorton as the result of the death of Harold Holt and for Turnbull, the political demise of Tony Abbott at the hands of his party room. The blame attributed to the leaders was further agitated by the failure of Gorton and Turnbull to give sufficient attention to the policy areas seen as the strongest suits for their respective governments.[43] However, unlike Turnbull who said little about national security, Gorton did return to defence issues later in the election campaign, which may help explain the difference between the outcomes in 1969 and 2016.[44] Although there were differences, such as the simultaneous full Senate election in 2016 which was absent in 1969, the parallels are clear.

The election in 1969 was therefore important in many ways and although there was no change of government, it was certainly a crucial precursor to the immense change that was to come in 1972. Following 1969 the government, as with the final moments of *Don's Party*, was left exhausted and emotionally depleted, and many relationships were fatally exposed and irreparably wounded.

---

42 See Aitkin, 'The 1969 Federal Election'.
43 Ibid.
44 Hughes, 'Political Review', p.23.

INTERIM 1969–1987

After 23 years of conservative rule, Labor came to power in 1972 with a large and expensive reform agenda. Despite the 1973 oil crisis and subsequent recession, Whitlam persisted with his measures in the face of a hostile Senate where the DLP still held the balance of power. A double dissolution election was called for 18 May 1974. Despite the lowered quota, the DLP lost all five of their Senators, managing 3.6% of the Senate vote and just 1.4% in the House of Representatives. The Liberal leader, Billy Snedden, wrestled back three seats but Labor was comfortably returned with 66 to 61 in the 127 seat lower house and a two-party preferred vote of 51.7%.

Crucially, the 1974 election failed to give Labor control of the Senate. When Labor Senator Lionel Murphy resigned on 9 February 1975 to go to the High Court, conservative New South Wales Premier Tom Lewis broke a long-standing protocol by sending an Independent replacement in Cleaver Bunton rather than an ALP member. Months later, conservative Queensland Premier Joh Bjelke-Petersen did the same when Labor's Bert Milliner passed away. Rather than send another Labor nominee (as is now the law), Milliner was replaced with Patrick Field, a man with Labor links but a vocal opponent of Whitlam. The ALP challenged the legitimacy of Field's appointment but the opposition refused to grant a 'pair' during the dispute, giving the conservative parties a Senate majority and the power to block supply (despite Bunton ultimately voting with the government). This led directly to the 1975 constitutional crisis and Whitlam's infamous dismissal by the governor-general, Sir John Kerr.

Fraser was sworn in as prime minister and dutifully called another double dissolution election for 13 December 1975. Despite Whitlam's sense of injustice and call for supporters to 'maintain the rage', the ALP suffered a calamitous defeat, winning just 36 seats in the 127 seat lower house. The coalition retook the government benches with a majority in the Senate also. The year 1975 also saw the Northern Territory and Australian Capital Territory elect Senators for the first time. Whitlam maintained his leadership position and was determined to keep fighting. His defeat at the 1977 election, however, spelled the end of his colourful political career. Whitlam managed to win back just two seats and increase the two-party preferred vote to a still paltry 45.4%. In the aftermath, former Queensland police officer, and probably the best ministerial performer in the Whitlam government, Bill Hayden, took the reins of a flailing party. Meanwhile, under the leadership of former Liberal, Don Chipp, the Australian Democrats emerged as the new third force in Australian politics, winning 9.4% of the vote.

Hayden performed well and restored confidence in Labor as a viable alternative. At the 1980 election, Labor took back much of the ground it lost in 1975. In particular, strong gains were made in Victoria. While the ALP took 49.6% of the two-party preferred vote, the coalition retained a handy 23 seat majority in the House of Representatives, despite ceding control of the Senate with the Australian Democrats holding the balance of power. The ambitious former leader of the Australian Council of Trade Unions, Bob Hawke, entered parliament in 1980 as the Member for Wills in Melbourne. Hawke unsuccessfully challenged for the party leadership in 1982 but following a by-election in Flinders in which Labor polled disappointingly, loomed as an attractive alternative. Fraser sought to take advantage of the leadership tensions and called a snap election for 5 March 1983 (the third double dissolution in five elections and less than ten years, going back to 1974). On the same day as Fraser visited the governor-general, Hayden lost the support of caucus and resigned, leaving Hawke to assume the Labor leadership unopposed.

Labor returned to power in a comprehensive victory. The party secured 75 of 125 federal seats and a commanding 53.2% of the two party preferred vote (its highest post-war result). The Democrats saw their vote slide but still returned senators in five states. Having suffered the worst defeat of any non-Labor government, Fraser duly resigned as leader of the Liberal Party. Andrew Peacock defeated deputy leader John Howard to secure the leadership.

Australians returned to the polls less than two years later, on 1 December 1984, as Hawke sought to take advantage of his enormous personal popularity and his government's strong performance in a recovering economy. With both houses increased in size (to 148 in the House of Representatives and 76 in the Senate), the major parties increased their seat numbers. Labor's majority, however, was reduced and it was seen as a disappointing result. Nevertheless, Labor retained 51.8% of the two-party preferred vote. Peacock was plagued by internal divisions and sought unsuccessfully to have Howard removed as deputy leader. Frustrated by an apparent lack of support and internally outmanoeuvred, Peacock ended up resigning as leader in 1985. Howard was elected as leader unopposed and appointed Peacock shadow foreign minister.

Chapter 7

1987

LABOR MAKES IT THREE

Frank Bongiorno

The 1987 election does not immediately suggest itself as an election that changed Australia. It did not bring a new government to office. It did not see a large swing to one or another of the parties. It did not see many seats change hands. It was a double dissolution election, formally triggered by the Senate's rejection of a bill to introduce a national identity card. That issue, however, barely figured in the election. Yet for other reasons the 1987 election was arguably the most significant of the 1980s and one of the most consequential in the last quarter of the twentieth century. It was the election that announced, once and for all, that the Australian Labor Party was ruled by a hard pragmatism and a determination to do 'whatever it takes' to win elections. Labor had never won three federal elections in a row before. For the coalition parties, moreover, the election was hardly less significant. 1987 was the decade's 'New Right' election, the contest most affected by the 'radical' conservative revolt that had occurred in the two years that preceded the election. The contest is most commonly associated with the push by Joh Bjelke-Petersen, the Queensland National Party premier, to transfer to federal politics and seize the prime ministership. But Bjelke-Petersen's ambitions were not only a product of his own personal instability and of the eccentricities of Queensland politics; they were a result of the New Right's outflanking of the leader of the Liberal Party, John Howard, and of mainstream conservative politics more generally. The most significant effect of this destabilisation of John Howard and the coalition during 1985-7 was to help extend Labor Party rule for almost another decade. It was not until the defeat of Fightback! *in 1993 that the New Right genie was returned to its bottle.*

ELECTIONS MATTER

Background

The Joh-for-PM (or Joh-for-Canberra) crusade is recalled by many as the salient episode of the 1987 election campaign. During 1985 Bjelke-Petersen won a stunning if brutal victory against striking electricity workers in his state, a dispute now recalled as one of several victories across the nation for industrial relations hardliners associated with the New Right. After his unexpected outright victory at the Queensland state election held in November 1986 – the Nationals having discarded their Liberal coalition partners in 1983 – The National Party was able to govern alone. John Howard, watching Bjelke-Petersen claim victory on television, turned to his wife Janette and declared with unerring accuracy: 'We'll have trouble with this lunatic now'.[1]

There had been rumours of a switch to Canberra for some time, a move being encouraged by a group of Gold Coast entrepreneurs known as 'the white shoe brigade'. These men, of whom the most prominent was the flamboyant former car-dealer and current property-developer, Mike Gore, had a number of preoccupations. They still loathed John Howard for his role as treasurer, in the Fraser government, in introducing retrospective legislation designed to shut down 'bottom of the harbour' tax schemes. They also probably harboured the ambition of installing the obese and corrupt Gold Coast politician Russ Hinze as Queensland premier.[2] A further factor that entered their calculations is that they had little to fear from a

---

1   Paul Kelly, *The End of Certainty: Power, Politics, and Business in Australia* (Sydney: Allen & Unwin, 1992), p.297.

2   John Howard, *Lazarus Rising: A Personal and Political Autobiography* (Sydney: HarperCollins, 2010), pp.155-6; Rob Borbidge, Interviewed by Roger Scott and Maree Stanley, *Queensland Speaks*, Accessed online. <www.queenslandspeaks.com.au/rob-borbidge>

pro-business Labor government in Canberra, some of whose leading members were openly identified as friends and supporters of such thrusting entrepreneurs.

By Christmas 1986 it was clear enough that Bjelke-Petersen would soon make a move. At a rally in Wagga the following month, the Queensland premier warned that those who did not support him and his policies would find their seats contested at the next election. The Queensland National Party powerbroker Robert Sparkes, who was quite unable to contain Bjelke-Petersen's increasingly unhinged behaviour and inflated ambitions, now felt he had little choice but to throw the weight of the state party branch behind the premier. In February 1987 a meeting of the Queensland Nationals at Hervey Bay agreed to back the Joh-for-PM campaign, and called on federal National Party leader Ian Sinclair to withdraw from the coalition and, if he refused, for the Queensland Nationals to go their own way. At a National Party federal council meeting in Canberra in March, Bjelke-Petersen memorably thrust his arms into the air and announced his 'good news' that the coalition was finished.[3] Bjelke-Petersen was attracting the support, or at least the praise, of prominent Australians. Geoffrey Blainey, prolific historian and media pundit, considered him 'one of the quiet giants in our political history', a man 'like the legendary tortoise racing the hare'. 'I think he will be a more serious challenger than most media-people are suggesting', Blainey suggested, a prediction that turned out to be accurate in the unlikely event that Blainey had in mind the Queensland premier's capability to derail his own side of politics.[4] In announcing the formal break-up

---

3   Paul Davey, *Joh for PM: The Inside Story of an Extraordinary Political Drama* (Sydney: NewSouth Publishing, 2015), p.78.
4   *Herald* (Melbourne), 19 February 1987.

of the federal coalition, in March, Howard again accurately predicted that Bjelke-Petersen 'will clearly go down in history as the coalition wrecker and he has no chance of ever becoming prime minister'.[5]

The Bjelke-Petersen thrust has sometimes been presented as the product simply of the idiosyncrasies of the ageing and corrupt megalomaniac that he was, or of the peculiarities of Queensland politics. But even leaving aside the various agendas being pursued by his supporters, the Joh-for-PM push was rather more complicated, in fact being very much a product of the fluid character of Australian economic and political change in the mid-1980s. The style of consensus politics pursued by Bob Hawke from the time he assumed leadership of the federal Labor Party in early 1983 stimulated political entrepreneurship of various kinds on the right. Blainey's campaign against the pace of Asian immigration in 1984, and the mining executive Hugh Morgan's against Aboriginal land rights in the same year, were followed by agitation of the so-called New Right in favour of anti-union and anti-arbitration industrial relations reform, lower taxes, government spending cuts and even lower wage growth than the government had achieved via its Prices and Incomes Accord with the union movement. At a time of rapidly declining farm incomes, a rural revolt led by the National Farmers' Federation, with wealthy South Australian grazier and businessman Ian McLachlan at the helm, added potency to the chatter of city-based dining clubs, employer organisations and barristers' chambers. The views of the New Right appeared frequently in the op-ed columns of the country's newspapers, especially the *Australian,* and the confidence of these new militants found expression in a series of high-profile industrial disputes,

---

5   John Howard, 'The Coalition', Press Release, 28 April 1987, in 'Joh Crusade' Folder, Liberal Party Federal Secretariat Papers, National Library of Australia (NLA) MS 5000, Box 1363.

culminating in a lock-out of workers at Robe River on the Pilbara iron-ore field in Western Australia in 1986.[6]

While Andrew Peacock had performed creditably at the 1984 federal election, with the coalition reducing Labor's majority in an enlarged House of Representatives, his leadership did not survive the rivalry with John Howard, who replaced him the following year. Howard had every reason to hope that the intellectual influence being exercised by the New Right outside the parliament would help him to reshape the political agenda. Having rather unfairly had to bear much of the opprobrium for the perceived failures of the Fraser era, he wished to forge a legacy of his own that would draw to some extent on the kinds of free-market policies being pursued in Britain by Margaret Thatcher and in the United States by Ronald Reagan. The Liberal Party divided into a 'dry' faction, which supported this direction and was influenced by the ideas of the New Right, and a 'wet' faction that identified more strongly with a statist tradition that some traced to the early prime minister Alfred Deakin, and which looked more to Peacock than Howard as its favoured leader. Peacock's name, however, was also mentioned in connection with the Joh-for-PM push, underlining the role of personal rivalries and animosities beyond whatever ideological differences existed on the conservative side of politics. Howard's problem was that his leadership was being destabilised from within, as well as from without, where he was being out-flanked by the increasingly adventurous policies of the New Right.[7]

---

6   Frank Bongiorno, *The Eighties: The Decade That Transformed Australia* (Melbourne: Black Inc, 2015), chs 3 and 6.
7   Ibid., ch. 6; Howard, *Lazarus Rising*, pp.155-6.

Labor had been behind in the polls in late 1986 and early 1987 and party insiders, who after the election reported that Labor had been trailing by eight percentage points just ten months before, clearly expected defeat.⁸ The government had experienced a most difficult year in 1986, when the bottom had fallen out of the dollar and Keating had warned that unless Australia was able to turn itself around it faced a future as 'a banana republic'.⁹ A document drafted for the party's campaign committee in October 1986 and based on commissioned market research, reported 'seething anger and resentment' in middle Australia about the government's economic management, while its traditional supporters seemed to think the government was deriving 'a sadistic pleasure out of their hurt', as if they were receiving 'deserved punishment'.¹⁰ But by May 1987, with the economy showing many signs of improvement and Howard's leadership being destabilised by the Bjelke-Petersen push, as well as continuing 'wet' disaffection, Labor was beginning to overtake the opposition in opinion polling. An Economic Statement announcing a $4 billion cut in the budget deficit, delivered by the treasurer Paul Keating on 13 May, gained a favourable reception in the media and polls. And just two weeks later, Hawke secured a double dissolution election for 11 July. Keating has claimed much of the credit for the decision to go to an early election, an indication of the significance he attaches to the subsequent victory as the moment on which the place of the government in Australian political history would so largely

---

8   'Paul Kelly: where we go from here: Labor', *Australian*, 13 July 1987.
9   Bongiorno, *Eighties*, pp.158-9.
10 Draft Report for Campaign Committee: Government's Electoral Standing – Strategy for 1988 Election', pp.3-4, October 1986, Bob Hawke Papers, RH18/2/F52 (Box 2), Bob Hawke Ministerial Library, University of South Australia.

hinge.¹¹ Hawke, understandably, presents the decision to go to an early election as his own doing, the timing of elections ultimately falling under the prime minister's prerogative.¹²

Bjelke-Petersen was in the United States when the election was called. This famously shrewd political operator badly underestimated the temptation to an early election that his own erratic behaviour had posed. After returning to Australia and failing in an effort to secure the support of the National Farmers' Federation, he made himself look even more foolish by announcing that he would not be going to Canberra after all. Howard flew to Brisbane and managed to secure a joint statement with Bjelke-Petersen that they would agree to work together to defeat the government, but Bjelke-Petersen candidates ran in several seats where there were already official opposition candidates, thereby confusing voters and contributing to a sense of chaos on the conservative side of politics.

Campaign

The new ruthlessness and professionalism of the Australian Labor Party (ALP) was no better illustrated than in its decision to replace its previous advertiser, Forbes MacFie Hansen, with John Singleton Advertising. Singleton was not widely regarded as a friend of the Labor Party but, instead, recalled for his role in undermining the Whitlam government with an unpleasant advertising campaign in 1974. But the choice, for which Hawke took full credit in his memoirs, was inspired, giving rise to a campaign slogan that did seem to capture the feelings of many voters towards the government. 'Let's stick together' might have been the title of a Bryan Ferry song, but in

---

11   Kerry O'Brien, *Keating* (Sydney: Allen & Unwin, 2015), pp.298-301.
12   Bob Hawke, *The Hawke Memoirs* (Melbourne: Mandarin, 1996 [1994]), pp.392-3.

this case it was followed by an exhortation 'Let's See it Through'. Just what 'it' was, the jingle did not really specify, but the balance of payments crisis and plunge of the dollar during the previous year seemed a fair assumption. Electors received the advice that 'nobody ever got anywhere changing horses in midstream' – although the ALP had clearly thought otherwise when it hired Singleton.[13]

The other piece of advertising genius that emerged from this campaign was 'Whingeing Wendy', as she became known, or Wendy Wood. She was the wife of one of Singleton's friends and as a character named Beryl Timms sometimes featured on his radio program as a rough but honest working-class everywoman. Wood was a committed Labor supporter and when she looked into the camera and asked in her broad Australian working-class accent where John Howard was going to find the money to pay for his tax-cuts, she looked and sounded as though she really meant it.[14]

The Labor campaign did not go off without a hitch but Hawke's only major error – the promise that '[b]y 1990, no Australian child will be living in poverty' – was not one for which he would pay heavily in the short-term. The line appeared in the speech by mistake; Hawke was apparently supposed to say that because of the government's new Family Allowance Supplement, there 'would be no financial need for any child to live in poverty'.[15] Perhaps this over-compensation had much to do with the accusation, increasingly heard by 1987, that this was not a real Labor government but one for the wealthy and

---

13 Ibid., pp.398-400.
14 Gerald Stone, *Singo, The John Singleton Story: Mates, Wives, Triumphs, Disasters* (Sydney: HarperCollins, 2003), pp.217-20. See also 'Mrs. Wendy Wood Challenges Mr. John Howard', *Age*, 7 July 1987.
15 Hawke, *Hawke Memoirs*, pp.403-4.

powerful.[16] The Family Allowance Supplement was the product of collaboration between Hawke, Keating and left-aligned social security minister Brian Howe, and it was shaped by policy advice from the social policy academic Bettina Cass.[17] As a conspicuous effort to assist low income earners, it was especially timely in mid-1987 for, despite the sacrifices that government was demanding of ordinary voters, the very wealthy seemed to be doing better than ever. That year's *Business Review Weekly* Rich List announced Australia's first two billionaires, in Kerry Packer and Robert Holmes à Court, and the stock market was booming. Hawke's praise during the campaign for businessmen such as Packer and Alan Bond, and their apparent endorsement of him, would contribute to a growing chorus of criticism about 'rich Labor mates' in the years ahead, criticism that especially bit once the stock-market collapsed in October 1987 and many of yesterday's heroes became today's shysters.[18] But for the time being, Labor's families package and Hawke's extravagant promise about ending child poverty might have helped convince some wavering voters that the government still had a Labor heart. Laurie Oakes judged that the $300 million family payment 'should really be called Labor's social conscience package', a measure aimed at getting 'rid of the idea that Labor is no different from the Liberal Party in its values'. There had been a flirtation with the idea of providing a payment for all parents with children under six. But in the straightened economic times, the government did not pursue this option, a brave decision in view of the need to keep middle-income voters onside.[19]

---

16 Brian Toohey, 'The Death of Labor', *Eye*, July 1987, pp.8-11.
17 David O'Reilly, '"Conservative" Hawke takes a radical risk', *Bulletin*, 30 June 1987, p.19; George Negus, 'Hawke and the poverty factor', *Bulletin*, 14 July 1987, p.61.
18 Bongiorno, *Eighties*, pp.129, 185-7, 263-80.
19 Laurie Oakes, 'Hawke goes back to the basics for his platform', *Bulletin*, 23 June 1987, p.25.

The Liberals' errors, by way of contrast, were costly. Their campaign was disorganised, with the state branches exercising considerable autonomy tempered by minimal central direction until near the end.[20] They went to the election advocating drastic cuts to income tax, notably a top rate of 38%, in contrast with Labor's recent decision to cut the top rate to 49%. They also promised to reduce company tax rates, abolish the capital gains tax introduced by the Hawke government, to make employees rather than their bosses responsible for paying the fringe benefits tax, and to make business entertainment tax deductible.[21] Bjelke-Petersen, advised by former treasury secretary and present Queensland National Party Senator John Stone, advocated a flat rate of 25%, which might have made the cuts being offered by Howard look moderate if anyone truly believed that Bjelke-Petersen had been likely to cut taxes so drastically. Howard ran into the problem, however, that he was vague about what expenditure he was going to cut to pay for his tax policy, and in any case the plan was to phase in such cuts over several years, thereby raising questions of the feasibility of the reductions in taxation. Financial journalists smelt political opportunism, while voters – encouraged by Labor advertising – had reason to wonder where the money was coming from. But the Liberals soon faced additional problems.[22] Keating accused them of a major arithmetical error amounting to $1.5 billion, a piece of double-counting which meant that funding cuts to the states were likely to be even more severe than those being proposed. Howard and his shadow treasurer, Jim Carlton, admitted

---

20   Dean Jaensch, 'The Liberal Campaign', in Ian McAllister and John Warhurst (eds), *Australia Votes: The 1987 Federal Election* (Melbourne: Longman Cheshire, 1988), pp.57, 82.
21   David Barnett, 'What the Liberal Party promises', *Bulletin*, 14 July 1987, p.29.
22   Amanda Buckley, 'Howard stakes his future on tax cuts' and Gregory Hywood, 'The Liberals did not get their act together', *Australian Financial Review*, 10 July 1987.

the mistake. There were other gaffes in the campaign but this one – perhaps the kind of error likely to be made by a party distracted by the Joh-for-PM crusade – was the most damaging of them.[23]

By way of contrast, commentators from both left and right were increasingly in awe of Labor's political professionalism. New South Wales Labor minister Bob Carr, admittedly a partisan, thought the campaign Labor's 'best ever peacetime effort. With the panache of a Menzies, Bob Hawke persuaded the swinging voters that the issue in this election was not the record of the Government but the performance of the opposition'.[24] Pro-Liberal commentator Gerard Henderson agreed: Hawke won the election 'because the ALP is Australia's only truly professional party'.[25] The media was also largely onside; where once the ALP could count on opposition from the press, at least in their editorial positions, in 1987 it benefited in most cases from either support or neutrality.[26] It was the Liberal and National parties that were now more likely to complain of media bias, but journalists could respond that they were not inventing the stories of division and confusion within the ranks; these were plain for all to see. Issues that had once posed dangers to the ALP, such as the perception that it was insufficiently committed to the alliance with the United States, had dissipated as problems. During the 1987 campaign, the US Ambassador Bill Lane announced 'the past year' as 'one of the best bilateral relationships in the 36-year history of ANZUS'. As a result of pre-scheduled arrangements, Hawke's close

---

23 David Barnett, 'Howard plumps for a plain man's message', *Bulletin*, 30 June 1987, p.18.
24 Bob Carr, 'Hawke has exorcised Labor's ghosts', *Australian*, 13 July 1987.
25 Gerard Henderson, 'Sheer professionalism won the day', *Australian*, 13 July 1987.
26 Sam Lipski, 'The election the press anointed Labor', *Bulletin*, 21 July 1987, p.61. For a contemporary discussion of the media and the election, see Pamela Bone, 'The Media Edge: Hawke or Howard?', *Age*, Green Guide, 2 July 1987.

friend Secretary of State George Shultz and Secretary of Defence Casper Weinberger visited Australia during the campaign; Hawke had insisted on the visit going ahead, and the Americans did not demur. None of this did the government any harm at all, providing welcome photo opportunities for Hawke, foreign minister Bill Hayden and defence minister Kim Beazley.[27] 'Howard is ploughing a more difficult furrow than prime minister Bob Hawke who was out on a golf course with US Secretary of State George Shultz on Sunday telling TV people that he was a statesman', reported David Barnett in the *Bulletin*. By way of contrast, in the wake of the double-counting fiasco, 'Howard fought it out with the media, an ashen-faced and silent Carlton at his side'.[28]

But it was not just that Hawke himself was engaged, focused and indefatigable, performing far better than in 1984 and seemingly gaining new energy from the daily campaign round. It was also the skill of the party machine itself: Bob McMullan, as party secretary in Canberra head office, pollster Rod Cameron, and the advertiser John Singleton, were influential members of a formidable campaign team. McMullan and Cameron, however, were also central to the formulation and implementation of what former Hawke staffer Stephen Mills has called an incumbency strategy. It was no longer just a matter of such figures becoming active at campaign time. They were also involved in government between elections, helping to develop a plan for winning the next election and remaining in office.[29] In particular, Labor successfully targeted marginal seats – those it held

---

27   Laurie Oakes, 'Labor gets tacit US support', *Bulletin*, 30 June 1987, p.22; Stephen Mills, *The Hawke Years: The Story From Inside* (Melbourne: Viking, 1993), pp.163-4.

28   David Barnett, 'Howard plumps for a plain man's message', *Bulletin*, 30 June 1987, p.18.

29   Stephen Mills, *The Professionals: Strategy, Money & the Rise of the Political Campaigner in Australia* (Melbourne: Black Inc, 2014), pp.130-1.

by a slender margin, such as several in Victoria, and those it hoped it might win elsewhere, such as in Queensland – and with considerable success. As Paul Kelly put it, Labor 'focused during the campaign on the swinging voter and it got the swing where it mattered'.[30]

McMullan gave a young party organiser, Gary Gray, the responsibility for marginal seats. Gray then proceeded to spend a quarter of a million dollars on computers capable of storing the details of voters in each target electorate, and laser printers that would, at the mighty rate of four pages per minute, produce letters for direct mail-outs.[31] These went into eleven of the most marginal seats. The party also installed another new-fangled device, the fax machine, in the offices of marginal seat candidates to ensure rapid communication, especially when the prime minister's travelling circus was visiting the electorate. The research, planning and technological support that underpinned Labor's 1987 campaign victory was, by Australian standards, unprecedented and prodigious.[32]

Outcomes

The outcome was superficially undramatic but this is a case of the numbers telling only a small part of the story. The 1987 election must be considered as more meaningful when set in the wider context of modern Australian political history. Labor, it appeared, had shaken off a sense that it was 'the party of occasional government'.[33] While leading commentators resisted the idea that the ALP had now become the natural party of government, there was a feeling that a 'historical pattern' had 'been broken'; that in the not-too-distant

---

30 'Paul Kelly: where we go from here: Labor', *Australian*, 13 July 1987.
31 Mills, *Professionals*, pp.195-6.
32 Ibid., p. 135; David O'Reilly, 'The New Face of Politics', *Bulletin*, 21 July 1987, p.20.
33 Bob McMullan, quoted in Mills, *Professionals*, p.128.

past, in such an economic situation, the ALP would have faced electoral annihilation.[34] Hawke's 'return defied all established nostrums of Australian politics', according to David O'Reilly in the *Bulletin*. 'He ran on his record, in winter, and promised the electorate almost nothing.'[35] The coalition achieved a small swing in the two-party preferred vote of 1% but even if it had been uniform, it would have been insufficient get the opposition parties over the line since Labor's buffer was 2.3%. As it happened, the Liberals and Nationals failed to achieve a swing in marginal seats that they needed to win, with the result that Labor picked up four extra seats, increasing its tally from 82 to 86.[36] In New South Wales, the Liberal and National parties gained swings of between 5% and 7% in seven safe Labor and two safe National Party divisions – votes that were of no use whatsoever so far as winning seats was concerned. As we have seen, such an outcome was the result of a deliberate, careful and successful Labor strategy of targeting of marginal seats. In these places, where there were seats to be won or lost, Labor's complicated message – that the country was in economic difficulty and that it was the best party to deal with the problems – appears to have gained sufficient traction to get the government over the line. The chaos unleashed by Bjelke-Petersen in Queensland also appears to have benefited Labor, which picked up four seats in that state, more than making up for losses of a seat in each of Victoria and New South Wales.

There was widespread agreement that division within the coalition ranks had cost them dearly. Michelle Grattan of the Melbourne *Age* saw Hawke's victory as a 'tribute to the electorate's common

---

34 'Paul Kelly: where we go from here: Labor', *Australian*, 13 July 1987.
35 David O'Reilly, 'The New Face of Politics', *Bulletin*, 21 July 1987, p.19.
36 John Warhurst, 'The ALP Campaign' and Malcolm Mackerras, 'Appendix: Election Results', in McAllister and Warhurst (eds), *Australia Votes*, pp.35, 252, 259.

sense, and a vindication of the political adage that division is death'.[37] Some post-election commentators rightly praised John Howard for his courage and grace under pressure, but they were uncomplimentary about his team. The shadow treasurer, Jim Carlton, was widely blamed for the accounting error but in reality, the coalition had failed to devote sufficient time to getting their policies right. Too much had been left to the last minute, and, as the *Australian Financial Review* put it, there was too much that smacked of 'half-baked policy proposals, ill-digested responses and just plain garbage'.[38] The Liberals went to the election with a messy policy of undoing Medicare's universalism and pushing all but the poorest and the most vulnerable into private health insurance. The proposal to charge families for the first $250 of their medical bills each year contributed to an impression that it could not be trusted on health. The elections of 1990 and 1993 further entrenched this idea, to the enormous electoral cost of the conservative parties.

It has been suggested that perhaps a fifth of the electorate changed its votes from 1984, but there was very likely a cancelling out of most votes as defectors from each side switched allegiance.[39] This perhaps reflects the degree of confusion that had come to surround party voting by the mid-1980s as well as the fierceness of competition between the parties. Yet, although it could not be fully realised at the time, and would become clearer in 1990, there was a gentle hint here of a future in which the major political parties would become more dependent on fragile, shifting and shrinking coalitions of voters assembled for the purposes of winning each election. And

---

37 Michelle Grattan, 'The People Prefer the Devil They Know', *Age*, 13 July 1987.
38 *Australian Financial Review*, 13 July 1987.
39 Ian McAllister and Alvaro Ascui, 'Voting Patterns', in McAllister and Warhurst (eds), *Australia Votes*, p.226.

where Hawke's performance had been widely criticised in 1984, this time there was more agreement that he was an asset to the Labor Party, accounting for 1.4% of the vote that would have gone elsewhere, according to one estimate.[40] His approval rating was 20 points ahead of Howard's.

If 1987 might be seen as representing a symbolic break of the Labor Party with the past as it steered its course through increasingly adventurous market reforms, the same was even more true of the Liberal Party. For the Liberals, the 1987 election was, in generational terms, arguably the last election of the Fraser era. The divisions of the period greatly weakened Ian Sinclair, one of three key Fraser allies in the National-Country Party (The others being Doug Anthony and Peter Nixon), and he would lose the leadership at the same time as John Howard was overthrown in 1989. There would also be a move after the 1987 election against several Liberal progressives – or 'wets' – such as Ian Macphee, who lost preselection, while figures from the era of Howard government such as Peter Costello and Kevin Andrews would enter the parliament at the beginning of the 1990s. Alexander Downer, later to become Australia's longest-serving foreign minister after a brief and inglorious time as party leader, was the Liberals' young environment spokesman in 1987, seeking to sell a policy that wanted to shift responsibility for most matters in his portfolio to the states – and then condemning the very same policy soon after the election.[41]

A major figure from the Fraser era, Andrew Peacock, would be marginalised in the 1987 election, and was widely rumoured to be flirting with the Joh-for-PM campaign; he would live on to fight

---

40   David O'Reilly, 'That Old Hawke Magic', *Bulletin*, 4 April 1989, pp.37-8.
41   Jaensch, 'The Liberal Campaign', pp.71-2.

another day as leader when he pushed Howard out in 1989, but would fail in 1990 as Howard had done in 1987. Joh Bjelke-Petersen would soon lose the premiership of Queensland and, at the hands of the Fitzgerald Royal Commission, what remained of his reputation as well. But for the time being, in the immediate aftermath of the election, there were some true believers. New Right commentator in the *Australian*, Des Keegan, a conspicuous Joh-for-PM supporter, would not let go, declaring that '[t]he Coalition was invited, cordially invited, to join the anti-socialist drive with Sir Joh. Jealous of potent promise, it spurned a winning offer'.[42] In retrospect, it seems marvellous that apparently sensible people offered their warm commendation and support to the Queensland premier's blatant charlatanism, but it is easy to under-estimate the strains of utopianism in the New Right during this era, the extent to which the Hawke government had created confusion among such people, and the enormous capacity of some of them for self-delusion and wishful thinking. After the election, however, most commentators thought Bjelke-Petersen's often unhinged and always self-centred behaviour had deeply damaged the conservative cause. John Howard, for one, devoted the remainder of his long and fruitful career to ensuring that he would never again suffer anything resembling the debacle of 1987.

The issue that had triggered the double dissolution election, the Australia Card, barely figured in the campaign. This was a foolish omission on the part of the opposition parties, because public opinion was turning against it. One post-election commentator remarked that the failure of the Liberal Party to make anything of the issue suggested 'the same lack of interest, if not contempt, for civil liberties

---

42   Des Keegan, 'Time for a Liberal spring clean', *Australian*, 13 July 1987.

as the Labor Party'.⁴³ A more likely explanation, however, is that the coalition simply failed to register the potential potency of the issue, in a climate in which economic matters seemed the most pressing. As it happened, the government abandoned its plans for the Australia Card before the end of the year when confronted with an explosion of public hostility.⁴⁴

The consequences of the disarray in conservative politics that the 1987 election both reflected and compounded have had powerful implications for Australian political history. This was an election that mattered. Labor's victory meant that it could press on with policies that, for its critics on the broader left, often amounted to the slaughter of sacred cows. Reform of the university system including the re-introduction of fees, tariff cuts, privatisation and a move towards more decentralised industrial relations all followed the election. While the coalition would have travelled down much the same path – possibly faster and further – if it had won the election, Labor's victory meant market-friendly reforms would be tempered by social and welfare spending of a kind to which the coalition parties remained unreconciled throughout the 1980s. For instance, when the Labor government moved to reform the university sector, it pursued a middle way by introducing a system of income-contingent deferred fees payable through the taxation system, rather than attempting a more vigorous shift towards full fee-paying or even a privatised system – something that the conservative parties may well have attempted if their 1987 policies are any guide. Labor's electoral longevity also helped ensure that when the shift away from centralised wage determination

---

43   David Potts, 'Howard: right policy, right man, wrong party', *Australian*, 13 July 1987.
44   Bongiorno, *Eighties*, pp.238-40.

occurred in the late 1980s, the unions were able to retain a central place in the system as agents in a collective, or enterprise, bargaining process. Through the Prices and Incomes Accord, they would play a major role in shaping compulsory superannuation. Labor's electoral success in 1987 – and its further victories in 1990 and 1993 – also preserved another policy that had been part of the ALP's agreement with the unions when it came to office in 1983, the system of health insurance called Medicare.

In the final years of the Hawke Government between 1987 and 1991, there would also be a decisive move towards stronger environmental protection. While Labor had a good record in this area stretching back to its success in preventing the damming of the Franklin River in Tasmania in 1983, the style of pragmatism that Labor had displayed at the 1987 election was critical in shaping its future actions. Labor courted conservation groups in the lead-up to the election, with right-wing powerbroker Graham Richardson, who would become environment minister after the election, being instrumental in this effort. The coalition policy, by way of contrast, was to return environmental issues largely to state government control.

Commentators puzzled after the 1987 election about whether Labor's success represented a decisive break with the patterns of twentieth-century electoral competition, which had seen the non-Labor parties dominate. Thirty years on, it is still not entirely clear whether this was the case, since the coalition has dominated federal politics since the end of the Hawke-Keating era. Increasing party competition, manifest especially in the growing number of marginal seats, ensured that Labor's ascendancy rested on much shakier foundations than the hegemony of the Menzies Government. The ALP's share of the primary vote dropped from 49.5% in 1983 to 47.5% in

1984 and 45.8% in 1987, and it then dipped below 40% in 1990. As a result, the government became increasingly dependent on the preferences of minor parties.

What If?

How would modern Australian politics have been different if the coalition had won the 1987 election? Inevitably, counterfactual history is a dangerous business, but the following scenario seems plausible. John Howard would probably have governed for two terms at least – the normal minimum since the demise of the Scullin Labor government in 1931 – but a coalition government would then have faced the challenge of guiding Australia out of a recession in the early 1990s. In the meantime, Howard is likely to have drastically cut expenditure in the effort to pay for his tax promises at the 1987 election and then balance the books in the context of declining economic activity from around 1990, as Australia entered a recession. With an empowered New Right outside parliament – and, no doubt, increasingly well-represented in it – supporting even lower taxes and lower spending, the pressures for dry economic policy and aggressive anti-union measures would have been powerful. The Liberal Party had decided not to take a consumption tax to the 1987 election, but perhaps it might have found it necessary to do so in 1990 or 1993, in the face of declining tax receipts from other sources. Having already abolished Medicare as a universal health scheme, a coalition government is likely to have sought to reduce health expenditure even further after 1987, and to have pursued a more aggressive policy of inserting market forces into higher education, as well as faster and more far-reaching privatisation of government assets.

All the same, the coalition would have still faced the barrier of the Australian Democrats in the Senate, a moderating influence, as well as resistance from a union movement that in 1990 represented about 40% of the paid workforce. A coalition might have lost government either in 1993 or in 1996. Perhaps a more experienced John Hewson, fresh from his ordeals as treasurer in a Howard Government, might have emerged as opposition leader against a Labor government led by Kim Beazley. It is hard to imagine Paul Keating having endured many years in opposition after his time as treasurer.

These are mere speculations; and, in truth, given the extent of agreement between the major parties in economic and foreign policy by the 1990s, the differences might not have been great in the end. Perhaps Australia would have had a *WorkChoices*-style industrial relations policy in the 1990s, but this would have been unlikely without conservative control of the Senate. Possibly a later 1990s Labor government might have been able to advance the cause of an Australian republic, but the same divisions as actually occurred in 1999 over the most appropriate model would not have evaporated with the career of John Howard.

Nonetheless, even amidst the uncertainties of counterfactual history, it is clear enough that there would have been greater pressures on a 1980s Australian social model that sought to balance freer markets and higher profits with a reasonably generous welfare state, environmental protection, and a continuing role for unions in industrial affairs. To that extent, 1987 was an election that mattered, one which ensured that even during a period of rapid global transformation, Australia tended to cleave to a 'middle way'.

INTERIM: 1987–1996

John Howard's dogged performance in the 1987 election was ultimately insufficient to allow him to retain the leadership of his party. His effort, during the bicentennial year of 1988, to shift the Liberals in a socially conservative direction through the *Future Directions* statement received some favourable reaction but also a good deal of criticism and even ridicule, much of it focussed on the nostalgic image of a family on the cover that was redolent of the 1950s. Some remarks in a radio interview that same year suggesting that the number of Asian immigrants arriving in the country might be more than could be readily absorbed by the Australian community seemed to further undermine his position.

In May 1989 his great rival of the era, Andrew Peacock, managed to regain the leadership in a party coup; Ian Sinclair lost the leadership of the National Party at the same time. But several of the coup-plotters then went on ABC television to provide the inside story of their overthrow of Howard, thereby immediately damaging the position of the new leader. The Liberal Party was also haunted through this period by the possibility – never realised – of a move into federal politics by John Elliott, one of the era's leading businessman and a major figure in Liberal Party affairs.

The Labor government entered one of its most adventurous periods of reform during the late 1980s, but in the context of a growing sense of unease within the community about the rapid nature of change. The government announced a big round of tariff cuts in 1988, and there was a revolution in the higher education sector, which included the reintroduction of student fees, intended to reshape it to meet Australia's future economic needs. The Bicentenary of 1988 was an occasion for celebration and pride, but also for reflection on the legacies of colonialism, acting as a reminder that Labor's performance in delivering justice to Aboriginal people was disappointing. Asian immigration remained contentious, as did immigration policy more generally, at the same time as Japanese investment produced overblown rhetoric about economic domination. Environmental issues were increasingly salient.

The 1990 election signalled a critical shift in Australian electoral politics. No government before this time had managed to win a majority in the House of Representatives with a primary vote of less than 40%. But this was Labor's achievement in the election, a result that the party had pursued frankly, especially through environmental policy, in the expectation that many disillusioned voters no longer prepared to give the government its primary vote would nonetheless offer a preference. The vote for minor parties such as the Australian Democrats and Greens and Independent candidates increased, but preference flows helped the ALP narrowly retain office. The Liberals' performance in the election campaign was poor, reflecting somewhat the fractiousness of the coalition's internal politics over the previous several years.

The politics of the early 1990s were shadowed by a deep economic recession and the intense rivalry between Bob Hawke, the prime minister, and Paul Keating, the treasurer. Keating managed to defeat Hawke in a party room ballot in December 1991 after an earlier, unsuccessful effort. The poor state of the economy, the government's declining standing and a resurgent opposition under the leadership of John Hewson, a professional economist before his entry into politics, appeared to spell the end for the long-standing government. Keating, however, gradually gained an ascendancy over Hewson, whose radically free market *Fightback!* manifesto proved a large target. The opposition's proposal for a Goods and Services Tax was particularly damaging to its popularity. After a superb campaign by Keating, Labor won a surprise victory in the federal election of March 1993.

Labor's good fortune could not last. Keating continued to emphasise Australia's relations with Asia, Aboriginal reconciliation, the arts and the republic, and the economy showed signs of recovery, but the accusation that the government was out of touch with voters gained increasing support. The opposition could not initially capitalise, as a fatally damaged Hewson was replaced as leader by Alexander Downer, who in turn gave way to John Howard in January 1995. Howard proved a stabilising influence and positioned the coalition for a return to government.

Chapter 8

1996

LAZARUS RISES

Jill Sheppard

Paul Keating has claimed that Australia would be a republic today if he had won the 1996 federal election, but change is hard. Public opinion was on his side in the republic debate, but his attempts to bundle the republic issue into a broad vision of large-scale social reform were less popular. Keating's government promised a new Australian identity: confident, outward-looking, socially progressive, not pitching to mass public opinion or apologising for its progressiveness. The landslide electoral result that brought John Howard's nearly 12-year government into power suggests that Keating's plan for Australia was too much, too fast, for most Australians. Howard's victory on a platform of minimal reform and traditional values, his remarkable tenure as prime minister, and the political approaches of subsequent Labor governments reflect Australian voters' inherent conservatism. For better or worse, 1996 was an archetype for the disciplined, 'small target' campaigns that so often win Australian elections. Political survival and risk minimisation now characterise Australian politics.

Retrospective accounts of the 1996 Australian federal election focus heavily on 'the race issue': it was, after all, the election at which Pauline Hanson entered parliament as the 'disendorsed Liberal' member for Oxley.[1] And undoubtedly, the persistence of Hanson

---

1 Simon Jackman, 'Pauline Hanson, the Mainstream, and Political Elites: The Place of Race in Australian Political Ideology', *Australian Journal of Political Science*, 33:2, 1 July 1998, pp.167–86.

as a thorn in the side of Australian multiculturalism points to the importance of 1996 as a pivotal moment for public discussions on race, Indigenous relations, and immigration in Australia. However, the 1996 election was about the repudiation of Prime Minister Paul Keating's sometimes lofty, and sometimes inclusive, rhetoric in favour of a former treasurer renowned as much for his quiet conservatism as for not being as hazard-prone as his immediate predecessors as Liberal leader.

Why, then, does a country discard a government with a declared vision for the nation, and presiding over post-recession economic growth, for an untested opposition, led by a bespectacled former solicitor on his second stint as the alternative prime minister? This chapter posits three broad reasons for the decline of the Keating government. First, Australians' innate (small 'c') conservatism, which results in voters choosing stability over change. Second, campaigns do not necessarily 'win' elections, particularly in a compulsory voting context such as in Australia, but egregious missteps can absolutely lose campaigns. The Liberal Party's 1996 campaign embraced discipline to an extent not previously seen in Australia. Finally, Keating's focus on 'blue sky' issues attempted unsuccessfully to change the nature of political campaigning in Australia, and has led to the subsequent reversion to more tangible political issues, namely economic management and immigration policy.

More than twenty years on, the legacy of the 1996 election is arguably only just being realised. Pauline Hanson is still part of the Australian political landscape, and immigration regularly features among surveys of Australians' 'most important issues'. Public support for immigration has increased steadily since 1996, but not since Keating's tenure has a major party unequivocally endorsed mass immigration and a multicultural society. The notion of becoming a republic – first floated as a serious prospect by Keating during his time as prime minister – sits persistently at the fringes of our political debate. Keating's passionate advocacy for a republic, coupled with public support, led opposition leader Howard to reluctantly commit to holding a 'people's convention', and eventual referendum, on the issue, in spite of his deeply-held monarchist views.[2] Chair of the Australian Republican Movement, Malcolm Turnbull, later became the 29th prime minister of Australia, representing the Liberal Party. In as much as the 1996 election was a testing ground for the policies, campaign techniques, and leadership styles central to Australian politics, the results reveal much about Australia's political culture.

The Keating Years

Previously an esteemed and immensely skilled federal treasurer in the Bob Hawke-led ALP government, Keating launched a second, and this time successful, challenge to Hawke's leadership in December 1991. The then opposition leader, the Liberal Party's John Hewson, had embarked on a bold strategy of announcing detailed, wide-ranging policies. While this approach culminated in the ill-fated *Fightback!* policy package that has since been described as a major failing of Hewson's 1993 election campaign, the newly installed prime minister faced an opponent with a comprehensive suite of policy positions.[3] It is easy to understand the sense of urgency that inspired Keating first to overthrow Hawke, whom Keating believed to be wasting his time

---

2   Ian McAllister, 'Elections without Cues: The 1999 Australian Republic Referendum', *Australian Journal of Political Science*, 36:2, 2001, pp.247–69.
3   Andrew Robb, 'The Liberal Party Campaign', in Clive Bean et al. (eds), *The Politics of Retribution: The 1996 Australian Federal Election* (Sydney: Allen & Unwin, 1997), pp.34–41.

and opportunity as prime minister, and then to set about declaring his own vision for the nation.[4]

The extent to which Keating immediately set to work outlining his ambitious plan for Australia is remarkable. Contemporary accounts indicate his frustration at having to wait as long as he did to become prime minister, withering in Hawke's shadow for eight years: 'Mate, I'm carrying such a crushing burden ... all this should have happened years ago', Keating is quoted by Paul Kelly as saying.[5] In 1992 alone, Keating delivered an infrastructure and economic policy statement designed at rebutting the Liberals' *Fightback!* manifesto, visited Indonesia in a bold declaration of his government's foreign policy priorities, and delivered the 'Redfern speech' acknowledging the deleterious effect of previous governments' policies towards Indigenous Australians and committing to reconciliation within a decade. Throughout the year, he signalled his preference for an Australian republic to an audience that included Queen Elizabeth II, and declared that the Australian flag should not 'have the flag of another country in the corner of it'.[6] These provocative social stances were balanced with savvy 'retail politics': Keating both positioned himself as 'de facto opposition leader', justifying his pivot to issues of grand social reform, and 'used incumbency ruthlessly' to deliver tax cuts and 'bonus' welfare payments to families in his first year as leader.[7]

Keating began 1992 trailing Hewson as Australians' 'preferred Prime Minister' by as many as 18 percentage points (Graph 1). By

---

[4] Pamela Williams, *The Victory: The inside Story of the Takeover of Australia* (Sydney: Allen & Unwin, 1997).

[5] Paul Kelly, *The March of Patriots: The Struggle for Modern Australia* (Melbourne: Melbourne University Press, 2009), p.54.

[6] Ibid., p.73.

[7] George Megalogenis, *The Longest Decade*, Second Edition, (Melbourne: Scribe Publications, 2009), p.65.

campaigning relentlessly against Hewson's economic proposals – primarily, his proposed 15% 'goods and services tax' (GST) – Keating's approval rating surpassed Hewson's for the first time as early as March that year. Learning from Hawke's 'disastrous' response to Hewson's GST proposal, Keating attacked Hewson on the detail of his policy to end 1992 with equal levels of support from the electorate.[8] The confusion surrounding the centrepiece of the opposition's economic package was 'a problem of Hewson's making'.[9] For all Keating's 'big picture' rhetoric throughout 1992, the issue that brought voters around to his government was uncertainty about a complex policy put forward by a comparatively unknown opposition leader. To the extent that voters knew Hewson, they knew he was a wonkish, Ferrari-driving economist with a PhD, and hell-bent on reform.[10] Graph 2 shows how drastically the ALP's electoral prospects shifted in late 1992 and early 1993. At the election on 13 March 1993, the ALP increased its majority in the House of Representatives, stunning pollsters, journalists, and Keating himself.[11]

Hawke gave Keating little credit for winning the 1993 election, sarcastically referring – on the night of the election, no less – to the GST as the 'Government Salvation Tax' and speculating that Howard, then Hewson's shadow minister for industrial relations, could have defeated Keating at the election.[12] Undeterred by Hawke's dismissive appraisal, Keating resumed his 'big picture' policy agenda following his unexpected election win. And here is where the image

---

8   Paul Kelly, *The End of Certainty: Power, Politics, and Business in Australia* (Sydney: Allen & Unwin, 1994); Megalogenis, *The Longest Decade*.
9   Ibid., p.84.
10 Paul 't Hart and John Uhr, *Public Leadership: Perspectives and Practices* (Canberra: ANU E Press, 2008), p.221.
11 Williams, *The Victory*.
12 Megalogenis, *The Longest Decade*, p.87.

ELECTIONS MATTER

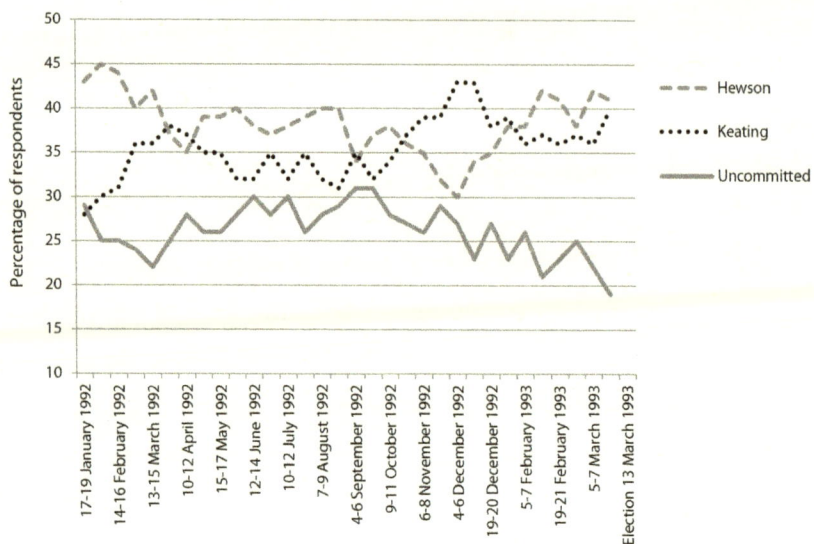

Graph 1: 'Who do you think would make the better Prime Minister?', 20 December 1991 to 13 March 1993.[1]

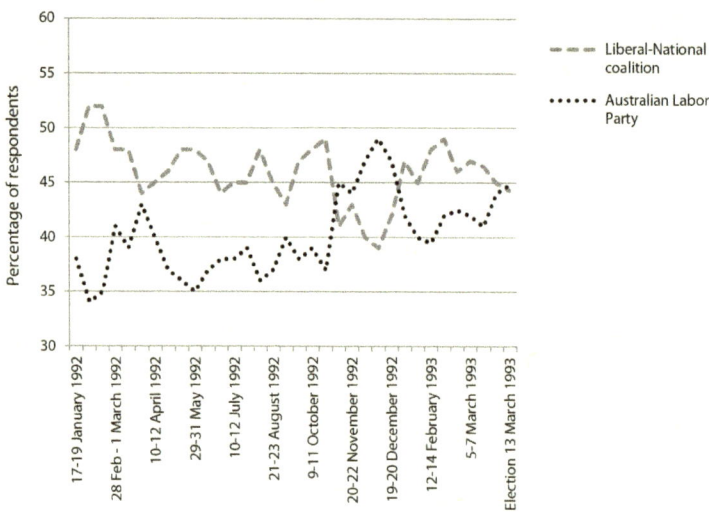

Graph 2: 'If a federal election for the House of Representatives was held today, which of the following would you vote for?'; two-party preferred, 20 December 1991 to 13 March 1993.[2]

---

1   'Opinion poll archive', *Newspoll*, Accessed online at < http://polling.newspoll.com.au>.
2   Ibid.

of the 1996 election begins to emerge more sharply. With the drudgery of the election behind him, and satisfied with his role in the government's victory,

> Keating wanted to open a fresh chapter of Australian history. Every song he sang was consumed by this thirst – from the Republic to the Redfern speech to competition policy.[13]

From 1993 onwards, Keating determinedly threw off the pragmatic politics that characterised Hawke's leadership between 1983 and 1991, and focused – to the apparent dismay of many of his advisers and party officials – on this 'fresh chapter'. Paul Kelly calls Keating's mindset at this time 'a blend of idealism, ambition and megalomania laced with a thread of plausibility'.[14] More generously, Carol Johnson notes that 'in speech after speech subsequent to becoming prime minister, Paul Keating drew a much broader vision of the Australian society he wished to create – multicultural, diverse, celebrating difference, benefitting everyone'.[15] Whichever characterisation better reflects Keating's intentions, with the benefit of hindsight his leadership on social reforms – as well as arguably less provocative microeconomic reforms – is remarkable in its audacity.

Perhaps foremost among Keating's social reform pillars was his focus on reconciliation with Indigenous Australians. In 1992, the High Court of Australia handed down its judgment on the landmark case of *Mabo v Queensland (No. 2)* striking down the concept of *terra nullius*: that is, the concept that Australian was 'nobody's land' when

---

13 Kelly, *The March of Patriots*, p.92.
14 Ibid., p.97.
15 Carol Johnson, *Governing Change: Keating to Howard* (Brisbane: University of Queensland Press, 2000), p.30.

European settlers arrived in 1788.¹⁶ This effectively cleared the way for Indigenous communities to lodge claims for continuously inhabited land and prompted a 'collective meltdown' among the resource and agricultural industries who feared for their mining and pastoral leases respectively.¹⁷ Australians had recently softened in their views towards issues such as Indigenous support and reconciliation, but remained generally unsupportive: following the 1993 election, 44% of Australians believed that government support for Indigenous Australians had gone 'too far' or 'much too far'. The last time they were asked whether Indigenous Australians' land rights had 'gone too far', were 'about right' or 'not gone far enough' (in 1987), 59% answered 'too far'.¹⁸

It was in this environment – industry lobbies in defence mode, and public opinion seemingly set against further support or land rights for Indigenous Australians – that Keating launched his campaign for reconciliation. George Megalogenis notes that Keating 'wanted to give Aboriginal Australians something they had never had before [i.e. native title] – and which a majority of the electorate thought he was crazy to even consider'.¹⁹ Moreover, his colleagues within the ALP grew increasingly frustrated with Keating's doggedness on the issue, encouraging him to yield to the mining and agricultural lobbies.²⁰ Whether Keating intended it or not, his defence of the Mabo decision in the face of business and public opposition marked him

---

16   Frank Brennan, *One Land, One Nation : Mabo – towards 2000* (Brisbane: University of Queensland Press, 1995).
17   Megalogenis, *The Longest Decade*, p.105.
18   Sarah M. Cameron and Ian McAllister, *Trends in Australian Political Opinion: Results from the Australian Election Study, 1987-2016*, (Canberra: Australian National University, 2016).
19   Megalogenis, *The Longest Decade*, p.107.
20   Ibid.

in voters' minds as a fundamentally different leader to Hawke, and someone with loftier interests than just day-to-day life in Australia.[21]

The characterisation of Keating as 'out of touch' contrasts with the rhetoric of embracing national identity he deployed between 1993 and 1996.[22] This is perhaps best typified in his emphasis on engagement with Asia, a second pillar of his broadly defined social reform agenda. Again, Keating attempted to lead public opinion – and in retrospect he foreshadowed a pivot in foreign policy that has since manifested in official government references to an 'Asian Century'.[23] For Australians in 1993, however, future plaudits were irrelevant: Keating's talk of all Australians as a collective 'we', and assurances of the nation's safety amidst its Asian neighbours, could not convince voters in the short term.

Keating found himself more closely aligned with voters on his desire for Australia to become a republic and, arguably more provocatively, to change the Australian flag. Picking up on arguments first floated before the 1993 election, Keating connected the anachronisms of the British Monarchy, and Australia's constitutional reliance on the Monarch as the country's head of state, with the increasing diversity of the population. Such a proposal was timely, argued Keating, because never before did so few Australians have cultural or genealogical ties to Britain.[24] Keating was correct on the demographics: net migration to Australia had increased rapidly during the

---

21 Williams, *The Victory*, p.46.
22 Stephanie Younane Brookes, '"Secure in Our Identity": Regional Threat and Opportunity in Australian Election Discourse, 1993 and 1996', *Australian Journal of Politics & History*, 58:4, December 2012, pp.542–56.
23 Hugh White, 'Power Shift: Rethinking Australia's Place in the Asian Century', *Australian Journal of International Affairs*, 65:1, 1 February 2011, pp.81–93.
24 James Jupp, 'From "White Australia" to "Part of Asia": Recent Shifts in Australian Immigration Policy towards the Region', *The International Migration Review*, 29:1, 1995, pp.207–28.

late 1980s and the population was more culturally and linguistically diverse than ever.[25] The Australian- and British-born population had hit a low of 83% of all Australian residents, down from 85% in 1986 and 87% in 1971.[26]

Further justification for Keating's push for a republic was the strong level of support among Australian voters. In 1993, 60% of voters favoured becoming a republic to remaining a constitutional monarchy, while 42% supported Keating's mooted plan to change the flag.[27] But he misread the mood of the population in favouring grand symbols over grassroots sentiment. Australians seemed effectively to decouple their opinions on becoming a republic from their opinions on immigration and multiculturalism. Where Keating saw a connection between republicanism and a larger, more diverse population, most Australians saw none. Following the 1993 election a full 70% of Australians thought the number of immigrants allowed into the country had 'gone too far': the highest number in the almost three decades that the question has been asked.[28] In 1996, 63% wanted immigration levels reduced either 'a little' or 'a lot', and 46% stated that the coalition was the party closest to their own view on immigration.[29]

---

25 Janet Phillips and Joanne Simon-Davies, 'Migration to Australia: A Quick Guide to the Statistics', text, Research Papers 2015-16 (Canberra: Parliamentary Library, Parliament of Australia, 2015), Accessed online. <http://www.aph.gov.au/About_Parliament/Parliamentary_Departments/Parliamentary_Library/pubs/rp/rp1516/Quick_Guides/MigrationStatistics>

26 James Jupp, '1031.0 Year Book Australia: Ethnic and Cultural Diversity in Australia (Introduction)' (Canberra: Australian Bureau of Statistics, January 1, 1995), Accessed online. <http://www.abs.gov.au/ausstats/abs@.nsf/0/49F609C83CF34D69CA2569DE0025C182?Open>

27 Cameron and McAllister, *Trends in Australian Political Opinion*.

28 Ibid.

29 Ibid.

Howard Rises Again

Keating's juxtaposition of closer ties with Asia, multiculturalism, and a republic (and potential flag change), while also supporting the rights of Indigenous Australians to claim native title, asked a lot more of the electorate than Hawke's agenda ever did. Where Hawke led with a 'folksy' style, at times obsessive about achieving the approval of voters, Keating required that Australians make the same connections and use the same length of foresight that he could.[30] In the meantime, voter disenchantment did not have an obvious resolution: Hewson had seen off a post-election challenge by John Howard to remain Liberal leader, before eventually succumbing to the 'dream team' of Alexander Downer and Peter Costello in May 1994. After a disastrous eight months as leader of the opposition, Downer resigned from the position in January 1995, clearing the way for Howard's return to the Liberal leadership, and Keating's first real challenge.

An introspective social and economic conservative, Howard had previously served inauspiciously as treasurer (from 1977 to 1983) in Malcolm Fraser's government and later as opposition leader from 1985 to 1989. Although the economic rationalist policies he pursued as treasurer were endorsed and adopted by subsequent governments of both major parties, 'Howard left office [in 1983] tarnished after the treasury misjudged the economic slowdown'.[31] As opposition leader (1985-89), he had withheld detailed policy in favour of slogans aimed at getting voters to think about their 'hip-pocket' interests. As discussed in the previous chapter, his lack of a cohesive message

---

30 Kelly, *The End of Certainty*, p.272.
31 Ibid., 102.

backed with credible policies had seen the Hawke government easily returned to power.[32]

This time around, Howard had a clearer idea of what a successful opposition leadership – understood as retention of the job and eventual electoral victory – would entail. However, the thing for which he was best known among voters – 'dry' economic reform – had been co-opted by the Hawke and Keating governments and provided no obvious point of differentiation between the new challenger and the incumbent.[33] Moreover, generational turnover in the federal press gallery meant that many journalists covering the new opposition leader knew little about him.[34] Accordingly, Howard embarked on a series of 'headland' speeches throughout 1995, setting out his alternative vision for Australian society. He spoke expansively on the role of government in Australian society, on 'Australian fairness', and in December 1995, on national identity. Not since Robert Menzies had a leader of either major party so deliberately laid out an overarching vision of Australian society; between 1992 and 1995, the leaders of both major parties embarked on such a strategy.

Immediately, Howard's stated vision fitted more closely with public opinion than Keating's ever did. Howard's references to 'individual freedom and dignity, fairer and more competitive enterprise, limited and more accountable government, and a more genuine sense of national community' contrasted sharply with Keating's statements of previous years.[35] Indeed, the differences between Howard's and

---

32 Clive Bean, 'The 1996 Australian Federal Election', *Electoral Studies*, 15:3, 1 August 1996, pp.422–25; Kelly, *The End of Certainty*, ch. 18.
33 Gerard Henderson, *A Howard Government?: Inside the Coalition* (Sydney: Harper Collins, 1995), p.98.
34 Megalogenis, *The Longest Decade*, p.162.
35 '1995 National Lecture Series: The Role of Government', June 6, 1995, Accessed online. <http://australianpolitics.com/1995/06/06/john-howard-headland-speech-

Keating's public statements prior to 1996 were more rhetorical than substantial: Howard lauded the benefits of trade with Asia, while warning that 'once we start disavowing our history, or disowning our values or changing our institutions simply because we think regional countries will respect us more for doing so, then we will be badly mistaken'.[36] On social services – an issue on which he was particularly vulnerable due to his longstanding support for economic rationalist reforms – Howard emphasised his conservatism:

> I give you this pledge: I want to do everything in my power to preserve the social fabric of this nation… No Government can make things perfect but the challenge for Government is to make things better. If the price of progress is human misery, it's not progress. If change makes people worse off, it's not reform.[37]

Besides appealing to voters' conservative instincts, Howard also placed lower cognitive demands on voters. Where Keating argued that Australia's future would be shaped by external forces – including Asia's emergence and the declining relevance of the British Monarchy – Howard declared that 'future constitutional arrangements or national symbols are exclusively a matter for Australians'.[38] He committed to hosting a 'people's convention' to explore options for constitutional change at some time in 1997, effectively deferring the issue of a republic until after the election. On national identity more broadly, he argued that 'the suggestion that we have yet to develop a proper identity, or that government can deliver us a new and improved one,

---

role-of-govt.html>

36   Ibid.
37   'Fair Australia' (Address to the Australian Council of Social Services, Sydney, October 13, 1995), Accessed online. <http://australianpolitics.com/1995/10/13/fair-australia-howard-headland-speech.html>
38   1995 National Lecture Series: The Role of Government.

treats us like children'.³⁹ And on immigration specifically, Howard had sent a clear, if unscripted message back in 1988, when as opposition leader he made a series of comments to the effect that a smaller intake of immigrants from Asia would improve social cohesion in Australia.⁴⁰

Lead up to the Election

In the three years leading into the 1996 federal election, political discourse in Australia converged on these few symbols: the country's place in the world (particularly in relation to Asia and Britain), the identity of its people, and its relations with its Indigenous population. Keating had been allowed to set the agenda in this regard, despite reluctance from his ALP colleagues, and Howard appeared willing to join the fight in 1995 on these broad terms. Where Keating emphasised the need to use international and domestic circumstances to embrace progress, Howard acknowledged those circumstances but urged against progress just for the sake of it. Unusually for Australian elections, the campaign looked as though it might be fought on these symbolic issues, as much or even more than the more usual 'hip-pocket' economic policies, health, and education.

Two decades on from the 1996 election, it is difficult to imagine an election campaign fought on such abstract, visionary issues. The accumulation of almost a century of research into voter behaviour has identified a number of explanations for voters' decision making. For instance, Downs' theory of spatial politics observes that voters use ideological shortcuts to identify which parties are 'closest' to

---

39 The Hon John Howard, 'Politics and Patriotism: A Reflection on the National Identity Debate' (Melbourne, December 13, 1995), Accessed online. <http://australianpolitics.com/1995/12/13/national-identity-howard-headland-speech.html>
40 Kelly, *The End of Certainty*, p.422.

their own positions.⁴¹ Campbell et al. emphasise the role of party identification, drawing on social psychological research into the relative effects of in-group and out-group membership.⁴² Alternatively, Stokes' critique of spatial politics argues that voters effectively make assessments based on the perceived competence of parties to manage the issues most salient to them personally.⁴³ Research has shown that Australian voters tend to assess the major parties' ability with regard to economic management, jobs, good governance, and border security policies.⁴⁴

Each of these theories notes the incentive for parties to attract voters who would not, in ordinary circumstances, cast their ballot for that party. In spatial terms, it might mean either moving more closely towards the ideological position of a critical mass of undecided voters, or deliberately obfuscating a party platform to induce irrational behaviour from voters. In social psychological terms, the challenge for parties is to convince voters that they are better off as party identifiers than not. In neither of these concepts of voter behaviour – which have between them informed the majority of subsequent voter research – is campaigning on broad themes of national identity and Indigenous reconciliation particularly advisable: voters do not regularly rate them as important enough issues to inform a vote decision. And in terms of valence politics, the most rational approach for

---

41   Anthony Downs, *An Economic Theory of Democracy* (New York: Harper and Row, 1957).

42   Angus Campbell et al., *The American Voter* (Chicago: University of Chicago Press, 1960).

43   Donald E. Stokes, 'Spatial Models of Party Competition', *The American Political Science Review*, 57:2, 1 June 1963, pp.368–77.

44   Ian McAllister, Jill Sheppard, and Clive Bean, 'Valence and Spatial Explanations for Voting in the 2013 Australian Election', *Australian Journal of Political Science*, 50:2, 3 April 2015, pp.330–46; Cameron and McAllister, *Trends in Australian Political Opinion*.

a party seeking government is to emphasise its competency in widely salient issues and not, generally, issues such as national identity.

It is within this context that the tactical success of Howard's foray into Keating's territory throughout 1995 becomes evident. The 16 percentage point swing towards the Liberals' Brendan Smyth at a March 1995 by-election in the seat of Canberra (the cause of which – Ros Kelly's forced resignation – was a minor victory for Howard's opposition) provided early signs of optimism. When the election campaign officially commenced on 29 January 1996, the coalition had led opinion polls of voting intention for a full year (see Graph 3). Howard had worked to assure voters that he had positions on each of Keating's 'big picture' issues, and that those positions were not radically different from Keating's positions. What differences existed, either rhetorically or substantially, placed Howard to the conservative side of Keating on Indigenous reconciliation, national identity, and immigration. The option remaining to Keating was to convince voters that his government, and his less conservative stances, were preferable to Howard's more cautious approach. Moreover, Keating's commitment to those totemic issues and his positions on them bounded what he could reasonably raise in the context of an election campaign. For Keating, substantially shifting his focus or positions would have risked alienating his existing supporters.

1996

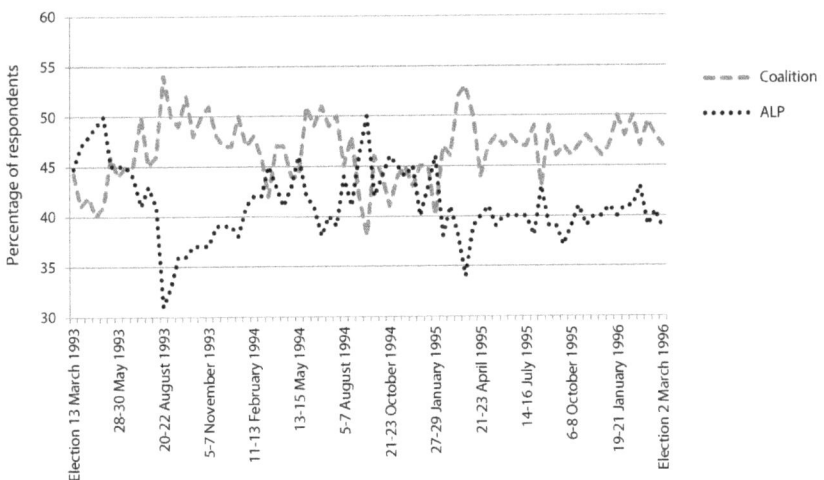

Graph 3: 'If a federal election for the House of Representatives was held today, which of the following would you vote for?'; two-party preferred, 1993 to 1996.[45]

Howard's rhetorical manoeuvres throughout 1995 were complemented – if not scripted – by a particularly astute Liberal Party organisation. Headed by eventual cabinet minister Andrew Robb, the Liberal Party secretariat of 1996 placed great stock in commissioned research identifying a bloc of established ALP voters who felt 'betrayed' by Keating's lofty ambitions for Australia.[46] Robb's campaign exploited the contrast between voters' 'economic insecurity' and 'news that land was being bought for Aboriginal people or ramps were being built for the disabled'.[47] Once the campaign proper was under way, any sense of bipartisan agreement on immigration or reconciliation was lost. In the final weeks of the campaign period, Howard went so far as to accuse the ALP of having a 'millstone' of political correctness around its neck.[48]

---

45 Opinion poll archive, *Newspoll*, Accessed online <http://polling.newspoll.com.au>
46 *Williams, The Victory*, p.50.
47 Marian Sawer, 'A Defeat for Political Correctness?', in Clive Bean et al. (eds) *The Politics of Retribution: The 1996 Australian Federal Election* (Sydney: Allen & Unwin, 1997), p.74.
48 Ibid., p.73.

The Hanson Factor

With the right-wing of the electorate targeted by Howard's conservative assurances, arguably the largest threat to the coalition's 1996 campaign came from that same quarter. Disciplined tactics and messaging could not have prepared the Liberal Party campaign machine for a candidate like Pauline Hanson. Preselected by the Liberal Party of Queensland in 1995 for a seemingly safe Labor seat, Hanson was subsequently disendorsed on 15 February 1996 after accusing previous governments of perpetuating racism by 'looking after Aborigines too much'.[49] The prospective member for Oxley presented a singular problem for Howard: how to disavow her comments on the basis of moral rectitude, but not confuse voters as to the validity of his previous conservative statements on Asian immigration (another target of Hanson's ire). The complexity of Howard's position was compounded by Hanson's candidacy in Queensland, the state with voters most likely to agree with her stance.[50]

Hanson's unapologetic expression of what might be called the 'anti-Keating' position on immigration and reconciliation – that white, working- and middle-class Australians were being left behind in the name of social progress – also posed a major problem for the ALP campaign. The same regular ALP voters whom Liberal researchers identified as likely to break ranks with the party over Keating's defiant progressivism had the issue of Asian immigration – and its ostensible impact on Australian society – placed at the forefront of their minds. As far as valence issues go in Australian politics, immigration is one

---

49 Williams, *The Victory*, p.245.
50 John Wanna, 'Queensland', in Jeremy Moon and Campbell Sharman (eds), *Australian Politics and Government: The Commonwealth, the States and the Territories* (Cambridge: Cambridge University Press, 2003), pp.74–103.

of the big ones: Hanson was increasing its salience, and a majority of Australians preferred the coalition's policies.[51]

Meanwhile, the ALP focused its campaign on health policy. Followers of Australian politics will observe how consistent ALP election campaigns are in this regard, and there is a clear reason for it: following the 1996 election, more than half of surveyed voters named the ALP as the party closest to their own position on health and Medicare.[52] Gone were the 'big picture' aspirations of 1992-5. Instead the party emphasised a $1.3 billion dollar plan to reduce the cost of private health insurance for families.[53] Typifying Keating's disastrous luck throughout the 1996 campaign, the marquee policy announcement was undermined by health minister Carmen Lawrence misquoting the Liberals' position on Medicare. Adding insult to injury, in the dying days of the campaign Treasurer Ralph Willis announced that he had inadvertently received two letters in his electorate office: purportedly addressed to Howard and written by Costello and Liberal Premier of Victoria Jeff Kennett, the letters suggested that Howard planned to cut existing payments of federal funds to the state governments.[54] Befitting the inauspicious Labor campaign, the letters were swiftly uncovered as frauds; the result of a practical joke devised by conservative students at the University of Melbourne, and Willis' credibility was devastated. Already in retreat on policy and vision for the nation, Keating's government had been publicly embarrassed by student politicians.

---

51 Jackman, 'Pauline Hanson'.
52 R. Jones, I. McAllister, and David Gow, 'Australian Election Study 1996 [Data File]' (Australian Data Archives, The Australian National University, 1996), Accessed online. <http://aes.anu.edu.au>
53 Williams, *The Victory*, 218.
54 Ian McAllister, 'The End of a Labor Era in Australian Politics', *Government and Opposition*, 31: 3, July 1996, pp.288–303.

The Result

With the campaign drawing to a close on 2 March 1996, Howard's Liberal-National coalition had a substantial lead in public opinion polls, and the result was a foregone conclusion. Four years earlier, when Keating promised to breathe new life into the established ALP government, the economy was recovering after the economic recession of 1990 and 1991, and Hewson was failing to inspire voters' confidence with his detailed economic policy manifesto. As voters went to the polls in 1996, the diminutive and sometimes bumbling Howard looked to unseat the urbane, visionary Keating. The campaign proved to be a victory for political scientists, as both major parties fell in lockstep with the small target, 'hip-pocket', and highly salient issues common in Australia political campaigns. Until 1996, Keating's strategy had offered something different in its ambitious vision. Once the election writs were issued, however, political survival tactics took over. Seven elections later, political survival continues to define Australian political campaigning.

Some of the key dynamics of the 2 March 1996 federal election are, ironically perhaps, best revealed in the atypical case of the working-class, Ipswich-based electorate of Oxley. Notionally disendorsed by the Liberal Party,[55] with Howard declaring that she would never be a member of the Liberal parliamentary party, Pauline Hanson nevertheless more than doubled the vote achieved by the Liberal Party's candidate in the previous (1993) election: she received 48.6% of the first preference vote, compared with 25.5% by the party's candidate in 1993. While a mere snapshot of the national mood, the Oxley

---

55 By the time Hanson made these remarks – the most recent in a string of provocative public comments – the Australian Electoral Commission deadline for nominating candidates (and party associations) had passed. Hanson was therefore listed on ballot papers as a Liberal Party candidate.

result shows the ideological distance between Keating and Australian voters. After five years of prime ministerial speeches and other statements about closer integration with Asia and the need to realign the national identity, Oxley voters embraced the opportunity to vote for a candidate arguing for lower immigration and a halt to Indigenous reconciliation.

The national results were overwhelmingly clear: the Liberal Party won enough seats in the House of Representatives to govern in their own right, that is, without requiring the support of their coalition partner, the National Party.[56] The 5.1% national swing in 'two-party preferred' vote share from the ALP in 1993 to the Liberal-National coalition in 1996 was uncommonly large. The movement of voters from the ALP to the coalition was largest in Queensland, with an 8.6% swing. The ALP retained only two seats in Queensland. Even in Victoria, where the ALP polled well in 1993, there was a swing towards the coalition (albeit of only 1.6%). Including Hanson, five Independent candidates were elected to the House of Representatives (the most at one election since 1946), while five Australian Democrats candidates and one Australian Greens candidate were elected to the Senate. Neither major party held a majority in the Senate, with the Democrats, Greens, and Tasmanian Independent Brian Harradine (and soon thereafter Labor renegade Mal Colston) commanding the balance of power.

There is never one simple explanation for election results, and the 1996 election is no different. Two overarching reasons have been proffered. The first reason contends that Keating asked Australian voters to trust in his leadership, but failed to observe or ignored the

---

56 Bean, 'The 1996 Australian Federal Election'.

fact that he was deeply disliked.[57] The second reason holds that the issue of race relations (in the context of both Indigenous reconciliation and Asian immigration) was a successful 'wedge' that cut across traditional Liberal-ALP ideology, and shifted voters from the ALP to the Liberal Party.[58]

With the combination of a relatively uneventful campaign period, broad bipartisan agreement on many issues, and little movement in public opinion polls from the start of 1996, the result arguably supports existing research that campaigns have little effect on the final result.[59] However an alternative, and plausible, reading is that the ALP's dysfunctional and undisciplined campaign had a negative effect on the result (albeit not an effect that is easily measured). The head of the ALP organisation and ostensible campaign director, Gary Gray (like Robb, also a future federal minister), had a notoriously fractious relationship with Keating throughout 1996. Williams notes the frustration faced by Gray as he continually attempted to engage Keating in campaign strategy, only to discover Keating and his advisers following their own, ultimately doomed, plans.[60]

A more disciplined ALP campaign might have avoided the futile focus on Keating's leadership as a core campaign theme, knowing that voters' opinion of Keating was irretrievably poor.[61] Likewise, a more cohesive relationship between the leader and the party organisation might have led to a more sympathetic hearing for Gray's warnings that Indigenous reconciliation made suburban voters feel insecure,

---

57   Ibid.; Clive Bean and Ian McAllister, 'Short-Term Influences on Voting Behaviour in the 1996 Election', in *The Politics of Retribution*, pp.191–206.
58   Jackman, 'Pauline Hanson'.
59   Bean, 'The 1996 Australian Federal Election'.
60   Williams, *The Victory*.
61   Bean and McAllister, 'Short-Term Influences', p.203.

and that Keating's message should be tempered with acknowledgement of that insecurity.[62] In response, Keating argued that 'he always got a good response about the Government's Mabo reforms from the people he talked to'.[63] Perhaps no one example better exemplifies the problem that the ALP organisation faced in Keating, and the double-edged sword of Keating's remarkable confidence.

On the evening of 2 March 1996, the vanquished prime minister Keating declared:

> I've got to say, not once did I tackle or take a second-best option. I always went for the big ones and people may say 'the big picture' and call into question but in the end it's the big picture that changes nations. And whatever our opponents say, Australia has changed inexorably for the better.[64]

Perhaps unsurprisingly, given what is now known about Keating's reluctance to take counsel and his legendary self-confidence, he acknowledged neither the ALP organisation nor his predecessor, Hawke. Perhaps more startlingly, Keating allegedly told colleagues that if he had the chance to run the campaign again, he would not do anything differently.[65] Retiring from the parliament in April 1996, he spent the first few years following his prime ministership in quiet repose. When he returned to public view, the full extent of his often abrasive character was on display: as well as caustic appraisals of Howard's prime ministership, he has since shared harsh words about the ALP governments led by Kevin Rudd and Julia Gillard. In an unapologetic display of his renowned iconoclasm, in 2011 he

---

62 Williams, *The Victory*.
63 Ibid., p.47.
64 Ibid., p.318.
65 Ibid., p.329.

published a collection of his speeches on issues ranging from the ALP to architecture, classical music, and Indigenous affairs.[66] However, the distance he maintained from the ALP organisation has restricted him from the ongoing political influence of Hawke.

Howard led his coalition government to three further election victories, and became the second longest serving prime minister in Australia's history, after his idol, Menzies. Under Howard and Treasurer Peter Costello, the government continued Hawke and Keating's policies of economic liberalisation, while putting the brakes on social liberalisation. Aside from substantial microeconomic reform in 2000, with the introduction of a goods and services tax five years after Hewson's failure to do the same, the nearly 12-year government did not embark on drastic economic or social change. Howard upheld his pledge to conduct a 'people's convention' to explore potential pathways to becoming a republic; the resulting constitutional convention in 1998 recommended a 'minimalist' republic model that ultimately failed at a referendum in 1999.[67] It is impossible to say whether Keating could have overseen a successful referendum campaign. While Howard was determinedly monarchist, and as a result the 'yes' campaign did not receive fully bipartisan support, referendums on constitutional change in Australia rarely succeed, and this one posed a particularly complex question to voters.[68]

---

66 Paul Keating, *After Words: Post-Prime Ministerial Speeches* (Sydney: Allen & Unwin, 2011).
67 Helen Irving, 'The Republic Referendum of 6 November 1999', *Australian Journal of Political Science*, 35:1, March 2000, pp.111–15.
68 McAllister, 'Elections Without Cues'.

Conclusion

When the Howard government was finally defeated in 2007 – in a landslide that even removed Howard from his seat in the House of Representatives – it was by an ALP leader who positioned himself as almost as conservative as Howard. By describing himself as an 'economic conservative', Kevin Rudd sought to emulate Howard's successful campaign of 1996: minimise the differences on issues favourable to the other party, and use rhetoric to amplify the differences in issues favourable to your own party. And that, in summary, is the overarching lesson from the 1996 federal election.

Keating's ALP had promised a new vision for Australia: a confident, outward-looking, socially progressive national identity that did not pitch to the 'lowest common denominator' of public opinion or apologise for its boldness. Keating's defiant defence of his government on the night of his defeat typifies the kind of politics that he tried, and largely struggled, to impose on the Australian public. Howard's victory, his remarkable tenure as prime minister, and Rudd's eventual victory in 2007 demonstrate that Australian voters are inherently conservative. Further, while campaigns might not have observable effects on election results in Australia, voters can absolutely tell when a prime minister has stopped listening to them. And not since 1996 has a successful campaign attempted, as Keating's did, to run ahead of public opinion. For better or worse, 1996 was an archetype for the disciplined, conservative, and 'small target' focused campaigns that win Australian elections.

INTERIM 1996–2001

After the coalition's victory in 1996, John Howard prosecuted the culture wars against left-wing 'élites', but his efforts were thwarted when he was outflanked on the right by the election of the Independent right-wing populist Pauline Hanson as the member for a normally safe Labor seat in Queensland. Howard did little to counter her appeal or to criticise her anti-Asian and anti-Aboriginal statements. After a mass shooting at the Port Arthur historic site in Tasmania in April 1996 that resulted in 35 deaths, the government tightened Australia's gun laws. It also cut public spending, partially privatised Telstra, limited the legal fall-out from a High Court decision in favour of native title, and formed an alliance with an aggressive stevedoring company to destroy union power on the waterfront. Australia managed to weather the Asian economic crisis as well as the collapse of the dotcom boom.

After a High Court decision that invalidated several state taxes, the government took to the 1998 federal election a proposal for a Goods and Services Tax (GST), like one that had contributed to the coalition's failure at the 1993 federal election. Facing a Labor Party led by Kim Beazley which opposed the tax, the coalition in 1998 received a smaller share of the two-party preferred vote than the opposition, but won a majority of seats. Its majority in the House of Representatives was cut to 12. The second Howard government (1998–2001) legislated a GST and introduced significant changes to the federal funding of schools, reforms widely seen to favour private over public institutions. The government also made changes to health insurance, establishing a system of penalties and incentives aimed at encouraging Australians to take out private cover, and it sold what remained of Telstra.

The quest for the republic now reached its dénouement. In November 1999, following an earlier convention comprising a combination of elected and appointed delegates held in Canberra, the government conducted a referendum on two proposals to amend the constitution: the insertion of a new preamble and the replacement of the monarchy with a republic. Both the proposal for a new preamble and that for a republic were comfortably defeated, with 55% of voters opposing the republican amendment.

While the successful staging of the 2000 Olympic Games in Sydney generated national goodwill and contentment, by the early months of 2001 the Howard government was trailing in public opinion polls and seemed unlikely to survive another election. In August a Norwegian tanker, the MV *Tampa*, picked up a group of refugees whose boat was sinking and made for the Australian territory of Christmas Island, to deliver them to safety. With an election looming, the Howard Government decided to take a stand, and it refused to allow the *Tampa* to land its human cargo. Howard was in Washington at the time of the terrorist attacks on the World Trade Centre in New York and the Pentagon in Washington DC on 11 September 2001, and he invoked the ANZUS Treaty for the first time. These dramatic events greatly assisted the incumbent government as it faced the election due before the end of the year.

Chapter 9

2001

BOATS, TERROR AND LEGACY

Marija Taflaga

2001 is one of those election years Australians remember, but not because of the campaign. The political contest between the coalition and the Australian Labor Party (ALP) was disrupted by two significant external events: the arrival of the MV Tampa *and the September 11 terror attacks. These important intrusions into Australian politics wrong-footed the ALP, which had geared up for a domestically focused campaign centred on the GST and a significant skills package. For the coalition, it allowed the Howard government to capitalise on its incumbent position and months of ceaseless efforts to placate an angry electorate. The debate surrounding* Tampa *brought the issue of asylum seekers to the forefront and provided an avenue to bring the most fraught aspects of immigration policy into the heart of contestable politics. When Howard secured a third term, he cemented his place in the Australian political pantheon and turned the corner in his prime ministership, coming to dominate and awe his government. For Labor, the election would prove fateful and saw the party wander ever deeper into the wilderness. However, the events surrounding the* Tampa, *the 'children overboard affair' and the foreign policy consequences of the terror attacks on the United States would arm Labor with a significant moral argument against the Howard government. The* Tampa *would prove to be an important memory milestone in how Australians understood themselves and a formidable lesson in politics. Would our contemporary debate on asylum seekers be possible without* Tampa *and what would Australia look like had Labor won in 2001?*

The 2001 election is remembered mainly for the dramatic events preceding and following the campaign proper. It was an election year where a change of government was a live possibility and a constant source of discussion by the political commentariat. As the dramatic events of the *Tampa* and the attacks on September 11 2001 reshaped the political landscape, all this changed. This election was another telling reminder of the power of incumbency and its impact on electoral politics. John Howard and his Liberal-National coalition were 'dog meat' at the beginning of the 2001.[1] The coalition had only just managed to slide back into power in 1998, winning a majority of seats; but it lost the popular vote and had weathered the storms and inevitable teething problems of implementing the Goods and Services Tax (GST). Small business owners felt 'a sense of betrayal' as they dealt with the impact of the GST changes and the complexity of filling out their quarterly Business Activity Statements.[2] The lowly paid, unemployed and pensioners saw more of their fortnightly income slip through their fingers at the cashier as they paid tax on many everyday essentials, gaining little from the price drop of luxury goods and consumer durables.[3] For months the polls had made for depressing reading for government members.[4] The conventional wisdom making the rounds at Australia Day barbeques was that Kim Beazley, leader of the Australian Labor Party (ALP), would be in government by year's end.

---

1 Kim Beazley, Personal communication with the author, 16 March 2017.
2 Peter Switzer, 'A Sense of Betrayal That's Hard to Miss', *Australian*, 21 March 2001.
3 Emma McDonald, '500,000 Jobless, Students Below the Poverty Line: ACOSS', *Canberra Times*, 10 May 2001.
4 Murray Goot, 'Turning Points: For Whom the Polls Told', in John Warhurst and Marian Simms (eds), *2001: The Centenary Election*, UQP Australian Studies (Brisbane: University of Queensland Press, 2002), pp.65-69.

ELECTIONS MATTER

Background

Beazley was the likeable former defence minister and deputy prime minister during the Hawke-Keating government. He shared his name with his father, a long-serving Labor politician and minister in the Whitlam government. The younger Kim Beazley represented the West Australian seat of Brand and, like his father, was universally known as a 'good bloke'. He had a long-held and deep fascination with American history and a taste for Kentucky Fried Chicken on the campaign trail. Since its near win in 1998, Labor promised to 'roll back' the GST and reinvest in social welfare. It launched an ambitious policy proposal of large-scale investment in human capital, anticipating the significance of the nascent 'knowledge economy'. But in 2001, Beazley faced a pragmatic and determined opponent. John Howard would bring to bear his accumulated experience of almost three decades in public life and demonstrate shameless policy flexibility in the face of voter anger, alongside his trademark resoluteness. In 2001 the times suited him and Howard found the right formula and pursued his course of action to electoral victory. Howard delivered a third consecutive term in office and a favourable swing of 2% towards his government.

The man who had long banked on his ordinariness was beginning to deliver on his promise of a 'relaxed and comfortable' Australia. Under Howard's stewardship, the Australian economy was performing better than the rest of the world, which was picking through the debris of the Asian financial crisis and the 'tech wreck'. In the second half of 2001, the official unemployment rate came down and interest rates were cut successively to reach 30-year lows.[5] Australians were

---

5   Virginia Marsh, 'Australian Leader Gets Jobless Lift,' *Financial Times*, 12 October 2001; Zoe Daniel, 'Interest Rates Drop to 30-Year Low', *PM* (Australian

beginning to spend big with reports noting that they were saving only 70 cents out of every 100 dollars.[6] It was the beginning of the good life that would come to signify the Howard years of popular memory.

In March, the loss of the somewhat middle-class Brisbane seat of Ryan in a by-election to the ALP came on the back of an electoral wipe-out for the coalition in the Queensland state election a month earlier. In the electoral wash-up, angry Queensland state and federal MPs vented to federal Liberal Party president, Shane Stone, who in turn wrote a single copy of a secret memo for Prime Minister Howard. The memo's contents were explosive. MPs felt that the government was seen as 'mean', 'too tricky' and not listening to Australians. While the memo specifically named the treasurer, Peter Costello, and deputy prime minister, John Anderson, Stone's personal annotations argued that Howard was guilty 'by association'.[7]

Aware of the challenge that his government faced (even without the memo), Howard was determined to show the Australian people that he was listening. Often over-riding the objections of his colleagues, in the months leading up to the budget Howard backflipped or steamrolled over several policy problems, including bailing out HIH insurance policy holders, supporting One.Tel employees' entitlements after the company's collapse, cutting politicians' superannuation, freezing the indexation on petrol and simplifying

---

Broadcasting Corporation, 3 October 2001).
6   Zoe Daniel, 'Big Spending, Low Saving Australians', *AM* (Australian Broadcasting Corporation, 7 June 2001).
7   Fran Kelly, 'Scathing Liberal Memo', *The 7.30 Report* (Australian Broadcasting Corporation, May 1, 2001), Accessed online. <http://www.abc.net.au/7.30/content/2001/s286916.htm>

processes around GST reporting.⁸ The solutions were often inelegant or outright policy vandalism, but as Peter Reith noted in his diary, Howard wanted to fix problems before they would be forced to make 'a change anyway but get no credit for doing so'.⁹ However, when the secret memo was leaked three weeks before the budget, it led to a furore and questions surrounding how such a damaging document found its way into the press underscored the existing tensions between Howard and Costello.[10]

In the May budget, the government bet three billion dollars on hand-outs for disgruntled voters. Pensioners and self-funded retirees would receive a one-off $300 payment, and there was additional money for GPs, regional communities and natural heritage groups to name a few.[11] Costello argued it was 'good policy and pensioners deserve[d] it'.[12] The spending splurge left only a modest $1.5 million surplus. By late August, the government's polling position had recovered to the extent that Reith noted in his diary that the coalition was 'in a better position than we were at the same time out from the election in 1998'.[13] By contrast, Labor had foreshadowed its election platform would centre on the party's GST 'roll back', but the party had withheld the details of the plan until the election campaign. Beazley ran a traditional small-target strategy in order to maximise the media

---

8   John Howard, *Lazarus Rising: A Personal and Political Autobiography* (Sydney: HarperCollins, 2010), ch. 30.

9   Peter Reith, *The Reith Papers* (Melbourne: Melbourne University Press, 2015), p.303.

10 Peter Costello, *The Costello Memoirs: The Age of Prosperity* (Melbourne: Melbourne University Press, 2008), p.159. Howard, *Lazarus Rising*, p.369.

11 Ivor Ries, 'Try This Fistful of Dollars for a Real Golden Oldie', *Australian Financial Review*, 23 May 2001; Jason Koutsoukis, 'Bridging the Rural Gaps: Anderson', *Australian Financial Review*, 23 May 2001; Jason Koutsoukis, 'Heritage Trust Lands $1bn Five-Year Boost', *Australian Financial Review*, 23 May 2001.

12 Costello, *The Costello Memoirs*, p.159.

13 Reith, *The Reith Papers*, p.307.

impact of his policy announcements during the election campaign and to limit the media's capacity to attack Labor's plans which were characteristically expansionary and redistributive.

The Tampa Affair

On 26 August a sinking boat laden with 438 asylum seekers was picked up by the Norwegian freighter the *MV Tampa*. Australia's reaction to Captain Rinnan's request to land at Christmas Island was hostile and the Australian government engaged in intensive lobbying to secure agreement to offload the asylum seekers in Merak, Indonesia. Learning that they would be returned to Indonesia, a delegation of aggravated asylum seekers delivered an ultimatum: they would engage in a hunger strike or jump off the ship if they did not continue on to Christmas Island. Such were the extraordinary circumstances of the *Tampa* that both the Department of Immigration and Multicultural Affairs and Australia's rescue authority *Coastwatch* were continuing to monitor the vessel's progress out of Australian waters when they first learnt that the freighter was again heading towards Christmas Island.[14] This led to fears in Canberra that the ship had, at worst, been hijacked or, at best, that the asylum seekers were attempting to impose themselves upon Australia. The net effect was to embolden cabinet and harden its resolve to prevent the freighter entering Australian waters.[15] Howard's government refused the *Tampa* entry, and an international standoff ensued between Australia, Norway and Indonesia. As the *Tampa* was a vessel acting under the authority of a fellow government – unlike the rickety boats of

---

14   David Marr and Marian Wilkinson, *Dark Victory*, 2nd ed (Sydney: Allen & Unwin, 2004), pp.25–27.
15   Paul Kelly, *The March of Patriots: The Struggle for Modern Australia* (Melbourne: Melbourne University Press, 2011), p.551.

asylum seekers – the specific circumstances of the rescue provided the government with the capacity to respond to unauthorised arrivals in a new and muscular way.

While the specific circumstances of the *Tampa* and the international stalemate it engendered were a bolt from the blue, the issue of refugees and asylum seekers was a regular fixture of the Australian political landscape. Historically large numbers of refugees began arriving again on Australia's northern shore in 1999 and continued in high numbers through to 2001, totalling 8300 people before the *Tampa* arrived.[16] By comparison, between 1989 and 1996 around 2000 asylum seekers, mostly Cambodian and Sino-Vietnamese, had arrived by boat.[17] It was the influx of these refugees that saw the Keating Labor government establish Australia's system of mandatory detention in 1992. The continued political pressure of boat arrivals also saw the Keating government remove references to legislated time limits on detention, effectively paving the way for indefinite detention.[18] Australia's policy of holding people until their claims were processed was a breach of the United Nations convention and out of step with international practice.

The Hawke-Keating government's approach was an echo of the course pursued by the Whitlam government in 1975 – the preservation of Australia's right to arbitrate the entry of non-citizens.[19] Further back, the Chifley government predicated its decision to take

---

16   Kelly, *The March of Patriots*, p.541.
17   Amy Nethery, '"A Modern-Day Concentration Camp": Using History to Make Sense of Australian Immigration Detention Centres', in Klaus Neumann and Gwenda Tavan (eds), *Does History Matter?* (Canberra: ANU Press, 2009), p.66.
18   Nethery, 'A Modern-Day Concentration Camp', p. 66.
19   Klaus Neumann, 'Oblivious to the Obvious? Australian Asylum-Seeker Policies and the Use of the Past', in Neumann and Tavan (eds), *Does History Matter?*, p.53.

refugees on selecting the 'best ones' before they were all taken.[20] Indeed, the Fraser government's response to the Vietnamese crisis was built on similar logic – namely maintaining control over the flow of people into the country.[21] Fraser's support for refugees was structured around the anti-Communist credentials of the Vietnamese boat people, but even this did not inoculate this cohort of refugees from suspicion that they were economic migrants and claims that they should come to Australia by the 'proper' channels.[22] The bottom line remained that refugees would be processed offshore and selected in strict compliance with Australia's desired specifications, regulations, and above all, in an orderly manner.

The Howard government had struggled to manage the numbers of boats arriving for much of its second term. Its policy settings consisted of, first, temporary protection visas – a Howard government innovation. Second, there was mandatory detention, which was increasingly in isolated locations and in facilities designed to appear more like prisons. Third, the government attempted, with limited success, to block asylum seekers' access to legal recourse, which saw the Federal Court clogged with cases.[23] Last, the Howard government had reconfigured the refugee program as zero-sum: every unauthorised arrival found to be a refugee would directly reduce Australia's capacity to take a person from a refugee camp overseas. The

---

20   Jayne Persian, '"Chifley Liked Them Blond": DP Immigrants for Australia', *History Australia* 12:2, 1 January 2015, pp. 80–101.

21   Marr and Wilkinson, *Dark Victory*, p.45. See also Claire Higgins, *Refugees by Boat: Origins of Australia's Refugee Policy* (Sydney: NewSouth Publishing), 2017.

22   Rachel Stevens, 'Political Debates on Asylum Seekers during the Fraser Government, 1977–1982', *Australian Journal of Politics & History*, 58:4, 2012, pp.526–41.

23   Kelly, *The March of Patriots*, pp.544–46.

approach dovetailed with the presentation of asylum seekers arriving by boat as 'queue-jumpers'.

Throughout 2001, the mainstream press was replete with stories of new boat arrivals, riots in detention centres, and reports of overcrowding and human rights concerns in the detention network.[24] The immigration department had been obliged to build new detention centres as the numbers swelled because they were committed to their policy of detention as deterrence. By August 2001, Australia's detention system was severely stretched and at capacity. Asylum policy was already a weeping wound for the government.

When the *Tampa* presented itself as a dilemma to Australian policy-makers, processes and ideas about how 'suspected illegal entry vessels' ought to be managed were well established. The Howard government, and Phillip Ruddock as immigration minister, had spent the last two years running a hard line on immigration. With some important exceptions, the overall thrust of maintaining the Australian government's right to arbitrate over the movement of non-citizens had the support of the Labor leadership (though this position was hotly contested by the left faction of the Labor Party). Behind the scenes, the Howard government was already heavily engaged in a search for the means to halt the flow of boats. These discussions ranged from empowering the Australian Federal Police to work with the Indonesians, to deploying the defence force, or seeking to

---

24 For examples see Catherine McGrath, 'Family of Protestor Attacks Immigration Department', *The World Today* (Australian Broadcasting Corporation, May 29, 2001); Tanya Nolan, 'Kuwaiti Asylum Seekers Threaten Suicide over Australia's Detention System', *AM* (Australian Broadcasting Corporation, June 16, 2001); Catherine McGrath, 'Judge Attacks Immigration Department over Treatment of Asylum Seekers', *AM* (Australian Broadcasting Corporation, July 28, 2001); Jo Mazzocchi, 'Villawood under Fire', *PM* (Australian Broadcasting Corporation, July 23, 2001); Shane McLeod, 'Refugee Guidelines to Be Tightened', *PM* (Australian Broadcasting Corporation, August 13, 2001); Julie Posetti, 'Safety Concern at Woomera Increases', *AM* (Australian Broadcasting Corporation, August 27, 2001).

establish a deal with Indonesia similar to Fraser's and Keating's offshore processing solutions.[25] The trouble was there was no clear path forward with any of these proposals.

The government's reaction to the MV *Tampa* was shocking because by refusing to allow the rescued asylum seekers to land on Christmas Island, Australia shifted the burden on to Indonesia or Norway. The government argued it could refuse entry because the ship was under the flag of Norway and therefore it could be directed by the Norwegian government, despite the reality that it was a commercial liner.[26] After three days the *Tampa* was running out of food, grossly overcrowded, several people were suffering serious medical conditions (a claim disputed by the Australian government) and the captain had declared a distress situation. After both Indonesia and Norway refused to accede to Australia's demands to take responsibility, the *Tampa*'s Captain made the decision to cross over into Australian waters to seek medical assistance and arrest the crisis on board his ship. The Australian government's response was swift and decisive: the elite Special Air Service regiment was ordered to board the now distressed vessel.[27] This decision and its implications saw the military drawn into a previously civilian domain of operation, which blurred the lines of communication and responsibility between civilian and defence arms of the bureaucracy. The militarisation of this issue has continued down to the present.

Standing at the dispatch box later that day to update parliament on the unfolding situation, Howard reminded the House of Representatives that Australia 'continued to be a warm, generous

---

25 Kelly, *The March of Patriots*, pp.548–49.
26 Marr and Wilkinson, *Dark Victory*, pp.98, 102.
27 Kelly, *The March of Patriots*, pp.554.

recipient of refugees' but argued that the nation had become 'increasingly concerned' about the 'increasing flow of people'. Howard would neither resile nor apologise for his tough stance in handling the situation. 'Every nation has the right to effectively control its borders and to decide who comes here and under what circumstances, and Australia has no intention of surrendering or compromising that right,' he argued. He reiterated that his government would 'take whatever action is needed – within the law, of course – to prevent that occurring'.[28] The difference between previous instances and the *Tampa* was that the government was able to demonstrate the seriousness of its intent in a way that it could not with a leaky boat sinking in the middle of the ocean. This was despite the reality that Australia failed to shift responsibility to either Norway or Indonesia and by boarding the *Tampa*, Australia would become ultimately responsible.

Labor's Response

In the first instance, Beazley backed the government's hard-line approach, despite concerns on his backbench. Colin Hollis, a Labor MP from New South Wales, pointed to the absurdity of the situation when he asked what would happen had the *Tampa* been a tourist vessel and whether, in refusing the ship's entry, the government was sending 'a message to every captain on the high seas they should let asylum seekers drown rather than rescue them'.[29] Beazley responded to Howard's statement in parliament by agreeing that the government had acted 'on the basis of international law', and that there was 'no change' in government policy in the way refugees 'coming illegally to this country ought to be treated'. Beazley further agreed that

---

28 John Howard, CPD 29 August 2001, p.30516.
29 Alan Ramsey, 'Beazley Is Not About To Rock Refugee Boat', *Sydney Morning Herald*, 29 August 2001.

it was 'quite clear' that 'in this particular case', the *Tampa* should disembark in Indonesia, 'regardless of whatever duress or pressures are placed on the captain of the vessel, his crew, the Norwegian government or the shipping line'.[30] Beazley also invoked Australian history in his critique, noting that the Howard government had seen 11,000 people arrive since 1996, compared with far smaller numbers under Labor. He concluded that while this was a 'serious problem', it was not a 'national catastrophe'.[31]

However, when the government sought to bring in a bill later that afternoon, which would indemnify public servants retrospectively for their actions in dealing with the *Tampa*, the bipartisan approach broke down. The bill was drafted in very broad terms that extended beyond the specific circumstances of the *Tampa*. It would allow Australian personnel not only to board or remove boats from its territorial waters but also to take actions against people on board in virtually any circumstance with minimal legal scrutiny.[32] Beazley opposed the bill because it 'changes policy'. As he explained further, on the basis of this legislation 'no matter what the circumstances, it will be a reasonable and authoritative thing for an Australian officer to take a boat that is sinking, and in which there are life threatening situations involving the people on board, and order it out' to sea.[33] Indignant, Beazley accused the government of engaging in 'wedge politics', and linked the government's approach on this bill to its actions on industrial relations or native title. That is, Beazley was accusing the government of playing politics and went on to criticise the government's handling of Australia's regional relationships,

---

30   Kim Beazley, CPD 29 August 2001, p.30518.
31   Ibid.
32   Kelly, *The March of Patriots*, p.55.
33   Kim Beazley, CPD 29 August 2001, p.30570.

which had led to a situation where Australia would have to take such extraordinary actions because it could not find a regional solution.[34] Howard saw Beazley's sudden reversal as 'remarkable' and his accusations of politicisation as 'political hysteria'.[35] Howard's overture of a sunset clause was rebuffed, which he interpreted as the result of internal political pressure from the left faction.[36] Interviewed for this project, Howard argues that the *Tampa* was a policy dilemma in need of a solution, and if anything, Beazley's refusal to back the bill was an act of politicisation.[37]

The public agreed with Howard. The government labelled Beazley a 'flip-flopper' and the perception stuck.[38] This was despite Labor's vindication three weeks later when the government presented a redrafted bill which took into account Beazley's concerns. Despite Labor's announcement that it backed the government's approach and its announcement that if elected it would establish a coast guard to patrol Australia's northern boarders, both public and internal polling showed a collapse in Labor's support.[39] Government backbenchers were delighted with the turnaround in the government's fortunes, with only quiet murmurings of dissent.[40] The story had consumed an overwhelming proportion of public attention and allowed the Howard government to gain maximum advantage from their

---

[34] Ibid.
[35] Howard, *Lazarus Rising*, p.400.
[36] Ibid., p.401.
[37] John Howard, Personal communication with the author, 16 March 2017.
[38] Louise Dodson, 'Poll Shows Howard On A Winner', *Age*, 4 September 2001.
[39] Marr and Wilkinson, *Dark Victory*, pp.122–123; Kim Beazley, Personal communication with the author, 16 March 2017.
[40] Alexandra Kirk, 'Coalition Backbenchers Revel in Support for Government Stand', *PM* (Australian Broadcasting Corporation, 30 August 2001).

incumbent position as resolute problem solvers with a clear position about how to defend Australia's national interest.

At every stage, Howard refused to back down on his initial stance, forcing the government to scramble to come up with an alternative to bringing the asylum seekers to Australia for processing. This lurching from consequence to consequence necessitated improvisation and, given the government's mood for 'radical action', helps explain why events unfolded so dramatically. However, in another way, its response was already framed by a limited set of possible actions given the way that decisions over decades, and more importantly, the previous two years, had narrowed the imaginations of policy-makers.

The fact that Labor was broadly supportive of the principle, though not all of the means, speaks to this shared historical context which both parties chose to draw on to make their case and rationalise their decisions. It was yet another step in line with Australian policy-makers' favoured approach of asserting their right to arbitrate over the entry of unauthorised maritime arrivals. The result was the birth of a set of singular public policy experiments known as the 'Pacific solution', which included Australian-managed, large-scale offshore detention in third party countries, the excision of Australian territories such as Christmas Island and Ashmore Reef from the migration zone, and the direct involvement of the navy, which would be empowered to tow boats back out to sea when patrolling Australia's waters to the North (Operation Relex).

Despite weeks of intense political focus the *Tampa* crisis was not over, and the dispute moved to the courts. A case brought by Civil Liberties Victoria resulted in a ruling that the *Tampa*'s removal from Australian waters was illegal.[41] Indeed, on the morning of September

---

41   The government appealed and the ruling was overturned a week later.

11 2001, John Howard was in Washington DC convening a press conference about the result of the court's *Tampa* decision when it became obvious to Howard's security detail that the United States of America was under attack.

September 11

The terrorist attacks of September 11 transformed the political landscape overnight. Politicians and ordinary citizens were transfixed by the surreal and horrifying images of collapsing towers and dusty rescue teams picking through piles of rubble in the heart of gleaming New York. In the immediate days that followed, no one knew if this was the first of a series of worldwide attacks on prominent Western targets. The world was gripped by the tragedy of the large loss of life and scrambled to learn all it could of Al Qaeda and its leader Osama Bin Laden. Not even the collapse of an Australian icon, Ansett Airlines, made much dint in the rolling coverage of the initial disaster, or of America's swift recourse to punish its enemies and avenge its victims.

In response to the attacks on the US, Australia invoked the ANZUS treaty for the first time. Upon his return to Canberra, the prime minister unveiled a new raft of security legislation, and significantly, the issue of asylum seekers, who were mainly arriving from Iraq and Afghanistan, was subsumed into a far wider security paradigm. Together, *Tampa* and September 11, two unexpected events, had shifted the terms of debate away from domestic issues to a broader security agenda. The circumstances favoured incumbents, and the specific context linked neatly with the government's recently demonstrated strengths on security and border protection, consolidating Howard's post-budget poll recovery.

The Campaign

John Howard announced the start of the 2001 election campaign on 5 October in the prime minister's courtyard. Relaxed and authoritative, he explicitly linked the decision voters would make to the unfolding global security crisis: 'This is not a time to change to either a prime minister or to a party that finds it difficult to articulate a clear view on the great issues that challenge the Australian nation'. Howard lashed Beazley's lack of clear-eyed vision, arguing that:

> he's had five-and-a-half years to define himself to the Australian public ... and I don't believe the Australian people have any clearer view now than they did in March of 1996 what he or the Australian Labor Party stands for.[42]

No sooner had the prime minister fired the starting gun, he was sharing a platform with Beazley as they waved off troops heading to the Middle East to support the US military campaign in Afghanistan. It would not be the last time either, and similar scenes would regularly punctuate the campaign. America was at war, bombing an already war-ravaged Afghanistan, and Australia was marching alongside.[43]

Nor did the issue of boat people fade away during the campaign. Instead, the issue would continue to play a significant role in shaping the campaign as the flow of boats continued unabated. In the first half of the campaign, there were reports of an imperilled boat, the SIEV 4, where it appeared that parents had 'thrown their children overboard' in order to stop the navy from turning the boat around. These

---

42 John Howard, 'Howard Calls November 10 Election', (Canberra, 5 October 2001), Accessed online. <http://australianpolitics.com/2001/10/05/howard-calls-election-wont-commit-to-serving-full-term.html>

43 'Watching The Towers Fall', *Age*, 16 September 2001.

reports were the cause of much shock and indignation among the political class and dominated the news headlines.[44] Halfway through the campaign, another boat sank, drowning 353 men, women and children. As news trickled in of the disaster, Beazley's attempts to shift the discussion of boat people back on to Howard's failure to deliver a regional solution was decisively rebuffed by Howard who accused Beazley of seeking to score political points off the dead.[45] Despite the reality that the government's new policy response to boat people was *ad hoc* and raised several important and concerning questions of public administration, the issue of asylum seekers continued to damage Labor electorally, even when the stories were negative for the government.[46]

This was Australia's first wartime campaign since the mid-1960s, and the dramatic turn of events wrong-footed the ALP. Labor had counted on a domestically focused campaign – just as every campaign had been for the previous 35 years. Labor's platform emphasised its traditional strengths in health and education. Its television advertisements saw Kim Beazley striding authoritatively to the strains of heart stirring music as he told voters that he 'could not stand by while John Howard takes away the chance for every Australian child to excel'.[47] The coalition attacked Labor's education platform: Peter Costello dubbed its *Knowledge Nation* policy 'Noodle Nation' because of the complex diagram designed by former MP Barry Jones, who had insisted on including it in the package.

---

44   Kelly, *The March of Patriots*, pp.596–97.
45   Marr and Wilkinson, *Dark Victory*, p.316.
46   Patrick Weller, *Don't Tell the Prime Minister* (Melbourne: Scribe Publications, 2002), chs 3 and 4.
47   Australian Labor Party, *Education: That's What I Stand For*, Accessed online. <https://www.youtube.com/watch?v=QhzVf8lfgS8>

While not quite 'betting everything on black', the ALP had taken great comfort in the electoral trouncing of parties who had introduced consumption taxes overseas. The party ran GST-themed ads noting that the consumption tax had been increased again in New Zealand and in the UK, asking voters if they 'could afford another surprise from John Howard?'.[48] When it finally announced its policy, it was less of a 'roll back' and more a pledge to simplify the GST, removing the tax from a number of essential goods, such as electricity, long-stay caravan park rentals and tampons.[49] Interviewed after the policy's announcement, the shadow treasurer, Simon Crean, had to defend Labor's focus on the GST and domestic politics in light of international events. He argued that the issue remained important because 'a vast majority of people don't consider themselves better off' and that the blame could be sheeted home squarely to the government, which had 'deceived' the Australian people 'about what the true impact of the GST would be'.[50]

The coalition's electoral spending spree was not over. Howard announced a doubling of the first home owners grant, the first iteration of the government's 'baby bonus', $100 million to tackle drugs, and just above $400 million was found for the aged care system, which had enveloped the minister, Bronwyn Bishop, in a rolling series of scandals.[51] The government came under pressure in regional

---

48 Australian Labor Party, *Another GST Surprise*, Accessed online. <https://www.youtube.com/watch?v=gz5vqD58ZH0>

49 Australian Labor Party, 'Kim Beazley's Plan For A Fairer GST', 19 October 2001, Accessed online. <http://parlinfo.aph.gov.au/parlInfo/download/library/partypol/AF756/upload_binary/af75610.pdf;fileType=application%2Fpdf#search=%222000s%20alp%202001%20GST%2010%2019%22>

50 Catherine McGrath, 'Shadow Treasurer Simon Crean Explains the Roll Back Policy', *PM* (Australian Broadcasting Corporation, 19 October 2001. Accessed online. <http://www.abc.net.au/pm/stories/s395647.htm>

51 'Campaign Launch: Policy Speech' (Sydney, October 28, 2001), *Museum of Australian Democracy*, Accessed online. <http://electionspeeches.moadoph.gov.au/

Australia over Costello's slip that the portion of Telstra still government owned would likely be sold. This caused great difficulties for the Nationals, who lost a week to battling the negative publicity it engendered.[52] Labor also focused on the thorny issue of the relationship between Howard and Costello. The party ran advertisements attempting to convince voters that a 'vote for John Howard was a vote for Peter Costello'. Even Pauline Hanson piled in on the attack, saying that she thought Australians would not be 'very happy' if Costello replaced Howard.[53] As for Costello himself, he declared that he was 'happy' to remain the treasurer after Howard committed to serving out a full term.[54]

Despite a clear victory in the first, and only, leader's debate, Beazley struggled to cut through the din of coverage of the war and asylum seeker crises. In the US, envelopes filled with powdered anthrax were delivered to government offices over the course of several weeks, resulting in deaths and widespread panic. Adding to the palpable sense of insecurity were several anthrax hoaxes in Australia.[55] Howard's campaign launch reflected this reality, which focused on the usual round of domestic election handouts but went on to discuss national security at length. In a blistering critique of his opponent, Howard again reminded voters of the uncertainty of the times and the importance of wise heads and clear-sighted focus on Australia's

---

speeches/2001-john-howard.>

52 Gaye White, 'The National Party Campaign', in John Warhurst and Marian Simms (eds), *2001: The Centenary Election* (St Lucia, Qld: University of Queensland Press, 2002), p.138.

53 'Hanson Wants Howard Commitment', *AAP*, 6 October 2001.

54 Katherine Murphy and Steve Lewis, 'Costello "happy" to Stay on as Treasurer', *Australian Financial Review*, 8 October 2001.

55 Marian Simms, 'The Media and the 2001 Election: Afghans, Asylum Seekers and Anthrax', in John Warhurst and Marian Simms (eds), *2001: The Centenary Election* (Brisbane: University of Queensland Press, 2002), p.98.

interests. Howard repeated his declaration from his parliamentary speech several weeks before, insisting that 'we will decide who comes to this country and the circumstances in which they come', unlike Labor, whose Left faction members had 'darkly muttered' that if the ALP won the election, the laws would change.[56] The coalition had a 'single irrevocable view' on border protection.[57] The contrast of the major parties' slogans summed up the disjuncture in the campaign. Labor's pitch was squarely focused on the domestic and promised 'A fair share for all Australians. Jobs. Health. Education.'. The coalition instead invoked the recent past and the rapidly unfolding security context with 'Putting Australia's interests first: Certainty, Leadership, Strength'.

The coalition's response to the *Tampa* had consolidated the government's modest polling recovery and the events of September 11 displaced the prominence of domestic agenda items. A study of television coverage found that terrorism, refugees and related issues featured more frequently than domestic issues combined in every Australian state except for the ABC news in Perth and Brisbane.[58] Similar results were found in an analysis of print media.[59]

In the dying days of the campaign a major scandal erupted over the claims made by the government about whether parents on the sinking boat, SIEV 4, had really thrown their children overboard. Accusations of a cover-up by the government drowned out all attempts to discuss other issues. Fearing these claims, the government released

---

56 Howard, 'Campaign Launch: Policy Speech'.
57 Ibid.
58 David Denemark, Ian Ward and Clive Bean, 'Election Campaigns and Television News Coverage: The Case of the 2001 Australian Election', *Australian Journal of Political Science*, 42:1, 2007, p.95.
59 Simms, 'The Media'.

footage which revealed that children had not been thrown overboard. Despite the damaging appearance of deception, the 'children overboard affair' thwarted Labor's attempts to capitalise on a modest surge at the end of the campaign. As Beazley put it, the issue demonstrated even when the discussion is negative, it does not matter because 'if it's your issue, you win'.[60]

The Result

The findings of the Australian Election Study (AES) confirm the importance of both terrorism and asylum seekers to the eventual result. However, as Ian McAllister argued, it was terrorism that proved more potent than asylum issues.[61] In his analysis of polling over the course of 2001, Murray Goot argued that the 2001 budget saw a significant turnaround in the government's position, that its response to the *Tampa* helped the government draw level with Labor, and that it was the attacks on September 11 that saw the government establish a significant lead over its opponent.[62] In all, Howard achieved a third term, with a significant 2% swing in the government's favour. The Liberals sought to downplay the importance of immigration issues, emphasising instead Howard's domestic leadership and response to global security issues.[63] Beazley, Labor argued, had saved the furniture, reducing the scale of the electoral drubbing that the party had expected when the campaign launched.[64] In both

---

60 Kim Beazley, Personal communication with the author, 16 March 2017.
61 Ian McAllister, 'Border Protection, the 2001 Australian Election and the Coalition Victory', *Australian Journal of Political Science*, 38:3, 1 November 2003, pp.445–63.
62 Goot, 'Turning Points'.
63 Lynton Crosby, 'The Liberal Party', in John Warhurst and Marian Simms (eds), *2001: The Centenary Election* (Brisbane: University of Queensland Press, 2002), pp.116-117.
64 Geoff Walsh, 'The Australian Labor Party', in ibid., p.129.

cases, the parties *said* they believed that the election and the campaign had mattered.

For the smaller parties, the 2001 election represented mixed results. The Nationals won government, but lost the seats of Farrer, to a Liberal, Sussan Ley, and New England, to an Independent, Tony Windsor. At the time, the Democrats viewed the election as a repeat of the 1998 election result, and despite a drop in their Senate vote, the party was pleased that they had weathered the odium of their part in the GST negotiations. They believed, erroneously as it turned out, they had confirmed their place as the 'third political force' in Australian politics.[65] One Nation saw their vote share drop and complained that the government had taken advantage of the international circumstances to capitalise on their policy strengths.[66] Only the Greens saw the 2001 election as an outstanding success for their party. They were proud of the clear stance they took on refugee issues, which they argued was a 'watershed' for the party's public recognition. Flush with the success of doubling their vote and representation within the Senate, the party tentatively (and accurately) predicted that they would take over the role played by the Democrats.[67]

What If?

Of course, it is impossible to know exactly how Australia might be different had the coalition lost in 2001. Labor's approach in several policy domains represented a significant difference from the coalition. On the environment, Beazley's Labor had pledged to ratify

---

65 John Warhurst, Marian Simms and Andrew Bartlett, 'The Australian Democrats', in ibid., pp.142-43.
66 Frank Hough, 'Pauline Hanson's One Nation', in ibid., pp.153.
67 Ben Oquist, 'The Greens: The Success Story of the Election', in ibid., pp.145, 150.

the Kyoto protocol on greenhouse emissions.[68] Whether or not that translated into a workable, effective and consolidated carbon pricing mechanism is, as recent history of climate politics demonstrates, another matter entirely. Labor also emphasised a future Australian economy based on a significant investment in human capital to arrest 'the brain drain' and harness the emerging 'knowledge economy'. Labor's *Knowledge Nation* argued Australia's future prosperity would be built on research and development and the integration of new online technologies and businesses. The 'knowledge economy', it was said, would secure Australia's long-term high living standards in the twenty-first century, in an uncanny prequel of the debates around innovation, the impact of the internet and the future of work we are wrestling with today.[69]

Then there are the other policy domains which would prove decisive during the Howard government's third term. Labor refused to support Australia's involvement in the Iraq war under the leadership of Simon Crean. Beazley too is contemporaneously on the record opposing the war. Beazley continues to maintain that a Labor government would not have supported the war, and that this would have caused a significant deterioration in the relationship between Australia and the US. He argues that perhaps at most, a Labor-led Australia might have 'rebadged' the nation's patrol in the Persian Gulf as part of the American Fleet in support of the Iraq war.[70]

Victory in 2001 consolidated Howard's leadership and he joined the rarefied ranks of prime ministers who successfully won a third

---

68   Australian Labor Party, 'Labor's Plan for Environment and Heritage', 3 November 2001, Accessed online. <http://parlinfo.aph.gov.au>
69   Australian Labor Party, 'Kim Beazley's Plan for the Knowledge Nation', 31 October 2001, Accessed online. <http://parlinfo.aph.gov.au>
70   Kim Beazley, Personal communication with the author, 16 March 2017.

term. After 2001, Howard emerged as the dominant figure in his government, his political instincts and his campaigning strategy vindicated. However, his unquestioned primacy and the almost blind faith in his ability to pull a rabbit out of a hat at each election would not become legend until after the 2004 election. For Labor, defeat in 2001 sent the party into another round of recriminations and disagreements over the party's policy approach and communication strategy. Beazley stepped down after the election, ushering in Labor's long period of leadership instability.

Was there a cost to such a long-lived coalition government? In recent times, it is not uncommon to hear that there were two Howard governments. The first was the muscular reform-orientated outfit that reigned from 1996 to 2001, which slashed the budget, reformed the waterfront, introduced a new industrial relations and public administration regime, acted on gun control and introduced the GST. The second, is characterised as intellectually exhausted, and benefiting from both global insecurity and the enormous economic windfall of a once in a century mining boom. [71] With Treasury successively underestimating sky-high revenues, government decisions were not contested as they had been in the past – Australia could afford a policy paradigm of 'no losers' and could spend generously on the government's favoured constituents. The coalition was arguably content to just 'keep Labor away from the treasury benches'.[72] Finally, in its desperation to win the 2007 election, and in a reprise of a strategy that it had deployed so effectively in 2001, the Howard government proposed yet another tranche of significant cuts to income tax, which

---

71   For an example see George Megalogenis, *The Australian Moment: How We Were Made for These Times* (Melbourne: Penguin Group Australia, 2012), chs 18 and 19.
72   Peter Van Onselen, 'Libs with Little Room to Move', *Australian*, 29 January 2016.

would eventually help break the national budget.[73] Of course, it was Labor's decision under Kevin Rudd to support and implement the move for electoral purposes that was crucial.

Unsurprisingly, Howard rejects this argument. He counters that the government was largely preoccupied with foreign affairs between 2001 and 2003. Moreover, he notes that between 2004 and 2007, the government revisited its reform handbook, seeking to capitalise on its surprise success in winning control of the Senate in 2004.[74] Determined not to be seen to squander its opportunity, the government worked at breakneck speed through its agenda of unfinished business that it had been unable to get through in its previous terms because of Senate opposition. On the other hand, there is no way of knowing how Labor would have managed the enormous mining boom windfall. This question asks us to assume that a government faced with surpluses that for years dramatically exceeded Treasury's forecasting would act prudently and think over the very long term. Except for a handful of rare cases, global history suggests otherwise.

Interviewed for this book, Beazley mused that he probably would not have lasted long as prime minister and would have had 'a hell of a time'. This he attributed to his likely difficult relationship as a result of Australia's refusal under his government to participate in the Iraq War.[75] However, perhaps the responsibility of having to make the decision, in light of all the consequences of failing to join the war, might have changed the calculation for him. As our recent history of prime ministerial departures shows, few who gain the job are capable of relinquishing it lightly.

---

73 George Megalogenis, 'Balancing Act: Australia between Recession and Renewal', *Quarterly Essay*, 61 (Melbourne: Black Inc, 2016), ch. 3.
74 John Howard, Personal communication with the author, 16 March 2017.
75 Kim Beazley, Personal communication with the author, 16 March 2017.

No aspect of the 2001 election has loomed as large as the legacy of the *Tampa* and the 'children overboard' scandal. The words *Tampa* and 'children overboard' are shorthand for the difficult and poisonous discussion of asylum policy in Australia. The confluence between 'turning back' the *Tampa* and the start of the 'War on Terror' marked a turning point in Australian history. Yet, these were all external shocks to Australia's politics. Their very striking deviation from 'politics as usual' overshadowed the expected contest over the exact distribution of wealth, jobs and economic growth that typically characterise Australian politics.

Almost two decades on, the biggest unanswered question is whether or not immigration and asylum debates might be conducted differently had Labor won office in 2001. Would prime minister Kevin Rudd's decision on the eve of the 2013 election, to take out full page advertisements notifying the Australian public that his 'PNG Solution' would guarantee that that asylum seekers arriving by boat would never be settled in Australia, be imaginable without the *Tampa*?

After the 2001 election, the *Tampa* and the children overboard scandal gave the Labor Party a powerful moral argument against the Howard government. In the lead up to the 2007 election, opposition leader Kevin Rudd penned an essay in the *Monthly* entitled 'Faith in politics', highlighting the 'great ethical concern' that the Howard government's policy approach raised for Christian believers and churches.[76] Having won office, Labor dismantled the Howard government's 'Pacific solution'. For a brief moment, the parliament sat down together to find *'A New Beginning'* on immigration detention

---

76   Kevin Rudd, 'Faith in politics', *Monthly*, October 2006, Accessed online. <https://www.themonthly.com.au/monthly-essays-kevin-rudd-faith-politics--300>

and Australia's response to asylum seekers.[77] However, this bipartisan consensus dissolved rapidly after boats began appearing on the horizon in ever-larger numbers from late 2008 onwards. Parliament was consumed by years of ugly and bitter debate over the issue. When Labor failed to win a majority in the lower house in 2010, its capacity to act on the issue was severely curtailed and the hot-house atmosphere of the hung parliament inflamed an already torrid debate.[78] The Abbott-led opposition was relentless in its pursuit of the issue, blocking Labor's policies even when they were more akin with its own positions than those Labor had set out to implement in 2007.

There is no clear line of sight from the *Tampa* through to the poisonous and deadlocked discussion of immigration and refugees today. The 'PNG solution' was as much the culmination of the Labor government's inability to manage the return of large numbers of arrivals after an almost virtual stop, as it was the result of the Abbott opposition's choice to pursue the issue for maximum political effect. Moreover, given the long-established preference for government policy-makers to guard fiercely against any weakening of its power to determine the entry of non-citizens into the country, it is difficult to argue that Australia's response to asylum seekers would have taken a 180 degree turn if 2001 had panned out differently.

Today, Beazley states that had he been prime minister at the time, he would have 'turned back' the *Tampa*, and processed the refugees offshore.[79] Beazley does not resile from the Keating government (and

---

77   Joint Standing Committee on Migration, *Immigration Detention in Australia: A New Beginning* (Canberra: The Parliament of the Commonwealth of Australia, 1 December 2008.), Accessed online. <http://www.aph.gov.au/binaries/house/committee/mig/detention/report/fullreport.pdf>

78   Paul Kelly, *Triumph and Demise: The Broken Promise of a Labor Generation* (Melbourne: Melbourne University Press, 2014), ch. 26.

79   Kim Beazley, Personal communication with the author, 16 March 2017.

incidentally, the Shorten opposition's) position of mandatory detention. Where he would draw the line, he says, would be the 'Pacific solution', which he argued 'undermined' Australia's standing and made the nation look like a 'needy and begging power' in the Pacific.[80] Yet, when asked this question in April 2009 for Paul Kelly's *March of the Patriots,* Beazley said that 'the *Tampa* would have made landfall and the people would have been processed in Australia'.[81] Importantly, he qualifies the remark by adding that 'we would have done whatever was required to keep agreement with Indonesia. If we had to pay big money, then we would have paid.' He reiterated, 'I believe in effective border protection. A hard line is essential.'[82]

Beazley made the above comments in 2009 after Labor had dismantled the 'Pacific Solution' with highly qualified support from the coalition and before boats started arriving again.[83] By contrast, Beazley's most recent reflections on the issue were made in the current context of an extreme ratcheting up of rhetoric and policy formulation over the last eight years. In 2009 Beazley could not have known how Australia would be affected by the largest displacement of peoples since World War II. But more importantly, in both instances Beazley insists that under his leadership Labor would have retained its commitment to finding a regional solution. With regard to Australia's right to prevent the settlement of irregular arrivals, Labor might never have gone to the extent of the 'Pacific solution' and perhaps without this foundation, Australia would not have progressed to the 'PNG solution'. But Australia's policy approach would most likely have retained its broad general direction.

---

80   Ibid..
81   Kelly, *The March of Patriots*, p. 564.
82   Ibid.
83   'Fed: Coalition Happy to "Wear" End of Pacific Solution', *AAP*, 24 February 2008.

Conclusion

What is certain is that the *Tampa*, enmeshed almost indistinguishably with the memory of the 2001 election, has had a profound legacy for the way people think about politics. For a substantial number of Australian politicians, particularly in the coalition, the *Tampa* was a lesson in politics: Australians will back a government which unashamedly asserts its right to guard its borders. An emphasis on perceived legal and procedural fairness – ensuring people come 'the right way' – and more contemporaneously, an emphasis on safety, is a formula that allows easy deflection of the many troubling issues that Australia's policy settings raise. An electorally successful and politically palatable formula was found to bring the most fraught aspects of immigration policy into the realm of constable politics, where previous attempts to raise the subject in the 1980s had utterly failed and Pauline Hanson's attempts a few years beforehand could not escape the odium of race politics.[84]

For Australia's progressive commentators and researchers, *Tampa* and the 'children overboard' scandal became significant planks in their moral critique of the Howard government. While almost forgotten now, Australia's treatment of people in immigration detention (particularly the deportation of Australian citizens Cornelia Rau and Vivian Solon and Australian permanent resident, Dr Muhamed Haneef), was an important dimension of Labor's argument that it was time for a change of government in 2007. The *Tampa* unleashed a flood of commentary and academic research critical of the Howard government's behaviour or searching for an explanation for why

---

84 Frank Bongiorno, *The Eighties: The Decade That Transformed Australia* (Melbourne: Black Inc, 2015); Simon Jackman, 'Pauline Hanson, the Mainstream, and Political Elites: The Place of Race in Australian Political Ideology', *Australian Journal of Political Science*, 33:2, 1 July 1998, pp.167–86.

Australia had ended down a dark alley.⁸⁵ *Tampa* came to symbolise the opening of the floodgates on race politics, which unleased a mode of politics that many progressives saw as illegitimate and not befitting a civilised and liberal society. It represented the triumph of a brutal politics over what they imagined were Australians' best selves. It was a '*Dark Victory*', normalising a taboo and legitimating the cynical political exploitation of desperate people risking their lives to seek asylum.⁸⁶

The events overshadowing the 2001 election demonstrated Australia's place in an increasingly globalised and inter-connected world. In spite of being at a far off corner of the map, Australia's politics could still be significantly shaped by events abroad and the country could not block out the sound of the world, with all its problems, knocking on its doors. Yet it also demonstrated Australia's tentative relationship with the implications of globalisation. Politicians on both sides could on the one hand try to invoke an Australia open to the globe, and particularly its economic opportunities, yet on the other reflexively return to the language of nationalism and insularity.

The 2001 election demonstrated the power of incumbency, timing and a little dose of luck. Howard, the consummate politician, instinctually knew how to respond. This election win was an important milestone in the life of the Howard government, cementing its legacy for good and ill. More broadly, the 2001 election was also significant for Australia because it represented an important juncture in the

---

85 Guy Rundle, 'The Opportunist: John Howard and the Triumph of Reaction', *Quarterly Essay*, 3 (Melbourne: Black Inc, 2001); Ian Ward, 'The Tampa, Wedge Politics, and a Lesson for Political Journalism', *Australian Journalism Review*, 24:1, July 2002, p.21; Robert Manne, 'Sending Them Home: Refugees and the New Politics of Indifference', *Quarterly Essay*, 13 (Melbourne: Black Inc, 2003); Peter Gale, 'The Refugee Crisis and Fear: Populist Politics and Media Discourse', *Journal of Sociology*, 40:4, 1 December 2004, p.321-340.

86 Marr and Wilkinson, *Dark Victory*.

nation's political discussion of immigration. It was a threshold that brought the subject fully into the realm of the cut and thrust of political debate. Immigration policy, which, with only occasional lapses, had been essentially bipartisan for decades, was now fair game.

INTERIM 2001–2010

Australia experienced a period of unparalleled economic prosperity in the 2000s, based on the sale of minerals to China, which paradoxically combined with a continuing sense of insecurity. John Howard's coalition government benefited from the salience of security issues at home and abroad, with Australia joining a 'coalition of the willing' in a US-led invasion of Iraq. United States president, George W. Bush, praised Howard as a 'man of steel', and Howard had little difficulty in gaining an ascendancy over Simon Crean, who had succeeded Beazley as Labor Party leader after the 2001 election defeat.

Crean, the son of the Whitlam government treasurer and himself a former president of the Australian Council of Trade Unions, would never have the opportunity to fight an election, for he was replaced by a younger successor, Mark Latham, at the end of 2003. Latham mounted a strong challenge to the government during 2004, but the wily Howard succeeded in instilling doubts about the Labor leader's reliability on national security and economic management. At an election held late in 2004, the Liberal-National Party coalition not only won an even larger lower-house majority than in 2001; for the first time since the 1970s, a government managed to gain control of the Senate. The victory gave Howard the opportunity to implement policies long thwarted by his opponents. The government soon introduced a large and complex new set of laws under the banner of *WorkChoices*, which were legislated once it controlled the Senate from mid-2005. These were mainly designed to reduce the influence of trade unions, which conducted an aggressive and damaging campaign against them through to November 2007.

At a time when all state and territory governments were controlled by the Labor Party, the Howard Government now entered a period of decline. The wars in Afghanistan and, particularly, Iraq were increasingly unpopular, and the government was dogged by the rivalry between Howard and his long-serving treasurer, Peter Costello. But there was also declining confidence in the ability of Beazley, who had returned to the Labor leadership after the 2004 election, to lead his party to victory. Late in 2006 Labor's foreign affairs spokesman, Kevin Rudd, formed a ticket with rising frontbencher Julia Gillard to challenge Beazley successfully for the leadership. Rudd gathered momentum during 2007 and, emphasising his personal appeal under the slogan of *Kevin 07*, Labor easily won the election held on 24 November 2007. Howard became the first prime minister since Stanley Melbourne Bruce in 1929 to lose his own seat at a federal election.

The new Rudd government ratified the Kyoto Protocol on climate change, and Rudd made a formal apology to the 'Stolen Generations' of Indigenous people. The government also promised to revive the country's infrastructure in a renewed nation-building effort, wound back *WorkChoices*, and adopted a less severe policy towards asylum seekers. By the final months of 2008, the government faced a more urgent challenge: the global financial crisis, to which it responded successfully through stimulus spending. Australia technically avoided a recession.

Amid criticisms of autocratic leadership and chaotic decision-making, the prime minister's ambitions for a major policy breakthrough increasingly focused on the United Nations Climate Change

Conference to be held in Copenhagen, Denmark in December 2009. The government was committed to a Carbon Pollution Reduction Scheme (CPRS), but its bills had run into problems in the Senate. Rudd therefore sought and – in November 2009 – received the cooperation of the leader of the Liberal Party, Malcolm Turnbull, who had succeeded Brendan Nelson as opposition leader in September 2008. In a party-room ballot on 1 December 2009 amid growing dissent from the party's position on the government's climate change policy, Tony Abbott, from the Liberal Party's conservative wing, defeated Turnbull by one vote to become leader. The Liberal Party now took a stronger stand against the government's emissions trading scheme (ETS) proposal, thereby ensuring that it would be defeated in the Senate. Rudd was also bitterly disappointed by the inability of the Copenhagen summit to arrive at a comprehensive agreement, and in April 2010 he announced that the government would defer its ETS.

Early in May 2010 a review of the taxation system was released, and the government was soon publicly committed to one of its key proposals, a Resource Super Profits Tax, which provoked a fierce campaign by the mining industry. The standing of the government and the prime minister declined, with the resumption of asylum-seeker arrivals by boat also eroding public confidence. On the evening of 23 June, Rudd and Gillard met in Canberra to discuss the Labor leadership. It soon became clear that Rudd no longer had the support of most of caucus and when it met the following morning, Gillard was elected without Rudd even standing for the leadership. Gillard, describing Rudd's administration as a good government that had lost its way, quickly arrived at an agreement with industry leaders for a more acceptable Minerals Resource Rent Tax and called an election for 21 August 2010.

Chapter 10

2010

ANOTHER HUNG PARLIAMENT

Isobelle Barrett Meyering

On any assessment, the election on 21 August 2010 was a remarkable one. Two and a half years earlier, on 24 November 2007, the Labor Party returned to office in a decisive victory, even ousting the former Liberal prime minister, John Howard, from his seat. When voters went to the polls in 2010, the party lost eleven seats, one of the largest ever losses for a first-term government. Much of the blame for the result has been laid on the controversial decision of the Labor Party to remove Kevin Rudd in favour of Julia Gillard two months earlier and the handling of the leadership change. The circumstances of Gillard's ascension to the role of prime minister overshadowed Labor's campaign. Nonetheless, these difficulties did not provide the coalition, led by Tony Abbott, with sufficient traction to defeat Labor. Instead, the election produced a hung parliament, the first since the 1940 wartime election, and Gillard was successful in forming a minority government with the backing of three Independents and the Greens. The election brought into sharp relief the hazards of the increasing 'personalisation' of election campaigns in recent decades and highlighted the crucial role that small parties and Independents play in contemporary politics. The election's additional significance as the first to be contested by a female prime minister and subsequent debate about her mistreatment ensure that it will be remembered as a crucial juncture in Australian political history.

On the morning of 24 June 2010, when Julia Gillard first faced the press after winning the leadership of the Labor Party, she promised to call an election soon so that 'the Australian people can exercise their birth right to choose their prime minister'.[1] Two months later, on 21 August 2010, voters went to the polls to deliver their verdict on the new leader and her opponent, Tony Abbott. The result was much closer than predicted at the outset of the campaign period, leaving neither Labor nor the coalition with the ability to form government on their own. Far from providing the public endorsement that Gillard had hoped for, the election instead placed her in a more precarious position. She succeeded in forming a minority government but, during the next three years of her term as prime minister, the view that she lacked a popular mandate proved difficult to shake. Attacks on the legitimacy of the government combined with a barrage of sexist commentary to significantly undercut Gillard's credibility. Meanwhile, internal division within the Labor caucus festered as Rudd's supporters manoeuvred his comeback.

Many factors contributed to the close result on 21 August 2010 and the subsequent difficulties faced by the Gillard government. However, the decision to call a quick election, as promised at Gillard's first press conference, was a crucial one. Political journalist Barrie Cassidy nominates it as Labor's 'worst tactical error', curtailing the opportunity for her government to 'shake itself free of the Rudd factor', a view he is far from alone in holding.[2] Yet Gillard has stood by the choice, reiterating that she 'did feel very keenly that the Australian public needed to get a say'.[3] Her decision illuminates one

---

1 Transcript of Joint Press Conference, Parliament House, 24 June 2010, Accessed online. <http://ministers.treasury.gov.au/DisplayDocs.aspx?doc=transcripts/2010/079.htm&pageID=004&min=wms&Year=&DocType=>
2 Barrie Cassidy, *The Party Thieves: The Real Story of the 2010 Election* (Melbourne: Melbourne University Publishing, 2010), p.239.
3 Jacqueline Kent, *Take Your Best Shot: The Prime Ministership of Julia Gillard* (Melbourne: Penguin Books, 2013), p.14. Gillard elaborates on her reasons for

of the central tensions of contemporary Australian politics. Voters do not, in fact, have a 'birth right' to choose their prime minister under the Westminster system. Nonetheless, the last two decades or so have seen the increasing 'personalisation' of election campaigns, with both sides of politics focusing heavily on party leaders.[4] This phenomenon reached new heights in Labor's *Kevin 07* presidential-style campaign, arguably reinforcing an expectation on the part of the electorate that they – not the party room – should determine the fate of leaders. The hazards of this approach became clear during the 2010 election, as questions over the leadership contest continued to weigh on Gillard's campaign.

Labor's decision to remove Rudd, a first-term prime minister, was an extraordinary one. The subsequent leadership instability that followed this decision, not just in the Labor Party but, later, in the coalition, makes the 2010 election a defining moment in Australian political history. Yet this is by no means the only feature of the election to make it merit its place in this collection. It is equally significant in having produced the first hung parliament since the 1940 wartime election. Minority government has long been a norm in comparable western democracies, and all state and territory governments have navigated minority governments at some point in recent decades.[5] However, the 2010 election was the first time that the dominance of the modern two-party system – established in 1909 with the Fusion and cemented in 1944 with the formation of the Liberal Party – was

---

calling a quick election in Julia Gillard, *My Story* (Sydney: Knopf, 2014), pp.32-33.

4 Ian McAllister, *The Australian Voter: 50 Years of Change* (Sydney: NewSouth Publishing, 2011), p.241.

5 Nicholas Horne, 'Hung Parliaments and Minority Governments', 23 December 2010, Australian Parliamentary Library, Canberra, Accessed online. <http://www.aph.gov.au/About_Parliament/Parliamentary_Departments/Parliamentary_Library/pubs/BN/1011/HungParliaments#_Toc320017745>

seriously challenged at the federal level. The resulting experiment in minority government has provided a test case that may well prove critical in future years, as both of the major parties struggle to maintain their support base.

Finally, the significance of the 2010 election as the first to be contested by a female prime minister – and, moreover, a woman who had no children, was in a de facto relationship and openly identified herself as an atheist, in contrast to Rudd, one of the most religious political figures in recent years – cannot be ignored. Gender was a prominent issue in the election and would only become more so in the subsequent years of the Gillard government. Indeed, by the end of her term as prime minister, it was apparent that one of its lasting legacies would be to generate a public debate about the status of women in Australian politics and the existence of what prominent feminist commentator Anne Summers has described as the 'misogyny factor'.[6] The Labor and coalition campaigns during the 2010 election provided a foretaste of some of the controversies to come. Moreover, the election outcome was itself an important factor in shaping the direction of gender politics.

The exceptional circumstances of the 2010 election have ensured that it has already emerged as a crucial juncture in the making of modern Australia, attracting an unusual level of attention, from insider accounts to academic appraisals.[7] While a full assessment

---

6   Anne Summers, *The Misogyny Factor* (Sydney: NewSouth Publishing, 2013).

7   For example, Cassidy, *The Party Thieves*; Bob Ellis, *Suddenly, Last Winter: An Election Diary* (Melbourne: Viking, 2010); Brenton Holmes and Sophia Fernandes, '2010 Federal Election: A Brief History', 6 March 2012, Research Paper no. 8 2011-12, Australian Parliamentary Library, Canberra, Accessed online. <http://www.aph.gov.au/About_Parliament/Parliamentary_Departments/Parliamentary_Library/pubs/rp/rp1112/12rp08>; George Megalogenis, 'Trivial Pursuit: Leadership and the End of the Reform Era', *Quarterly Essay*, 40 (Melbourne: Black Inc, 2010); Paul Howe, *Confessions of a Faceless Man: Inside Campaign 2010* (Melbourne: Melbourne

of its legacy awaits future historians, this chapter traces some of the key arguments that have emerged thus far about the importance of these three factors – the leadership contest, the hung parliament and gender politics – in the 2010 election and their role in shaping our political culture.

Rise of the Ruddbot

On 24 November 2007, the Labor Party, led by Kevin Rudd, with Julia Gillard as his deputy, won office after almost twelve years in opposition. Labor's victory was a decisive one: the election saw a swing of 23 seats to Labor in the House of Representative and Liberal prime minister John Howard lost his own seat of Bennelong. The path from Labor's victory in 2007 to minority government in 2010 in itself makes the latter an unusual election. The loss of seats – down from 83 to 72 in the House of Representatives – was for a first-term government exceeded by only 1931 and 1998, and Labor's primary vote fell from 43.38% to 37.99%. It is all the more remarkable given Rudd had been an extremely popular leader.

A former bureaucrat and diplomat, Rudd was elected to the federal parliament in 1998 and trod a 'lonely' path to leadership.[8] He located his politics in a Christian social justice worldview, a key tenet of which he argued was advocacy for 'the marginalised, the vulnerable and the oppressed'.[9] Despite his nerdish image, the 'Ruddbot' as

---

University Press, 2010); Mungo MacCallum, *Punch & Judy: The Double Dissolution Election of 2010* (Melbourne: Black Inc, 2010); Marian Simms and John Wanna (eds), *Julia 2010: The Caretaker Election* (Canberra: ANU E Press, 2012).

8   David Marr, 'Power Trip: The Political Journey of Kevin Rudd', *Quarterly Essay*, 38 (Melbourne: Black Inc, 2010), p.40.

9   Kevin Rudd, 'Faith in Politics', *Monthly*, October 2006. https://www.themonthly.com.au/monthly-essays-kevin-rudd-faith-politics--300 See also *Kevin Rudd, Not for the Faint-Hearted: A Personal Reflection on Life, Politics and Purpose* (Sydney: Pan Macmillan Australia, 2017).

popular political writer Annabel Crabb named him, was surprisingly charismatic and considered to be a skilled networker.[10] His ability to connect with voters was evidenced during the high-powered *Kevin 07* election campaign, notable for its focus on the leader's personality and use of social media. According to the Australian Election Study (AES), his approval rating was the highest for a prime minister since Bob Hawke.[11]

With much staked on Rudd's popularity with the electorate, heads began to turn when his approval rating started to fall noticeably in late 2009 and into 2010. It reached a low point at the beginning of May 2010, with a Newspoll showing it had dropped to 39%, the first time it had fallen below 50%. Moreover, the coalition was now ahead of Labor on a two-party preferred basis by 51% to 49%.[12] The result came the week after Rudd announced that he was delaying the proposed emissions trading scheme (ETS), a signature Labor policy. The proposal was one which Abbott, elected to the role of opposition leader on 1 December 2009 by just one vote over Malcolm Turnbull, had relentlessly attacked. Despite having formerly supported the concept of an ETS under the Howard government, Abbott declared it to be a 'great big new tax' on 'everything', a mantra he would repeat in the 2010 election.[13] The Rudd government had also suffered a number of other setbacks, with scandals emerging around its home

---

10 Annabel Crabb, *Rise of the Ruddbot: Observations from the Gallery* (Melbourne: Black Inc, 2010).
11 Hawke attracted a rating of 6.23/10 in 1987, while Rudd attracted a rating of 6.31 in 2007. McAllister, *The Australian Voter*, p.249.
12 Dennis Shanahan, 'Record Drop in PMs Satisfaction after ETS Backflip as Coalition Moves Ahead', *Australian*, 4 May 2010. The result was echoed in a Nielsen poll a week later, which put Rudd's approval rating at 45%. Phillip Coorey, 'Rudd in Free Fall: Voters Lose Faith', *Sydney Morning Herald*, 10 May 2010.
13 Lenore Taylor, 'Next Policy: Anything But A "Great Big New Tax"', *Australian*, 2 December 2009.

installation scheme and school buildings program, and the issue of boat arrivals prominent in the news, prompting Rudd to announce a suspension of the processing of claims by Sri Lankan and Afghan asylum seekers on 9 April 2010, a hardening of Labor's line on refugees. Soon, the government was also facing a well-funded campaign by the mining lobby over its proposed super-profits tax, announced on 2 May.[14]

The Leadership Challenge

As fears of an impending election defeat mounted, there was speculation about Gillard succeeding Rudd at some point in the near future. Gillard had followed a more traditional political career. She was a leader in student politics and worked as an industrial lawyer before entering parliament, along with Rudd, after the 1998 election.[15] She was acknowledged as a talented debater and had long been mooted as a potential future Labor leader, including in an ABC *Australian Story* profile, *The Gillard Diaries* (2006), an updated version of which was screened on 21 June 2010 with uncanny timing.[16] The speculation was not misplaced, although many were nonetheless stunned when, three days later, on 24 June, Gillard was elected to the Labor leadership unopposed.

The events leading up to the leadership challenge remain contested. The degree to which internal divisions over Rudd's personality and style of governing played a role – a key part of the explanation later

---

14 For an overview of these policy issues and the fallout from them, see for example Cassidy, *The Party Thieves*, pp.36-39, 45-47, 53-56, 59-61.

15 On Gillard's political career prior to her ascension to the role of the prime ministership, see Jacqueline Kent, *The Making of Julia Gillard* (Melbourne: Viking, 2009).

16 Caroline Jones, 'She Who Waits', *Australian Story*, ABC, 21 June 2010, Accessed online. <http://www.abc.net.au/austory/content/2007/s2933052.htm>.

given by Gillard and her supporters – is disputed by party insiders, as is the question of the extent to which the challenge was premeditated. Whether or not a deal was reached the night before, in which Gillard agreed to hold off, is also contested.[17] The existence of such a deal was first raised by journalist Laurie Oakes when Gillard spoke at the National Press Club on 15 July. The leak was an early sign of the disunity within Labor that would overshadow its election campaign.

In the interim, Gillard had positioned herself in 'caretaker mode', choosing not to move into the Lodge in Canberra. She also acted quickly to address several of the issues considered to be hurting Labor's electoral chances, including negotiating a compromise resources tax with the major mining companies, announced on 2 July 2010. When she duly called the election on 17 July 2010, Labor had cause for optimism about its prospects. Labor's ratings had improved in the weeks since Gillard had become prime minister and the first poll of the campaign, released by Newspoll on 19 July, confirmed the trend, putting Labor at 55% of the two-party preferred vote.[18]

The Campaign

Just two weeks into the campaign, there were signs that the election might not deliver Gillard the clear mandate she hoped for. On 31 July, a Nielsen poll found Gillard's approval rating had fallen from 56% to 51%, and put the coalition ahead of Labor in the two-party preferred vote, at 52% to 48%.[19] The poll followed a leak on 27 July

---

17   Gillard and Rudd, as well as other party insiders, provide their rival accounts in Sarah Ferguson, *The Killing Season: Uncut* (Melbourne: Melbourne University Press, 2016). See also Gillard's explanation of her reasons for challenging in Gillard, *My Story*, ch. 1.
18   Dennis Shanahan, 'Gillard Poll Gamble Paying Off – Newspoll Labor Grabs 55-45 Lead as New PM Builds Support on Boats, Climate', *Australian*, 19 July 2010.
19   Phillip Coorey, 'Abbott Seizes the Lead', *Sydney Morning Herald*, 31 July 2010.

that Gillard had opposed an increase to the old-age pension and the implementation of the paid parental leave scheme. Internal divisions over the leadership change were further underlined by another leak on 31 July that Gillard had sent a former security guard to national security meetings in her place. This followed a previous accusation on 22 July that Rudd had sent his chief of staff.

While the leaks were highly damaging, they were not the only factor that contributed to what many commentators considered to be a lacklustre performance by Labor. The campaign was also criticised as lacking big ideas, a product both of the short lead time and caution about the Rudd legacy. Several policy announcements drew particular ire. Gillard's professed support for a 'sustainable Australia' – in contrast to Rudd's 'big Australia' – announced at her first press conference for the election on 17 July, saw her accused of 'dog whistling' over the issue of immigration.[20] It was later blamed for a fall in the multicultural vote in Sydney electorates, although the result was not replicated in Victoria.[21] Gillard's subsequent announcement on 23 July that she would hold a citizens' assembly to consult on the issue of climate change was criticised as compounding the damage already caused by Labor's backdown on the ETS. Finally, while Gillard reiterated Labor's commitment to health and education spending, she waited until the last stages of the campaign to take up the issue of broadband, a potential 'game breaker'.[22]

---

20   George Megalogenis, 'A Sustainable Idea for Marginals', *Australian*, 19 July 2010. See also Megalogenis, 'Trivial Pursuit', pp.21-25.
21   James Jupp, 'Immigration Issues in the 2010 Federal Election' in Marian Simms and John Wanna (eds) *Julia 2010: The Caretaker Election* (Canberra: ANU E Press, 2012), p.274; Elaine Thompson and Geoff Robinson, 'New South Wales' in Marian Simms and John Wanna (eds), *Julia 2010: The Caretaker Election* (Canberra: ANU E Press, 2012), p.179.
22   MacCallum, *Punch & Judy*, p.213.

Difficulties in establishing Gillard's credibility were also evident in the wider campaign. The slogan, 'Moving Forward', drawn from Gillard's speech at the National Press Club on 15 July, quickly came to be derided as repetitive and clichéd. On 2 August 2010, Gillard announced a shift in Labor's strategy, stating that she wanted 'to throw away [the] rule book' and promising that the electorate would see more of the 'real Julia' in the remaining weeks of the campaign.[23] Commentators were universal in declaring the move – or at least the public proclamation of it – to be poorly conceived, with its implication that the prime minister had shown a fake front up until this point. Finally, efforts to address directly the leadership issue by involving Rudd in the campaign proved ineffective, including a staged meeting with Gillard arranged in Brisbane on 7 August, with reports noting that she and Rudd 'did not make eye contact or shake hands'.[24]

Labor's ongoing leadership tensions were a boon to the coalition and Abbott sought to make the most of them. Early in the campaign, during the televised leaders' debate on 25 July, he described the replacement of Rudd by Gillard as an attempt 'to trick the public that it's somehow different because it's changed the person at the top'.[25] Two weeks later, at his election launch speech on 8 August, he talked up the role of the 'faceless men' in the Labor Party who 'can execute a leader but … can't execute a programme'. Meanwhile, on policy issues, the coalition ran a largely negative campaign, promising

---

23 'The Real Julia Gillard', 702 ABC Sydney, 2 August 2010, Accessed online. <http://www.abc.net.au/local/stories/2010/08/02/2971264.htm>

24 'Gillard, Rudd Won't Campaign Together', ABC News, 7 August 2010, Accessed online. <http://www.abc.net.au/news/2010-08-07/gillard-rudd-wont-campaign-together/935832>

25 Transcript of 2010 Federal Election Debate, Herald Sun Online, 26 July 2010, Accessed online. <http://www.heraldsun.com.au/news/special-features/transcript-of-2010-federalelection-debate/news-story/a6802583f2db08b4e920b8d615a9ae3f>

to 'end the waste, pay back the debt, stop the big new taxes, stop the boats and help struggling families'.[26]

Yet Abbott's campaign was not without its own difficulties. The 2007 election defeat still hung over the coalition, particularly the subject of industrial relations. On the day the election was called, Abbott declared that *WorkChoices* was 'dead, buried and cremated', but the coalition's spokesperson on workplace relations, Eric Abetz, conceded that there might be some 'tweaking' of it, through ministerial directions or regulations.[27] The coalition also left itself open for criticism when a significant error in its budget calculations was exposed on 10 August, leaving an $800 million shortfall in savings it promised to make if elected.

Ultimately, even with the disunity within Labor over the leadership contest, the coalition did not achieve the traction required to win back government. In fact, although Labor's primary vote was one of the lowest on record, it still narrowly won the two-party preferred vote by 50.12% compared to the coalition's 49.88%. Nonetheless, Abbott could claim to have almost brought down a first-term government. His pleasure was in evidence on election night, as the vote was still being counted. While warning that it was no time for 'premature triumphalism', he confidently announced that the 'Coalition is back in business'.[28]

---

26 Tony Abbott, Election launch speech, 8 August 2010, Brisbane, Museum of Australian Democracy, Accessed online. <http://electionspeeches.moadoph.gov.au/speeches/2010-tony-abbott.Ibid>

27 Susan McDonald, 'Coalition Cannot Rule Out IR Tweaks', ABC News, 17 July 2010, Accessed online. <http://www.abc.net.au/news/2010-07-17/coalition-cannot-rule-out-ir-tweaks/908328>

28 Tony Abbott, 'Election night speech', Australian Politics, 21 August 2010, Accessed online. <http://australianpolitics.com/2010/08/21/tony-abbott-election-night-speech.html>

For Gillard, the failure to gain a clear win was a significant blow and, in the aftermath of the election, the question of whether Labor would have fared better had Rudd remained prime minister inevitably arose. The result in Queensland – where nine notionally Labor seats were lost – was cited as one that might have been prevented, although local factors also contributed to the outcome, including hostility towards Anna Bligh's state government.[29] That voters more generally were critical of the leadership change was confirmed in the Australian Election Study, which found that more than 70% of Australian voters disapproved of the way it was handled. Nevertheless, political scientist Ian McAllister, co-director of the survey, has cautioned that voter disapproval did not necessarily translate into a net loss of votes.[30]

Either way, the leadership contest and the fallout from it certainly damaged Labor's campaign. Moreover, it had repercussions ultimately extending beyond the election itself. The leadership contest was quickly linked to the 'New South Wales disease' of revolving leaders.[31] Sure enough, divisions continued within Labor over the course of Gillard's prime ministership until, finally, on 26 June 2013, the party reinstalled Rudd, only to be defeated three months later at an election on 7 September 2013. Labor's experience would subsequently come to be seen as seen as a cautionary tale to the coalition after disquiet emerged over Abbott's prime ministership.

---

29   John Warhurst, 'The Election Rudd Could Have Won', *Eureka Street*, 23 August 2010, Accessed online. <http://www.eurekastreet.com.au/article.aspx?aeid=22930#. V35Savl95hE>; Ian Ward, 'Queensland' in Simms and Wanna (eds), *Julia 2010*, p.225.
30   McAllister, *The Australian Voter*, p.250.
31   See for example Quentin Dempster, '"NSW Disease" Blamed for Labor Loss', *7.30 New South Wales*, ABC, 30 August 2010, Accessed online. <http://www.abc.net.au/news/2010-08-28/nsw-disease-blamed-for-labor-loss/961118>

Nonetheless, the coalition would end up replicating Labor's decision, with Turnbull replacing Abbott on 15 September 2015. The result is that Australia had four different prime ministers within a space of just over five years. What had seemed like an extraordinary decision in 2010 to remove a first-term prime minister had now been taken by both sides of politics.

Reactions to Abbott's ousting were more muted, leading some to conclude that there is now 'quiet acceptance' of the 'political reality' under the Westminster system that parties – not the electorate – determine their leaders' fates.[32] Of course, Abbott had never enjoyed the same degree of popular approval as Rudd. Moreover, Turnbull waited another nine months before going to an election on 2 July 2016, where he secured a narrow one-seat majority. Had Gillard too waited before calling an election, would the outcome of the 2010 election also have been a different one? If so, the hung parliament, the second of its distinctive features, might never have eventuated.

The (Protracted) Result

Late on the night of 21 August, Gillard addressed Labor supporters in Melbourne and told them that the election was still too close to call. She was calm and collected, and the crowd was surprisingly upbeat given the tight result. Emphasising that 'in our great democracy, every vote is important', she spoke of her past record of working 'productively' with the crossbench.[33] When the final result

---

32 Patricia Karvelas, 'Leadership Spills: We Now Realise this is Just the Westminster System in Action', *The Drum*, ABC, 23 September 2015, Accessed online. <http://www.abc.net.au/news/2015-09-23/karvelas-this-is-just-the-westminster-system-in-action/6797818>

33 Julia Gillard, Election night speech, *YouTube*, 21 August 2010, Accessed online. <https://www.youtube.com/watch?v=OPjNmggEsV8>

was declared, her comments on election night proved to be prudent. In the House of Representatives, Labor and the coalition had each secured 72 seats. The remaining six seats were held by four Independents, Bob Katter, Rob Oakeshott, Tony Windsor and Andrew Wilkie; one Green, Adam Bandt; and Tony Crook, a member of the Nationals in Western Australia but sitting on the crossbench. Their votes would determine who formed government.

The process of negotiation took a full seventeen days. Early in the process, on 23 August, a minor controversy emerged over a possible conflict of interest on the part of the governor-general, Quentin Bryce, in appointing the prime minister, given her daughter's marriage to Labor MP Bill Shorten. Any concern on constitutional grounds was, however, quickly quashed and the established conventions dictating the governor-general's role, including in the case of a hung parliament, were reiterated.[34] Meanwhile, Labor and the coalition continued their efforts to win over the relevant players.

Gillard announced an agreement first with the Greens on 1 September. The latter had achieved a historic result in the election. Bandt's victory in the inner-city seat of Melbourne – which long-time Labor member, Lindsay Tanner, did not contest – represented the party's first win in the House of Representatives at a general election.[35] It was also the first time the Greens had won a Senate seat in each state on a single occasion, giving them the balance of power. Overall, the Greens' result surpassed the record of third parties that have previously exerted a significant influence in Australian politics, namely

---

34 Brian Costar, 'Seventeen Days to Power' in Simms and Wanna (eds), *Julia 2010*, p.362.
35 The Greens had enjoyed a previous victory in the October 2002 by-election for the seat of Cunningham, when Michael Organ defeated Labor's Sharon Bird, despite receiving just 23% of the primary vote. Organ lost the seat at the 2004 election.

the Democratic Labor Party – which had made a surprise comeback at the election, securing a Senate seat for the first time since 1970 – and the Australian Democrats.[36] The success of the Greens meant that they were in a position to secure important concessions. Part of the deal included an agreement that Bandt and the Greens party leader, Senator Bob Brown, would meet on a weekly basis with Gillard during parliamentary sessions and that the Green's treasury spokesperson and Bandt would receive regular briefings from the treasurer and minister for finance. Gillard also agreed to establish a Climate Change Committee of experts and parliamentarians who recognised a need for carbon pricing.[37]

The Independents took longer to declare their positions. Wilkie, a former intelligence officer and whistle blower who had previously run as a Greens candidate, first against Howard in his Sydney seat of Bennelong in 2004 and then as a Tasmanian Senate candidate in 2007, announced his support for a Gillard minority government on 2 September. The rural Independents – quickly dubbed the 'three amigos' by the media – continued their negotiations together, but amidst increasing speculation that they might go in different directions.[38] Eventually, on 7 September, Katter announced that he had decided to support the coalition, citing the removal of Rudd – with whom he was friendly – as a factor in his decision. The fate of the parliament came down to Windsor and Oakeshott who held a joint press conference that same afternoon. Both were former members of the Nationals and it had initially been assumed that they would side with

---

36   Andrew Bartlett, 'The Greens' in Simms and Wanna (eds), *Julia 2010*, p.164.
37   'The Australian Greens & The Australian Labor Party – Agreement', 1 September 2010, Australian Politics, Accessed online. <http://australianpolitics.com/downloads/2010/10-09-01_labor-greens-agreement.pdf>
38   Lauren Wilson, 'Three Amigos Still Sing from Same Songbook, but not Necessarily in Tune', *Australian*, 6 September 2010.

the coalition. However, they also had significant grievances against the coalition and were cognisant that their influence would be curtailed in an Abbott minority government that lacked control over the upper house and would be more likely to call an early election.[39] At their press conference, they announced that they would support Gillard. To the frustration of those anxious to know the outcome, Oakeshott expounded on the reasons for his decision for almost seventeen minutes before declaring his intentions.

As the negotiations were taking place, speculation had quickly begun over the likely effect of the hung parliament. Some argued that it would lead to a climate of political uncertainty, while others, more optimistically, asserted that it would provide opportunities for more rigorous policy debate, greater accountability and the possibility of electoral reform.[40] Advocates of the latter position had some cause for hope in the process of deal-making itself, which saw both the Greens and Independents push for various reforms to parliamentary procedure, including a greater role for private members. Subsequently, the new parliament passed the *Evidence Amendment (Journalists' Privilege) Act* 2010, providing greater protections for whistle blowers. Sponsored by Wilkie, it was the first private member's bill initiated in the lower house to pass since 1999.

On several other measures the experiment in minority government might be described as a success. The Gillard government's legislative record is an impressive one. Over her time in office, more than 500 bills received royal assent, making her the most 'productive' prime minister in Australian history based on the number of bills passed

---

39   Costar, 'Seventeen Days to Power', pp.364-365.
40   Ibid., pp.357-358.

per day.⁴¹ This included several reforms that were quickly claimed as signature Labor initiatives, including the National Disability Insurance Scheme (NDIS) and the legislative arrangements for a new school funding model, developed in response to the Gonski Report. That said, her 'caution' when it came to social issues, such as asylum seeker policy, social security and same-sex marriage, was controversial.⁴² Gillard also succeeded in having her budgets passed with relative ease. This contrasts with the experience of the later Abbott government, which, despite having a comfortable majority in the House of Representatives, struggled to secure the support of the Senate for its 2014 budget measures.

At the same time, Gillard's minority government was not without difficulties. Gillard was hamstrung when it came to taking decisive action over political scandals involving Labor backbencher Craig Thomson, over charges of fraud in his previous capacity as a union official, and coalition defector Peter Slipper, alleged to have misused his travel entitlements and sexually harassed his former aide, James Ashby. Moreover, Gillard's deal with the Greens to introduce a fixed price on carbon for a three-year period before moving to an ETS, and her subsequent concession in a *7.30* interview on 24 February 2011 that it could be viewed as a 'tax', prompted claims that Gillard

---

41   Nick Evershed, 'Was Julia Gillard the Most Productive Prime Minister in Australia's History?', *Guardian*, 28 June 2013. Accessed online. <https://www.theguardian.com/news/datablog/2013/jun/28/australia-productive-prime-minister> For an extended analysis, see Gwynneth Singleton, 'The Legislative Record of a "Hung" Parliament' in Chris Aulich (ed), *The Gillard Governments: Australian Commonwealth Administration 2010-2013* (Melbourne: Melbourne University Press, 2014), pp.43-54.

42   Carol Johnson, 'The Credit She Deserved: Gillard and the Labor Legacy' in Samantha Trenoweth (ed.) *Bewitched & Bedevilled: Women Write the Gillard Years* (Melbourne: Hardie Grant Books, 2013), p.148.

had 'lied' to the Australian public in the election campaign.[43] The Greens themselves ultimately broke off their alliance with Gillard on 19 February 2013, citing disagreements on policy agendas, although they continued to guarantee confidence and supply. By this stage, some Labor figures were already publicly arguing that the alliance with the Greens had been a 'mistake'.[44] The perception that it had tainted the party's image was reflected in the 2016 election campaign, during which Labor leader Bill Shorten specifically ruled out any future coalition.

In the final event, Gillard's minority government arguably confirmed the biases of both those who saw it as an opportunity for a more deliberative form of government and those who predicted it would lead to instability. It now stands as a rare precedent and will no doubt serve as a reference point for any future minority governments. Indeed, as the prospect of another hung parliament was contemplated when the result of the 2016 election was still unclear, the experience of Gillard was quickly evoked (with mixed feelings).[45] While Turnbull narrowly avoided the same fate of Gillard and was returned with a one-seat majority, the 2016 election further underlined that the dominance of the two-party system can no longer be so easily assumed. Given the long-term decline in the primary vote

---

43 Heather Ewart, 'Gillard Explains Carbon Scheme', *The 7.30 Report*, ABC, 24 February 2011, Accessed online. <http://www.abc.net.au/7.30/content/2011/s3148281.htm>

44 'Labor-Greens Alliance Was a Mistake, Says NSW Labor Leader', SkyNews Australia, 12 July 2012, Accessed online. <https://www.youtube.com/watch?v=l7tjcY2QUgM>; Criticisms of the alliance by a range of Labor figures are canvassed in Paul Kelly, *Triumph and Demise: The Broken Promises of a Labor Generation* (Melbourne: Melbourne University Press, 2014), pp.40-42.

45 For example, Sid Maher, 'A Flop the First Time but Stars Return for Hung Parliament II', *Australian*, 4 July 2016; 'Previous Hung Parliament Proved Most Productive in Our History', *Canberra Times*, 7 July 2016; Jessica Sier, 'Hung Parliament Syndrome: Lessons from Gillard in 2010: Business Confidence', *Australian Financial Review*, 5 July 2016.

for the majority parties, another minority government at some point in the near future cannot be ruled out. In that case, we might have even greater cause to see the 2010 election as crucial turning point in Australian politics.

The 2010 election is remarkable both for the ousting of a first-term prime minister in the lead up and for the resulting hung parliament. That Gillard was also Australia's first female prime minister marks it as a truly historic occasion. This was not lost on the media. Even as the circumstances of Rudd's removal absorbed significant attention in the days immediately following the leadership contest and the commentary revealed a degree of ambivalence about Gillard's actions as an exercise in female ambition, much was made of the ascension of a woman to the role of prime minister.[46] The *Daily Telegraph*'s 'souvenir edition', featuring a full-colour front cover image of Gillard and published on the afternoon of 24 June, captured the momentous nature of the occasion.[47] Gillard was also quickly embraced by women's magazines who were 'unashamedly celebratory' in their portrayal of her rise to power.[48]

By contrast, Gillard sought to diffuse attempts to portray her as a champion for women or feminist role model. In her first press conference after deposing Rudd, she asserted that she 'didn't set out to crash [her] head on any glass ceilings'.[49] Gillard later told Anne Summers

---

[46] For a detailed analysis of the gendered responses to the leadership challenge, see Laura Hall and Ngaire Donaghue, '"Nice Girls Don't Carry Knives": Constructions of Ambition in Media Coverage of Australia's First Female Prime Minister', *British Journal of Social Psychology*, 52, 2013, pp.631-647.

[47] 'Julia PM: Rudd Stands Aside for Our First Female Prime Minister', *Daily Telegraph*, 24 June 2010.

[48] Susanne Gannon, 'Julia the Hottie and "You Go, Girl": Role Models for Girls and Young Women?', *Outskirts: Feminisms Along the Edge*, 23, 2010, Accessed online. <http://www.outskirts.arts.uwa.edu.au/volumes/volume-23/gannon>

[49] Transcript of Joint Press Conference, 24 June 2010.

that she did not feel it was necessary to draw further attention to her status as the first female prime minister. It was already 'so obvious' that she 'didn't need to hark on about it'.[50] A similar approach had been followed during the election campaign, in which Gillard 'studiously avoided' the subject of gender.[51] Perhaps most tellingly, Labor only released a full policy statement on women the day before the election and without a public announcement.[52]

The Gender Card?

One reason that Labor did not make more of Gillard's status as the first female prime minister was that the polls showed that she already enjoyed stronger support among women voters. Indeed, Gillard's apparent advantage over Abbott proved to be one of the key themes in the early election coverage. That Gillard enjoyed the benefits of the 'sisterhood' made the headlines on 20 July, after an Essential Research poll found that her lead over Abbott as preferred prime minister was double among women compared with men.[53] The *Australian* subsequently published previously unreleased data from Newspoll showing that Labor enjoyed a higher primary vote among women,[54] while the first Nielsen poll of the election, released on 24 July, found that on a two-party preferred basis, 58% of women supported Labor and 42%

---

50 Anne Summers, 'The Prime Ministership According to Julia Gillard', *Anne Summers Reports*, 3, July 2013, p.22. Also cited in Kelly, *Triumph and Demise*, p.403.

51 Marian Sawer, 'Managing Gender: The 2010 Federal Election' in Simms and Wanna (eds), *Julia 2010*, p.256.

52 Ibid., p.258.

53 53% of female voters nominated Gillard as their preferred prime minister and only 23% Abbott, a 30 point gap, whereas 47% of male voters preferred Gillard and 32% supported Abbott, a 15 point gap. Shane Wright, 'Sisterhood Gives Gillard Lift in Polls', *West Australian*, 20 July 2010. Accessed online. <https://thewest.com.au/news/australia/sisterhood-gives-gillard-lift-in-polls-ng-ya-204997>

54 Labor's primary vote was 44% among women and 39% among men, compared to coalition's primary vote of 33% and 42% respectively. Cameron Stewart, 'Coalitions Chances May Be Cruelled by Gender Drift', *Australian*, 22 July 2010.

the coalition, whereas men were split evenly.[55] *Sydney Morning Herald* journalist Peter Hartcher noted that if only women were permitted to vote, Labor 'would win in a landslide'.[56]

However, no sooner had Gillard's advantage among women voters been declared than there appeared to be signs that the gender gap might be closing. A Newspoll on 26 July reported a fall in Labor's primary vote among women since the previous week, from 44% to 40%, only just above that of men (39%).[57] The *Australian*'s Dennis Shanahan proclaimed that Gillard's 'honeymoon' was on the 'wane', a line that Abbott latched onto later in the day when interviewed on Fairfax radio.[58] The Labor leak about paid parental leave and the pension on 27 July compounded the trend downwards. Four days later, on 31 July, the Nielsen poll showed a dramatic drop in Labor support among female voters, with the coalition now slightly leading Labor on a two-party preferred basis of 51% to 49%.[59] Summers, who has since noted that the leak was 'calculated' to target Gillard as a childless woman, described its effect as 'deadly'.[60] Journalist George Megalogenis was even more scathing when he appeared on the ABC *Insiders* program on 8 August. Since the leaks, former Labor leader Mark Latham, now working for Channel Nine, had also entered the fray as a kind of Gonzo journalist. Reflecting on these developments,

---

55 Phillip Coorey, 'Women Give Gillard the Winning Edge But Labor Lags in Queensland and WA', *Sydney Morning Herald*, 24 July 2010.
56 Peter Hartcher, 'Gillard Can Count on the XX-factor', *Sydney Morning Herald*, 24 July 2010.
57 Dennis Shanahan, 'Coalition Narrows the Gap – Newspoll Gillard's Honeymoon Wanes as Women Shift Back to Abbott', *Australian*, 26 July 2010.
58 'PM Gender Honeymoon Over: Abbott', AAP General News Wire, 26 July 2010.
59 Phillip Coorey, 'Abbott Seizes the Lead', *Sydney Morning Herald*, 31 July 2010.
60 Anne Summers, 'A Wager on What Women Want', *Age*, 14 August 2010. See also Summers, *The Misogyny Factor*, p.133.

Megalogenis queried whether 'what we are actually seeing… is a lot of blokes trying to monster up a woman'.[61]

Despite these signs of a narrowing of the gender gap, it appears that Labor ultimately still ended up benefiting from a stronger vote among women. The spike in the coalition's two-party preferred vote among women in the 31 July Nielsen poll was not sustained and it quickly dropped back to the mid-40s, giving Labor the lead once again.[62] The AES also confirmed that gender was a factor in the election outcome. The survey found that Gillard was more popular with women than men, and that her popularity was correlated with a disproportionate number of women voting for Labor in the election.[63] Overall it showed that 44% of women compared to only 36% of men voted for Labor, while 41% of women and 50% of men voted for the coalition.[64]

The result stands in contrast to the traditional gender gap, which has seen women typically vote more conservatively than men. The shift, however, is not altogether new, with the previous three elections in 2001, 2004 and 2007 showing no gender differences in voting. The 2010 election was significant in so far as it represented not only a neutralising but a clear reversal of the traditional pattern.[65] The result was consistent with overseas developments showing a new trend of women voting to the left of men.[66] It was not, however, sustained at the 2013 election, in which no clear gender differences in the voting

---

61 *Insiders*, ABC, 8 August 2010, cited in Gillard, *My Story*, p.36.
62 See figure 21.2 in Sawer, 'Managing Gender', p.255.
63 McAllister, *The Australian Voter*, p.114.
64 Similar numbers voted for the Greens (12% of men, 13% of women) and other candidates (2% in both cases). Clive Bean and Ian McAllister, 'Electoral Behaviour in the 2010 Election' in Simms and Wanna (eds), *Julia 2010*, p.344.
65 McAllister, *The Australian Voter*, p.114.
66 Sawer, 'Managing Gender', p.253.

patterns were recorded for the major parties, although women were more likely to vote for the Greens.⁶⁷ At least in so far as the Labor vote was concerned, the pattern in 2010 had more to do with the option of voting for a female prime minister than a systemic change.

Importantly, the gender gap in the 2010 election also reflected women voters' reservations about Abbott. Marian Sawer has argued that the 2010 election was unusual in so far as the management of gender was an even greater problem for Abbott, whose 'hyper-masculine' image had proven effective as a counter to Rudd but required 'softening' against his new opponent.⁶⁸ That Abbott was a 'problem' for female voters was noted from the beginning of the campaign, when it was reported that he had even hired an advertising agency to work on the perception of female voters.⁶⁹ In particular, women were understood to be uneasy about Abbott's past record on issues such as abortion, including his decision to restrict access to the drug, RU486, while health minister in the Howard Government. Abbott's statement earlier in the year that he advised his daughters to treat their virginity as a 'gift' did not bode well either.⁷⁰

During the campaign Abbott took several steps to assuage these concerns. As early as 24 July, at a Liberal Party event in Western Australia, he spoke of the 'strong women' in his life, including his

---

67   According to the AES, 34% of men and 33% of women voted Labor and 46% of men and 45% of women voted for the coalition in the 2013 election. The Greens drew the vote of 7% of men and 10% of women. Clive Bean and Ian McAllister, 'Documenting the Inevitable: Voting Behaviour at the 2013 Australian Election' in Carol Johnson and John Wanna with Hsu-Ann Lee (eds) *Abbott's Gambit: The 2013 Australian Federal Election* (Canberra: ANU Press, 2015), p.414.
68   Sawer, 'Managing Gender', p.251.
69   See for example Cameron Stewart, 'Coalition's Chances May Be Cruelled by Gender Drift', *Australian*, 22 July 210.
70   On the reaction to his comments at the time, see for example Lauren Wilson, 'Abbott Confirms "Women's Worst Fears"', *Australian*, 27 January 2010.

wife and three daughters.⁷¹ On the policy front, he sought to appeal to women voters with his generous paid parental leave package, which was reannounced on 3 August with the promise of a lower levy on business to cover its cost. Abbott was also pushed to make a specific commitment not to alter abortion laws, stating the coalition had 'no plans whatsoever for any change in that area', after being challenged on the issue by the Health Minister, Nicola Roxon.⁷² Abbott would learn from the experience of the 2010 election, pursuing similar strategies in 2013, when his daughters were described as his best 'electoral weapon' and much was made again of his rival paid parental leave scheme.⁷³

Despite Abbott's efforts to appear more female-friendly, the 2010 election was not without controversy. Various comments during the campaign were interpreted as a sign that Abbott remained unreformed. A case in point was his appropriation of the phrase 'no means no' when Gillard challenged him to a second leaders' debate, sparking criticism that he was 'trivialising' the anti-rape slogan.⁷⁴ Abbott's emphasis on his wife and daughters was also interpreted as a slight against Gillard and her childless status – less explicit than Liberal Senator Bill Heffernan's infamous comment in 2007 that Gillard was

---

71 AAP, 'Abbott Thanks the Women in His Life', *News.com*, 24 July 2010, Accessed online. <http://www.news.com.au/finance/work/abbott-thanks-the-women-in-his-life/news-story/10a74833c3dcbf93dd100d27caef93f4>

72 Nicola Berkovic, 'Abortion Law to Stay', *Australian*, 10 August 2010.

73 'Tony Abbott's Daughters Say He's No Headkicker, Just a Daggy Dad', *Sydney Morning Herald*, 26 August 2013, Accessed online. <http://www.smh.com.au/federal-politics/federal-election-2013/tony-abbotts-daughters-say-hes-no-headkicker-just-a-daggy-dad-20130825-2sjgp.html> For a detailed analysis of the election, see Kristy McLaren and Marian Sawer, 'Gender and the 2013 Election: The Abbott 'Mandate'' in Johnson and Wanna with Lee (eds) *Abbott's Gambit*, pp.375-389.

74 Julian Drape, Abbott "Trivialises" Anti-Rape Campaign', AAP General News Wire, 3 August 2010.

unfit for leadership because she was 'deliberately barren', but nonetheless evidence that the coalition was 'running a subtle negative campaign around gender'.[75]

The election also confirmed feminist commentators' expectations that Gillard would be subjected to a significant degree of personal scrutiny by the media more generally. She was repeatedly queried about her relationship with her partner, Tim Mathieson, and whether they planned to marry, including in a front cover story in the *Australian Women's Weekly* that drew wide attention.[76] Her physical appearance was also the subject of ongoing attention, from her earlobes to her choice of outfits. This coverage did not necessarily damage Gillard in electoral terms and might even have been 'counterproductive'.[77] Nonetheless, it highlighted a double standard in the treatment of female politicians that would reach new levels during the remainder of her prime ministership.

Indeed, over the next three years, Gillard sustained an unprecedented level of sexist abuse. Documented elsewhere in closer detail, this manifested in a wide range of forms, from highly sexualised images that circulated online through to a controversial television satire, *At Home With Julia* (2011).[78] Gillard largely avoided being

---

75 'Heffernan "Deliberately Barren" Most Sexist Remark of 2007', AAP General News, 12 November 2007; Marcus Priest, 'Liberals Peddle Subtle Gender-Bending Tactics', *Australian Financial Review*, 27 July 2010.

76 Joe Kelly, 'Julia Gillard tells Australian Women's Weekly She Is "Wistful" Reflecting on Life Choices', *Australian*, 28 July 2010, Accessed online. <http://www.theaustralian.com.au/national-affairs/julia-gillard-tells-australian-womens-weekly-she-is-wistful-reflecting-on-life-choices/news-story/087d13fdf9925a620878a49f0efe6bf3>

77 Sawer, 'Managing Gender', p.256.

78 See for example Summers, *The Misogyny Factor*, ch. 5; Ana Stevenson, 'Making Gender Divisive: "Post-Feminism", Sexism and Media Representations of Julia Gillard', *Burgmann Journal*, 2, 2013, pp.53-63; Helen Pringle, 'The Pornification of Julia Gillard' in Trenoweth (ed.), *Bewitched & Bedevilled*, pp.68-81.

drawn into discussions over her treatment, until her now famous 'misogyny speech' on 9 October 2012.[79] Delivered during debate over the political future of Peter Slipper, the speech was specifically directed against Abbott and his record on women, including his own role in lending legitimacy to the attacks on Gillard. She later nominated Abbott's appearance at an anti-climate change rally on 23 March 2011, where he addressed the media in front of signs bearing slogans such as 'Ditch the witch' and 'Bob Browns [sic] bitch', as a moment that should have been 'career-ending'.[80]

What If?

In comparison to this period, Gillard's experience during the 2010 election was benign, if not the straightforward 'honeymoon' that the opinion polls might have suggested at the outset of the election. Crucially one of the key factors that changed the way gender politics played out was the election outcome itself. Much of the sexist commentary worked in tandem with a view that Gillard had failed to gain a popular mandate, resulting in more extreme views being tolerated. It is hard not to draw the conclusion that, had Labor secured a clear win and Gillard not been further destabilised by the ongoing leadership tensions, then the attacks on her would not have been as vitriolic. A majority government would also have reduced the need for post-election policy changes that perpetuated the 'Juliar' trope, coined by Alan Jones and used effectively by her political opponents.

The ensuing debates about the sexist treatment of Gillard are yet another reminder that Australian politics may well have taken a

---

79   Julia Gillard, Transcript of speech, *Sydney Morning Herald*, 10 October 2012.
80   James Massola, 'Julia Gillard on the Moment that Should Have Killed Tony Abbott's Career', *Sydney Morning Herald*, 23 June 2015, Accessed online. <http://www.smh.com.au/federal-politics/political-news/julia-gillard-on-the-moment-that-should-have-killed-tony-abbotts-career-20150622-ghug63.html>

different course but for the circumstances of the 2010 election. Much hinged on the fateful decision of the Labor Party to change leaders on 24 June 2010. Had the leadership contest never taken place and Rudd remained in power, Labor might have secured a second term in its own right. If so, the result might have been seen as a vindication of Rudd's leadership and helped to consolidate his position, much like Howard's close win at the 1998 election. Alternatively, Labor might have endured the loss some predicted and Abbott would have seized power three years earlier. Emboldened by the outcome of defeating a first-term government, Abbott could well have pursued an even more radically conservative agenda. Either scenario would have left Australia still waiting for its first female prime minister.

Instead, Australia did receive its first female leader, though any initial euphoria was remarkably short-lived. Labor went into the election under Gillard and ended up with a massive swing against it and a hung parliament. The repercussions extended well beyond the event itself. The election inaugurated a period of leadership instability on both sides of politics, brought into focus the precarious state of the major parties and put a spotlight on the treatment of female politicians. Despite talk of voter disengagement and apathy, the 2010 election underscored that much remains at stake when it comes to the ballot box.

CONCLUSION

A NEW NORMAL?

Benjamin T. Jones

In 2004 the Australian Labor Party, led by Mark Latham, was expected either to win or closely contest the upcoming election. Instead, John Howard's Liberal-National coalition secured a comfortable victory, increasing their majority in the House of Representatives and securing a majority in the Senate also. Addressing the Labor faithful, party elder Kim Beazley offered words of comfort. He reminded the audience that it had taken the coalition five attempts to oust the Hawke-Keating Labor governments and that Australians do not change governments quickly. With the turbulent Whitlam years seen as an exception to the rule (and even he secured successive victories), in post-war Australian politics, long terms in office were an expectation. This view might now be considered the old normal. Following the landslide *Kevin07* victory, many predicted that Kevin Rudd would be a long-serving prime minister, perhaps handing the reins to his popular deputy, Julia Gillard, in a third or fourth term. That he did not even see out one full term in office marked a new era in Australian politics.

Rudd's swift dismissal cannot be explained away by his personal traits or leadership style. With Australia's first female prime minister at the helm, Labor clung on to power following the hung parliament result of 2010 with support from nominally conservative rural Independents Tony Windsor and Rob Oakeshott. Once again, a new prime minister would not see out a full term with Rudd wresting back control after a second leadership challenge. This could perhaps be explained away as a particularly dysfunctional episode of Labor rule except the coalition would then follow the same pattern. In 2013, the newly elected Abbott government promised strong and stable government under coalition rule. 'The adults are back in charge', he smugly claimed. And yet, Abbott too would fail to see out his first term as prime minister, losing a leadership challenge to Malcolm Turnbull in 2015. Turnbull won the 2016 election by a single seat in the lower house and the coalition has consistently trailed Labor in the polls. As with the previous three terms of parliament, speculation is rife whether the same prime minister will survive till the end. This seems the new normal of Australian political life. John Howard in 2004-7 was the last prime minister to serve a full term in office and even he was plagued by persistent leadership rumours leading to a public promise that he would hand over power to his deputy Peter Costello. If Turnbull does fall victim to a leadership coup, it will mark the fourth consecutive term with a change of prime minister.

The new normal is marked by electoral volatility. The major parties can no longer take for granted a primary vote in the high 30s. As the Greens, Palmer United, One Nation, and the Nick Xenophon Team have shown, Australia is more willing than ever to cast large numbers of votes for minor parties as well as Independents. It is no longer a truism that Australians do not change government quickly. The old normal would presume that an incoming federal government will set the national agenda for a decade or more. Especially after the 2010 result, one-term governments are entirely conceivable. The

CONCLUSION

most pronounced feature of the new normal is the apparent ease with which a prime minster can be replaced. Turnbull's successful leadership challenge in 2015 marked five prime ministers in five years. The BBC dubbed Australia the 'coup capital of the democratic world'.[1]

Political pundits and the major parties themselves have invested a great deal of effort in understanding the creation of the new normal. One important factor is the power of elections and the way in which they shape the nation. Particularly in a nation such as Australia with a system that ensures consistently high voter turnout, the electorate is directly responsible for the shifts and changes in Australian political life. The case studies in this volume illustrate something of the ebb and flow of Australian politics. They reveal that just as recent elections have created a new normal, future elections can, and probably will, establish new norms once again. Elections are dynamic and ultimately driven by the political appetite of voters. Australians have a reputation for being politically apathetic but this defies the reality. Unlike the British system that sees five year terms, or the four-year terms of United States presidents, Australians participate in federal elections very regularly, every three years and, quite often, more frequently than that. Also unlike those nations, Australian citizens are legally compelled to show up at the voting booth. The old saying goes that in a democracy you get the government you deserve. This is particularly true of Australia with around 95% of the adult population taking part in federal elections. To this extent at least, and despite many signs of disillusionment, voters are empowered and elections do still matter.

---

1   Nick Bryant, 'Australia: Coup capital of the democratic world', BBC, 14 September 2015.

APPENDIX

HOW AUSTRALIANS VOTE

Michael Maley

If one of the senior officials involved in the conduct of the first federal election in 1901 could, by a miracle of time travel, be deployed to a modern federal election as an intertemporal observer, he would be stunned by what he would see.[1] At initial briefings, he might be surprised to hear that the House of Representatives and Senate had twice as many members as in his day, and territory representatives. During the campaign, he would wonder why so few public meetings and rallies were being advertised. He would be mystified by the large number of people who appeared to be voting at public offices before polling day. He would not know what to make of television, and of televised 30-second political advertisements appearing to contain dramatic slogans but, by the standards of his era, almost no information.

On election day itself, he would view with astonishment the enormous Senate ballot papers being marked by each voter with numbers, and the cardboard ballot boxes into which the ballots were being deposited. And on election night, he would be amazed to learn that within some four hours of the close of the polls on the eastern

---

1   The use of the masculine pronoun is deliberate here: at the time of federation, and indeed until the 1980s, all senior federal electoral officials were men.

APPENDIX

seaboard, it would be possible for someone with access to a computer almost anywhere in the world to be able to discover the number of votes polled by the various candidates in virtually every polling place in the country. He would return in the time machine to his own era conscious of enormous changes to the character of federal elections which would be taking place in the coming century. But he would not be able to tell his contemporaries how or when or why they had occurred.

The purpose of this Appendix is to explore the most important of the diverse developments which over time have influenced the evolution of Australia's federal voting system, including those relating to the activities and role of the federal electoral administration (variously known as the Electoral Branch from 1902 to 1973, the Australian Electoral Office from 1973 to 1984, and the Australian Electoral Commission, or AEC, since 1984). In the course of the discussion it will become apparent that electoral change and reform can be effected or driven by a range of different but often interacting factors, including the judicial or administrative interpretation of binding constitutional or legal provisions; deliberate legislative change; social, demographic or technological change; revision of the administrative practices of the electoral administration; changes in the broader political and normative environment, both national and international; and changes in the behaviour of political players in response to incentives associated with different aspects of the electoral system.

The account which follows is broadly structured to reflect the times at which different features of the Australian electoral system arrived on the scene, and deals with the following innovations:

- the franchise;
- the alternative vote;
- compulsory voting;
- proportional representation (PR) for the Senate, and its variants;
- electoral roll management;
- apportionment of seats, and redistribution;
- new approaches to polling;
- compilation of election results;
- the trend towards continuous electoral reform; and
- the changing role of the electoral administration as an institution
- of governance.

These broad topics by no means exhaust the list of federal voting system reforms; they rather seek to cover the main ones which have had political or representational rather than just administrative significance. Certain broader features of Australia's federal electoral processes are not addressed here, not because they are insignificant, but because they stand apart from the mechanics of the electoral process. For example, the management of political party funding and financial disclosure, which has been one of the major tasks faced by the AEC since 1984, is a discrete activity which affects campaigning by parties rather than the voting process. The focus of this volume being elections, the topic of federal referendums is also not addressed.

APPENDIX

The Franchise

Under sections 29, 30 and 31 of the Constitution, the 1901 election was conducted in accordance with electoral laws of the various states. The new parliament moved quickly thereafter to establish a uniform franchise by enacting the *Commonwealth Franchise Act 1902*, which gave the right to vote to all 'natural born or naturalized subjects of the King', male or female, who were not under the age of 21 and who had lived in Australia for six months continuously. It disqualified from voting persons of unsound mind; persons attainted of treason; persons who had been convicted and were under sentence or subject to be sentenced 'for any offence punishable under the law of any part of the King's dominions by imprisonment for one year or longer'; and 'aboriginal natives of Australia Asia Africa or the Islands of the Pacific except New Zealand' (unless entitled to vote under section 41 of the Constitution, a transitional provision which protected the federal voting rights of those individuals who were already entitled to vote at state elections prior to the establishment of the uniform federal franchise).[2] Major changes to the franchise have been few.

In 1949, the right to enrol and vote was extended to any 'aboriginal native of Australia' who was entitled to enrol for and vote at state elections or had served in the Australian Defence Force. In 1962, those rights were further extended to all Indigenous Australians, but on the basis that both enrolment and voting remained voluntary for them. Only in 1984 was the law finally amended to make enrolment and voting compulsory for them, placing them on the same footing as all other electors.

---

2   The transitional character of section 41 is not immediately apparent from its wording, but was confirmed by the High Court in 1983 in the case of *R v Pearson; Ex parte Sipka* [1983] HCA 6.

In 1973, the only change to date to the voting age was made, lowering it from 21 to 18.

In 1984, the law was again amended to change the basis of the franchise from British subject status to Australian citizenship. This flowed from the Report of the 1978 *Review of Post-arrival Programs and Services to Migrants*, often cited as the Galbally Report. When the change came into effect on 26 January 1984, the ongoing right to enrol and vote by any non-Australian citizen who had been on the roll on 25 January 1984 by virtue of his or her British subject status was preserved.

Also in 1984, the law was amended to limit offences giving rise to disqualification from voting to those punishable by imprisonment for five years or longer, rather than one year or longer. This remained the position until 1995, when a further amendment limited the disqualification to those *actually serving* a sentence of five years or longer. Then, in 2004, the critical length of sentence was again changed, from five to three years. In 2006, the most stringent disqualification of all was introduced, applying to any person who was serving any sentence of imprisonment for an offence against the law of the Commonwealth or of a state or territory. That final change was struck down by the High Court on constitutional grounds in the case of *Roach v Electoral Commissioner* [2007] HCA 43, a decision which restored the *status quo ante* under which a person serving a sentence of three years or longer is disqualified.

The Alternative Vote

In 1902, the parliament also moved to establish a federal electoral structure and laws, enacting the *Commonwealth Electoral Act 1902*.

APPENDIX

The Bill for this Act as originally introduced provided for the use of the alternative vote in single member electoral divisions for the House of Representatives[3] and for single transferable vote proportional representation to elect the Senate, but opposition within the parliament led to the substitution of the plurality ('first past the post') electoral formula for the House, and to the Senate being elected using a block vote plurality system with each state voting as a single electorate.[4]

The early years of federation were marked by a fractionalised party structure within the parliament and electorate, and it was not until the 1910 election that a relatively stable two-party system emerged. It is precisely when a polity has three or more relatively strong parties that the choice of electoral formula tends to have the greatest potential impact on election outcomes; and for that reason, the possibility of using the alternative vote remained in the minds of Australian political leaders. In 1906 the prime minister, Alfred Deakin, raised with the Labor leader Chris Watson the possibility of adopting it, to no avail at that point. Sir Joseph Cook's 1913-1914 Liberal government appointed a royal commission into the electoral system that recommended the use of the alternative vote for the House and proportional representation for the Senate, and those proposals figured

---

3   The alternative vote makes use of a ballot structure in which voters have to show an order of preference for some or all candidates, and an electoral formula (i.e., counting method) in which, if no candidate has more than 50% of first preference votes, the candidates standing lowest on the poll are successively excluded and their votes transferred to continuing candidates until one candidate has more than 50% of the votes still in the count. In Australia, this is often misleadingly called 'preferential voting', but in fact there are many different formulae by which preferentially-marked ballots can be counted. In the United States of America, the system has come to be widely known as 'instant runoff voting'.

4   For a detailed description of the prehistory of the alternative vote at federal elections, see B.D. Graham, 'The Choice of Voting Methods in Federal Politics, 1902-1918', *Australian Journal of Politics and History*, 8 (1962), reprinted in C.A. Hughes (ed), *Readings in Australian Government* (Brisbane: University of Queensland Press, 1968), p.202.

in Cook's campaigning for the 1914 election, at which his government was defeated.

Within Cook's Liberal Party, farming interests formed the spearhead for voting reform, and pressures came to a head when the Labor Party split in 1916 and the federal Nationalist Party was formed from the Liberal Party and pro-conscription elements of Labor loyal to Prime Minister William Morris Hughes. By-elections in 1918 in the divisions of Flinders and Swan highlighted the dangers posed to the non-Labor side of politics by the splitting of the vote between multiple candidates, and ultimately the *Commonwealth Electoral Act 1918* implemented the full alternative vote (that is, a system requiring voters to order *all* the candidates on the ballot) for the House, in time for a by-election in the division of Corangamite which saw the representative of the Victorian Farmers' Union elected (on Nationalist preferences) to the parliament.

The use of the alternative vote provided a basis for the subsequent rise of the Country Party as a second conservative grouping which could feasibly enter electoral contests without necessarily benefiting the Labor Party, and thereby facilitated the formation of the Bruce-Page government, founded on a coalition of what L.F. Crisp called 'the parties of town and country capital' which has substantially been in place since 1923. The alternative vote is now a thoroughly embedded feature of Australian elections. The Labor Party, conscious of the system's origins, long had a policy of return to the plurality formula, but that was abandoned prior to the election of the Whitlam government in 1972 in favour of a policy instead for 'optional preferential voting', under which voters would no longer be required to show a preference for every candidate on the ballot. As of 2018, the system is now essentially the same in its technical details as when it

APPENDIX

was first implemented, save that a scrutiny until only two candidates remain has since 1983 been conducted for every division, regardless of whether a candidate has already polled over 50% of first preference votes.

The long-standing use of the alternative vote has structured aspects of electoral contestation in a range of significant ways.

- Voters are able to cast expressive votes for minor parties or Independents without having to worry that doing so will in effect waste their votes by depriving them of the opportunity to influence which of the major parties will win in a division.

- Agreements between political parties to exchange preferences – in other words, to recommend to their supporters that preferences after their first be allocated to candidates who form part of the agreement – have become a prominent feature of Australian election campaigns.

- Also ubiquitous are the 'how-to-vote cards' distributed at polling places, through which parties' recommendations to their supporters are primarily made.

- The need to distribute preferences in closely contested divisions means that in the most extreme cases the winner may not be known until up to 13 days after polling day, when the scrutiny process can be finalised once all postal votes have been received by the electoral administration.

ELECTIONS MATTER

- The concept of the 'two-party preferred vote' has come to be widely used in electoral analysis in Australia, being routinely reported as an element of election results and opinion polling.

- The alternative vote formula only takes account of certain preferences on certain ballot papers, rather than giving weight in some way to all of them. For example, if a candidate polls more than one-third of the first preference votes he or she can never be excluded from the count, and the later preferences marked by his or her supporters therefore do not need to be looked at and have no effect on the result. From time to time this feature enables paradoxical situations to arise in which it is in a party's interest to reduce its own vote (which can be done through challenges by scrutineers at the count). This will most typically occur when a strong Independent or minor party candidate contests a division normally regarded as safe for one of the two main parties. In such a case, the other main party, while having no hope of winning the seat itself, may 'run dead' so as to ensure that its own candidate will be excluded, enabling his or her preferences to elect the Independent.

- The requirement for voters to number every candidate on the ballot paper has become increasingly onerous as the typical number of candidates for election has risen over time. This has contributed significantly to the level of informal voting for the House of Representatives, with successive surveys of informal ballot papers conducted by the AEC demonstrating beyond doubt the extent to which voters able to express a clear first preference have had their votes declared informal because of inadvertent numbering errors in later preferencing. This trend reached its nadir at the Bradfield by-election of 2009, when 22 candidates ran and the rate of informal voting reached 9%, largely because of numbering defects, despite the fact that never once in the history of the division (which dated back to 1949) had it been necessary to examine any candidate's second or later preferences in order to determine the winner.

This impact of the alternative vote on formality has been the primary motivator for the occasional consideration of the adoption of optional preferential voting as an alternative. Parties' attitudes to this have, however, tended to fluctuate over time, depending on their perceptions of whether it would be to their short-term advantage. The Labor Party, for example, appeared to lose interest in optional preferential voting at about the time when it started to see some of its vote taken away by the Greens. As of 2018, there appears to be no significant support within any of the major parties for a change from the version of the alternative vote which has been in place for almost a century.

Compulsory Voting

Compulsory voting was the next major innovation. It was put in place by the *Commonwealth Electoral Act 1924* (which had been submitted to the parliament as a private member's bill) and first applied at the 1925 general election. Its introduction was primarily motivated by a fall in turnout from 71.3% at the 1919 election to 57.9% in 1922. The broad elements of the scheme for its enforcement have gone largely unchanged since 1925: after an election, a person who appears not to have voted must be sent a notice demanding a valid and sufficient reason for failing to vote, and if such a reason is not provided, a penalty may be applied. Minor variations have included adding the option of imposing administrative penalties rather than requiring court action in all cases, and specifying that a religious objection to voting constitutes a valid and sufficient reason for failing to vote. Paradoxically, those on the electoral roll who fail to vote have in recent times been much more systematically penalised than those who fail even to enrol when qualified to do so.

Compulsory voting has been strikingly successful in achieving its objective of ensuring high levels of turnout, which returned to 91.3% at the 1925 election and have never fallen below 90% at any general election since.[5] (Turnout has, however, often been somewhat lower at by-elections, and also fell to 88.5% at the 2014 re-run in Western Australia of the 2013 Senate election.) Compulsion also enjoys widespread public acceptance. Ian McAllister, reporting in 2013 on a nationwide survey in which 68% expressed support for compulsory voting, 30% supported voluntary voting, and only 2% 'didn't know', notes:

> When the question was first asked in an opinion poll, in 1943, 60 per cent supported compulsory voting. That proportion gradually increased during the 1950s and 1960s, peaking at 77

---

[5] 'Turnout' here refers to the percentage of those on the electoral roll who actually vote. As a measure of electoral engagement or disengagement it needs to be approached with care, as it does not factor in those who have failed to enrol, or those who attend a polling place purely to avoid a penalty and deliberately cast an informal vote.

APPENDIX

per cent in 1969. Following the dismissal of the Whitlam Labor government in 1975, and some disillusionment with politics, support for compulsory voting declined to 64 per cent in 1987. Since then, support has gradually increased once again, peaking at 77 per cent in 2007. The figure of 68 per cent recorded in the current ANU poll is almost identical to the estimate for 2010, and reflects concerns among some voters about the experience of minority government between 2010 and 2013.[6]

The survey also identified that in the absence of compulsory voting 67% would still definitely vote, while a further 21% probably would.[7]

At the level of political elites, it has only been within the Liberal-National coalition, and only comparatively recently, that any serious resistance to the continuation of compulsory voting has arisen. Even there, opinion has been divided, with criticism of the status quo arising primarily from libertarian thinkers, but often encountering pushback from party colleagues on more pragmatic grounds. Arguments on the issue have been frequently put to the parliament's Joint Standing Committee on Electoral Matters, but to date that has not led to any serious moves towards the adoption of voluntary voting. The Committee's Report on the 1996 election actually recommended

---

6   Ian McAllister, *Attitudes to electoral reform – ANUpoll August 2013* (Canberra: ANU College of Arts and Social Sciences, August 2013), p.2, Accessed online. <http://politicsir.cass.anu.edu.au/sites/default/files/docs/ANUpoll-report-August-2014-attitudes-electoral-reform_0_0.pdf>

7   In the Australian Election Study of 2016, 70% of those surveyed supported compulsory voting, and 80% said that they would still have voted had it been voluntary. See Sarah M. Cameron and Ian McAllister, *Trends in Australian Political Opinion: Results from the Australian Election Study 1987– 2016* (Canberra: School of Politics & International Relations, ANU College of Arts & Social Sciences, 2016), p.55, Accessed online. <http://legacy.ada.edu.au/ADAData/AES/Trends%20in%20Australian%20Political%20Opinion%201987-2016.pdf>

the abolition of compulsory voting, but that was bluntly rejected by the Howard government.

The arguments for compulsory voting have by now been well rehearsed.[8] Its supporters most typically point to the level of political legitimacy which it helps to ensure; the political participation and engagement which it is said to foster; the manner in which it relieves parties of the burden of getting out the vote (and thereby, hopefully, makes them less dependent on funding from vested interests); and, finally, its effect on structuring political contestation as a battle for the votes of those in the centre, rather than a process of stimulating the interest of parties' base supporters further out on the political spectrum.

One final consequence of compulsory voting is worthy of mention. To the extent that it inevitably brings to the polls people who have no interest in politics, the phenomenon has long been noted of the 'donkey vote': a preferential vote for the candidates purely in the order in which they appear on the ballot. Prior to 1984, candidates were listed on the House of Representatives ballot paper alphabetically by surname, which gave parties the opportunity to secure the donkey vote by pre-selecting candidates with names early in the alphabet. This came to an end when alphabetical listing was replaced by the use of a random draw.

Proportional Representation (PR) for the Senate, and Its Variants

The introduction of single transferable vote PR for the Senate at the 1949 election represented the first significant electoral reform

---

8   For an outline of the arguments for and against, see C.A. Hughes, 'Compulsory Voting', *Politics* 1, 1966, reprinted in C.A. Hughes (ed) *Readings in Australian Government* (Brisbane: University of Queensland Press, 1968), p.225.

APPENDIX

in a quarter of a century. The background to its adoption has been researched in detail by John Uhr, and here only four of his key points need be noted.[9]

- First, PR did not appear out of the blue, but rather flowed from discussion about the appropriate way of electing the Senate which can be traced back to before Federation.
- Secondly, the adoption of PR was part of a package of parliamentary reforms, which also included the enlargement of the parliament, taking the Senate from 36 to 60 members.
- Thirdly, the electoral systems used for the Senate had by 1948 long been functioning in a 'winner takes all' manner, with the dominant party in a state typically winning all seats up for grabs. This had reached a point of near absurdity in the Senate constituted from 1 July 1947, in which there were 33 government senators and only three in the opposition: the Leader, the Deputy Leader, and the Whip. It was generally recognised that a Senate of 60 members so lopsidedly constituted would lack both public credibility and the capacity to function as an effective parliamentary chamber.
- Finally, the Labor government clearly realised that the use of PR, when combined with an increase in the size of the Senate, would in the short term guarantee its continued domination of the Senate after the 1949 election, which it was widely expected to lose.

---

9 John Uhr, 'Why We Chose Proportional Representation', in Marian Sawer and Sarah Miskin (eds), *Papers on Parliament No. 34 – Representation and Institutional Change: 50 Years of Proportional Representation in the Senate*, December 1999, Accessed online. <www.aph.gov.au/About_Parliament/Senate/Powers_practice_n_procedures/pops/pop34>

The single critical decision taken in 1949, which looks like a point of minor detail but in fact has fundamentally influenced all later developments, was that voters would be required to indicate preferences for all the candidates on a Senate ballot paper in order to cast a formal vote. Prior to the introduction of PR, it was virtually impossible for a candidate to be elected to the Senate from outside the ranks of the major parties. With PR, however, the Senate was transformed into a feasible battleground for minor parties as well, as became apparent with the ALP split in the mid-1950s, and the rise of the Democratic Labor Party. Successful minor party forays encouraged further candidacies from outside the mainstream, the number of candidates per vacancy trended upwards, ballot papers became larger, and the task faced by voters in numbering them all became more onerous. With the passage of time, voters came to be ever more dependent on 'how-to-vote' cards issued by the parties to get their numbering right (especially since party affiliations of candidates were not printed on ballot papers until 1984), but the informal vote percentage nevertheless grew inexorably, topping 9% nationwide at every Senate election from 1970 to 1983. The phenomenon reached its nadir at the 1974 Senate election in New South Wales, where 73 candidates stood for ten seats, and every voter had to number every candidate on the ballot paper: the informal vote reached 12.31%.

As I have noted elsewhere:

> The Hawke government, when it came to power in 1983, perceived the paramount need to address the problem of informal voting at Senate elections, but was constrained (by lacking a majority in the Senate) from being able to introduce its proclaimed policy of optional preferential voting, which would

APPENDIX

have relieved voters of the obligation to number every candidate. It accordingly opted for ... [a] ticket voting scheme, which in effect ... [enabled] a voter, by the marking of a single square on the ballot paper, to adopt in total the how-to-vote card of his or her party (as formally lodged with the Australian Electoral Commission).

...

Because it was apparent from previous election statistics that the vast bulk of voters had been following how-to-vote cards anyway, the change was not seen as being a particularly momentous one. But one important point was overlooked, and this was the issue which came to a head in 2013. Up until 1984, the only parties which were able to issue how-to-vote cards were those which had the membership base, field structure and resources to enable them to distribute cards physically at polling places. With ticket voting, on the other hand, every group of candidates on the ballot paper could provide voters with, in effect, a 'virtual' how-to-vote card. This ultimately led directly to the phenomenon of 'preference harvesting', which enables a host of 'micro-parties' to exchange preferences with each other for their mutual benefit.[10]

In response to the result of the 2013 election, which among other things saw a candidate elected in Victoria who had polled only 0.5% of the first preference votes, the Joint Standing Committee on Electoral Matters recommended, and the parliament ultimately adopted,

---

10   Michael Maley, *Senate Electoral Reform*, 29 September 2015, Accessed online. <https://auspublaw.org/2015/09/senate-electoral-reform/>

a major change to the Senate voting system, which saw the ticket voting scheme replaced with a form of optional preferential voting. This was first used at the 2016 election.

The impact of the adoption of PR on the role played by the Senate in the Australian system of government has been immense, and it would be impossible to do it justice here. In the broadest sense, however, it has clearly revitalised the Senate as an institution. While in 1971 two prominent observers of the parliament were able to note that in times past 'the Senate was regarded as a club for superannuated party hacks, old soldiers and others who could not have survived the rougher political tactics of the Representatives', such a description is now badly out of date; and the fact that governments now rarely dominate either the Senate as a whole or its committees has led to a far greater public focus on and recognition of the significance of the chamber.[11]

One final impact of PR has been on the filling of Senate casual vacancies. After 1949 it was rapidly recognised that the way in which that was done could have a significant impact on the extent to which the ongoing partisan composition of the Senate would remain proportional to votes polled. In the early 1950s, correspondence between state premiers gave rise to a convention that a departed senator who had been elected as a candidate of a political party should be replaced by someone from the same party. This arrangement was honoured until 1975, when it was blatantly breached by the premiers of New South Wales and Queensland following the appointment of Labor Senate leader Lionel Murphy to the High Court, and the death of Labor senator Bertie Milliner. These events ultimately gave rise to

---

11   Don Whitington and Rob Chalmers, *Inside Canberra: A Guide to Australian Federal Politics* (Adelaide: Rigby, 1971), p.247.

APPENDIX

an amendment of section 15 of the Constitution by referendum in May 1977 to give mandatory effect to the earlier convention. This represented the first recognition in the Constitution, and indeed in the electoral system, of the existence of political parties. A subtle element of the 1977 amendment was that a senator appointed by a state parliament to fill a casual vacancy would in future serve out the balance of the departed senator's term, rather than having to face the people at the next state-wide federal election, as had previously been required. Over time, this has had the effect of making the resignation of a senator almost completely cost-free from the point of view of his or her party, and far more senators are now taking their seats by appointment than was previously the case. Indeed, Senator Santo Santoro from Queensland managed to serve as a federal minister without ever facing election. On this phenomenon, I have noted:

> the case of Senator Bob Carr, who was elected in 2013 from the first place on the ALP ticket for a term due to begin on 1 July 2014, but resigned his seat on 24 October 2013, barely weeks after the declaration of the poll. He was replaced by (now) Senator Deborah O'Neill, who had not been a candidate for the Senate at all, but was rather a defeated ALP House of Representatives candidate, and whose term in the Upper House is now due to expire on 30 June 2020. One could hardly hope for a better example of 'bait and switch' in electoral processes.[12]

Electoral Roll Management

Australia has had permanent and continuously maintained electoral rolls since 1908. Keeping them up to date has for much of the

---

12   Maley, *Senate Electoral Reform*, noted earlier.

intervening period been the major activity pursued by the electoral administration between elections. Prior to the computer era, rolls were organised on the basis of subdivisions (geographical subsets of both federal and state electoral divisions, configured in such a way as to facilitate the use of a common roll for both levels of government). Full subdivisional rolls were regularly printed in bound form, and were used at polling places together with a supplemental roll identifying additions and deletions made since the print run. Compulsory enrolment, in place since 1911, was enforced by court action or administrative penalty, and in the last quarter of the twentieth century so-called habitation reviews – door-to-door canvasses conducted between elections – were used to update the rolls. A person could only be added to the roll on receipt by the electoral administration of an electoral enrolment form, which placed the onus firmly on the voters themselves to keep their enrolments current.

The inevitable introduction of computerised roll maintenance gave rise to two fundamental changes, one affecting political parties and the other affecting the voters. By the 1980s, parties had come to see the benefits of obtaining finely structured information about the electorate, and hardcopy 'habitation indexes' – rolls organised by street address rather than by voters' surnames – were coming to be valued. In addition, MPs were being supplied with envelope labels relating to newly enrolled electors in their divisions, enabling them to write welcoming letters, supposedly in their capacity as representatives rather than candidates. As the parties themselves developed more sophisticated databases, the rolls in electronic format came to be seen as a critical input; and eventually, the *Commonwealth Electoral Act 1918* was amended to require regular supply of roll data to registered political parties.

APPENDIX

For voters, the benefits of computerisation came much more recently. In 2010, electronic electoral enrolment was introduced, enabling voters to enrol or update their enrolments online, rather than by completing a hardcopy form. This was followed in 2012 by an even more fundamental modernisation, allowing the AEC to enrol an unenrolled person directly, or to update a voter's address on receipt of information indicating that the voter had moved.

Apportionment of Seats, and Redistribution

Section 24 of the Constitution requires the House of Representatives to be directly chosen by the people of the Commonwealth, and the number of members elected in each state to be proportional to the number of people in that state, except that at least five members must be chosen in each 'Original State'. The number of members of the House to be chosen in each state at the first election was explicitly set out in section 26 of the Constitution. Shortly after Federation, a number of details of how such proportionality should be maintained thereafter were clarified by the passage of the *Representation Act 1905* which, as subsequently amended in 1938, among other things:

- placed upon the Chief Electoral Officer of the Commonwealth the responsibility for ascertaining (using census data) and certifying the population of the Commonwealth and the various states as on designated 'Enumeration Days', and determining state representation entitlements;
- specified that only census days would be 'Enumeration Days'; and
- specified that an alteration in a state's representation entitlement resulting from the operation of the formula would have no effect

until the first general election after the electoral boundaries in the state had been changed so as to implement the required increase or decrease in the number of members to be chosen in the state.

In 1975, the *Representation Act 1905* came under scrutiny in the High Court. In the case of *Attorney-General for Australia (ex rel McKinlay) v. Commonwealth* [1975] HCA 53, the Court held the provisions outlined above to be unconstitutional. The basis of the court's judgement was its view that the constitution required that the populations of the states and Commonwealth be ascertained and representation entitlements determined during the life of each ordinary triennial House of Representatives, in time to permit elections based on the determination.

McKinlay's case led to substantial revision of the *Representation Act 1905* in 1977, and further changes in 1984 when the substance of that Act was incorporated into the *Commonwealth Electoral Act 1918*. Meanwhile, the related process of redrawing boundaries of electoral divisions (known in Australia as 'redistribution') had been coming under increasing pressure throughout the 1960s. Long gaps between redistributions had permitted considerable inequality to develop in divisional enrolments, and this trend was accentuated by the growth of new suburbs in Sydney and Melbourne. The reapportionment revolution in the United States had given new impetus to the intellectual arguments for the principle of one vote, one value, and vigorous efforts by Prime Minister Gough Whitlam to implement redistributions based on that principle were blocked by the hostile Senate during the period of his government.

Reform of these processes was therefore a priority for the Hawke Labor government when it came to power in 1983; and with

APPENDIX

painstakingly developed cross-party support it was able to implement changes in 1984 the effect of which was to make the processes of apportionment and redistribution almost wholly independent of government, and politically neutral in their basic character. The current redistribution process has five fundamental elements.

- The timing of redistributions proceeds according to a fixed and objective formula set out in the *Commonwealth Electoral Act 1918*, which among other things guarantees that a state or territory will be redistributed at least every seven years.
- Redistributions are conducted by independent and neutral bodies.
- Extensive opportunities are provided for transparent public input into the process.
- The criteria according to which boundaries are to be drawn are specified in detail in the law.
- A redistribution process once concluded is not subject to any governmental or parliamentary veto.

This approach to redistribution has been exceptionally successful. Gross disparities between voter numbers in different electoral divisions have been largely eliminated, and a process which was once intermittent and controversial has become regular and routine, with most federal parliaments now seeing at least one state or territory being redistributed. Australia's success in removing much of the politics from the process is especially striking when compared with the experience of the United States, where 'redistricting' is still a matter of the most bitter partisan division.

New Approaches to Polling

Until well into the 1980s, the vast bulk of votes were cast at polling places established on election day, with postal voting being made available as an exceptional arrangement for people who could not get to a polling place. One element of the reforms of 1984, however, was a significant expansion of different polling modalities. Mobile polling was introduced for the first time for hospitals, nursing homes and remote areas. Opportunities for people to vote overseas at Australian diplomatic missions were greatly expanded. Voting facilities were even provided at Australian Antarctic bases. And, most notably, voting in person at AEC offices prior to polling day was made ever more straightforward, with the process ultimately evolving into a pre-poll voting mechanism which for many voters these days is essentially the same as voting on election day. As a result, there is now, in effect, a polling period rather than just a polling day for federal elections and, at the 2016 election, there were more than 4.5 million early votes cast, representing more than 30% of the total votes counted. This reflects an increasing trend towards early voting across all Australian electoral jurisdictions and, indeed, world-wide, and has the potential to pose significant challenges for political parties in the timing and configuration of their campaigning.

Compilation of Election Results

The process of compiling and publishing the election results has changed radically over the last 50 years. As late as 1972, results of counting at polling places were still being phoned through to Divisional Returning Officers, accumulated, and phoned through again in consolidated form to the state head offices of the electoral

APPENDIX

administration for publication on manually maintained wooden tally boards at state and national tally rooms.

That process was enhanced by four separate leaps forward. First, in 1974, a computerised polling results processing package, run on a mainframe computer initially owned by the customs department, was introduced, enabling much more sophisticated analysis of data, including calculation of state and nationwide party totals and swing figures. In addition, it became possible to feed data directly to television networks' own computer systems. The system was used up to and including the 1984 election, after which the mainframe on which it ran was decommissioned. Thereafter, the AEC developed its own system, used for the first time in 1987. The second leap forward came in 1990, when the AEC first used an enhanced version of its new system to produce much more sophisticated swing figures, based on comparison of polling place results with results from the same polling places at the preceding general election, which largely eliminated the bias in early figures which had previously bedevilled election night analysis. The third leap came prior to the 1993 election, when the *Commonwealth Electoral Act 1918* was amended to enable certain preference counting to take place at polling places on election night, thereby clarifying likely results in many divisions where preference distributions would be needed. The final leap, which took place over a period of years, was the ongoing enhancement of the AEC's results system into a Virtual Tally Room generally accessible via the internet and so powerful as to make it unnecessary to continue to have a traditional tally room for the media (the last one of which was provided at the 2010 election).

ELECTIONS MATTER

The Trend towards Continuous Electoral Reform

In any account of the federal electoral framework, the year 1968 marks a critical turning point. Up until then, its evolution had been marked by the substantial reforms outlined above, separated by comparatively long gaps, and little change to the basic structure of polling. All of that was to change, however, in the decade and a half that followed, which was marked by a great intensity of electoral events and activities, as listed in the following table.

Year	Event
1968-69	Redistribution of electoral division boundaries in every state
1969	General election for the House of Representatives
1970	Half-Senate election, the last to date held separately from a House of Representatives election
1972	General election for the House of Representatives

Last election held concurrently with a House of Representatives election to fill a Senate casual vacancy (in Queensland) |
| 1973 | Referendums on federal power over prices and incomes |
| 1974 | First election following a double dissolution of the parliament since 1951, conducted in conjunction with four referendums

First joint sitting of both houses of parliament, passing laws providing for territory representation in the Senate, and changes to the rules for the drawing of electoral boundaries |
| 1974-75 | Redistribution of electoral boundaries in every state and the ACT, implemented in relation to Western Australia and the Australian Capital Territory, disallowed by the Senate (and reintroduced as legislation) in relation to New South Wales, Victoria, Queensland, South Australia and Tasmania. |
| 1975 | High Court ruling in *McKinlay's case*

Election following a double dissolution of the parliament |
| 1977 | Four referendums seeking alterations of the Constitution, conducted concurrently with a poll on the national song

Redistribution of electoral boundaries in every state

Concurrent House of Representatives and Senate elections |
| 1980 | Concurrent House of Representatives and Senate elections |

APPENDIX

1983	Election following a double dissolution of the parliament
	Establishment of the federal parliament's Joint Select Committee on Electoral Reform
1984	Implementation of a major package of electoral reforms, including the establishment of the Australian Electoral Commission
	Second only increase in the size of the parliament
	Redistribution of electoral boundaries in every state and the Australian Capital Territory
	Concurrent House of Representatives and Senate elections, conducted in conjunction with two referendums

Underlying these events was much political turmoil. Prime Minister Whitlam, in power from 1972 to 1975, had a long-standing personal interest in electoral reform. In 1974-1975, substantial legislation providing for relatively comprehensive electoral reform had been blocked in the Senate, and it came to be increasingly realised that Australia's federal electoral mechanisms were becoming seriously out-of-date. The Fraser coalition government was itself working towards the introduction of a package of electoral reforms, based on much research conducted by the then Australian Electoral Office, but these fell by the wayside with the government's defeat in 1983.

Critically, the Hawke Labor government that followed, conscious of the way in which the Whitlam government's reforms had been frustrated by parliamentary deadlock, opted for a different approach, establishing the parliament's Joint Select Committee on Electoral Reform. That decision had momentous and enduring effects. Not only did the committee produce a comprehensive report that formed the basis for the most substantial rewrite of the electoral law since 1918, but it provided a model for parliamentary consideration of electoral reforms which was consolidated after a short time by the creation of what has become the permanent Joint Standing Committee on Electoral Matters. That committee has been the focal point for an ongoing relationship between the AEC and the parliament, and has provided a forum for the political parties themselves to be able to consider potential reforms in detail and, crucially, to distinguish between those which are genuinely controversial and those on which agreement can be reached. As a result, the parliamentary deadlock which was a feature of the Whitlam government's time in office has essentially been broken, and the work done in 1983-84 has ushered in a new era in which electoral systems and processes have been able to be improved and fine-tuned on a continuous basis. This has been of particular importance given the technological advances of the last quarter century, many of which have been successfully taken up.

The Changing Role of the Electoral Administration as an Institution of Governance

By the early 1970s, the electoral administration was still in many respects remarkably similar to that which had been in place since shortly after Federation. The bulk of staff were to be found in a network of divisional offices, undertaking manual processing of vast volumes of forms, with typewriters rather than computers, and operating largely in an autonomous and decentralised way at election time. By standards of modern administration this sounds primitive, but it is worth bearing in mind that it proved to be a relatively robust arrangement that was able to cope effectively with the extensive challenges listed above, which arose in the period from 1968 to 1984. The turning point came with the establishment of the AEC in 1984 as an independent statutory body. Again, it is important to see this in proper context: because Australia's electoral laws have always been

APPENDIX

exceptionally prescriptive and because traditions of a neutral public service have long been well entrenched, electoral administration since 1902 had really been largely free from political interference in core activities. In effect, the AEC was not a new organisation, but a renamed and slightly reconfigured version of an organisation which had been in place for 82 years.

Two major changes did, however, flow from the independence of the AEC. First, it was able to function publicly as an independent voice and advocate for electoral reform, dealing directly with the parliament without being subject in its advice to any filtering by the executive government. Secondly, it was able, within the constraints of the law, to retool and modernise its administrative procedures.

In general, the AEC has functioned highly successfully, with a much greater public profile than the bodies that preceded it. Even in the aftermath of its one great operational disaster – the court-ordered rerun of the 2013 Senate election Western Australia – the Joint Standing Committee on Electoral Matters, in the aftermath of a forensic review, made no recommendations for any substantial change to the AEC's structure or functions.

In looking over the AEC's history since 1984, a number of trends can be identified.

There has been a steady move away from the old model under which divisional offices operated autonomously, in effect conducting separate elections. Organisation-wide systems are now extensively used for roll management, election planning and management, public relations, employment of staff, training of polling officials and results compilation. Many functions which were once performed manually are now computerised. Divisional Returning Officers who were once like feudal lords are now, to a much greater extent, cogs in a machine. These developments have produced massive efficiencies and improvements in service but there are risks associated with such arrangements too. In particular, a significant problem with a nation-wide system will have the potential to affect an entire election, rather than having only a limited local effect. A consequence of this trend is that the national office of the AEC contains a greater proportion of the organisation's total staff than was the case with its predecessor organisations.

Notwithstanding the AEC's formal independence, it is now more integrated into the broader Australian Public Service than in the past. In particular, its staffing profile is far more representative of the wider community than was once the case, with many more women in key positions. Until the mid-1970s, senior electoral officials tended to be individuals who had worked their way up through the electoral administration, with extensive knowledge and experience of election processes. The last Chief Australian Electoral Officer who fitted that profile, Frank Ley, was responsible for nine national electoral events in the period from 1959 to 1976. Since 1984, no executive head of the AEC has run more than four national events. At the time of the 2016 election, the AEC's two top officials had fewer such events under their belts than the comparable officials in the electoral authority of East Timor.

In the period immediately following its establishment, the AEC was unquestionably a leader in innovation among its state and territory counterparts. This partly reflected the fact that it was mandated to implement the extensive reforms legislated in 1984, but it was also a function of dynamic leadership. In more recent years, that trend has been reversed. The reasons for this are complex, but one important factor is that a three-year parliamentary term is slightly too short to

APPENDIX

accommodate readily processes of post-election review, parliamentary inquiries, governmental responses, drafting of legislation and the implementation of new systems. Internal project management processes adopted by the AEC have also contributed to some extent to risk aversion and a loss of agility. To give but one example, paper lists of voters were still being widely used for polling at the 2016 election, despite the fact that legislation making it possible for lists on electronic devices to be used had been enacted in 2010. This contrasts greatly with the situation in 1984, when every innovation mandated by the legislation that came into effect on 21 February of that year was implemented in time for the 1 December election. On the other hand, the AEC in 2016 did an outstanding job in implementing major changes to processes for counting Senate votes which were made necessary by legislation that commenced less than two months before the parliament was dissolved.

Finally, looking ahead, at least two major strategic challenges to Australia's electoral administration can be identified. First, while it is clear that at least in the short term elections will continue to be paper-based, it is becoming increasingly difficult to find people with the logistical skills needed to handle the very large volumes of paper that an election generates. Secondly, there is a risk of a slow loss of electoral knowledge within the AEC, because the key events through which staff can build up personal experience take place only every few years, and then over a short period of time. This is a particular challenge for the AEC's national office in Canberra, a city where mobility between jobs in different Australian Public Service bodies is both easy and encouraged; and the impact of the loss of a person who might have worked on a particular system for years is likely to be more keenly felt as systems become more sophisticated and complex. Overall, it is increasingly unlikely that AEC staff will have great depth of electoral experience, and this will give rise to a need for new processes of knowledge management.

INDEX

A

Abbott Government (2013–15) 238, 250
Abbott, Tony
   2010 election campaign 231–3, 244–5
   2013 election campaign 245
   attempts to appear female-friendly 244–6
   as health minister 244
   leadership of Liberals 221, 223
   loss of leadership 133, 234, 250
   misogyny 247
   as opposition leader 227, 231–3
   as prime minister 69, 133, 234
Abetz, Eric 232
adult suffrage, in colonies 7
Afghanistan, US invasion 203, 220
Age (newspaper) 33
age pensions 11, 98, 102–3
Aitken, Don 122
Alexander, Joe 61, 63
ALP *see* Australian Labor Party
amusement tax 49, 50, 52, 57, 60
Anderson, John 191
Andrews, Kevin 152
Anstey, Frank 50
Anthony, Doug 152
Anti-Communist Labor Party (ACL) 113
Anti-Socialists 24, 25
ANZUS treaty 147, 202
arbitration system 53, 54–5, 59, 60, 61
Ashby, James 238
Asian immigration 140, 159, 178–9
asylum seeker policy 194–8, 195–6, 199–200, 213–15, 220, 228
Australasian Federation Leagues 6
Australia, relationship with British Empire 74–7, 88–9
Australia Card 137, 153–4

Australian Democrats 135, 136, 157, 159, 181, 209, 236
Australian electoral system
   alternative vote 256–61
   apportionment and redistribution of seats 271–3
   in colonies 3–10
   compilation of election results 274–5
   compulsory voting xi–xiii, 46, 261–4
   continuous reform 276–8
   electoral administration as institution of governance 278–82
   electoral roll management 269–71
   evolution 252–4
   franchise 255–6
   polling 274
   proportional representation for Senate 264–9
   see also voting systems
Australian Free Trade and Liberal Association (AFTLA) 12
Australian Greens 159, 181, 209, 235–6, 239
Australian Labor Party
   1901 election results 16, 18–20
   1940 election results 85–6
   1972 election campaign 116
   1987 election campaign 143–4, 147, 148–9
   1996 election campaign 179, 182–3
   2001 election campaign 192–3, 204–5, 206, 207, 209–10
   2007 electoral campaign 224
   advertisers 143–4
   conferences 33–4
   factionalism 114
   first federal election win 27, 33
   intervention in Victorian branch 129–30
   Knowledge Nation policy 204, 210
   Lenin's view of 44

organisation 35–6
platform 18, 102
professionalism 43, 147
reform 129–30
religious affiliation of members 20
rise of 33–6
socialisation objective 102
split over communism 95, 96, 97–8, 109–11, 112, 113, 120
split over conscription 20, 45
split over economic policy during Depression 66, 80, 83
war policy 75
White Australia policy 17
Australian Labour Party Non-Communist (ALPNC) 80, 83, 85, 86
Australian Liberal Association (ALA) 12, 13, 18
Australian Liberal and Protectionist Organisation (ALPO) 12, 13
Australian Natives Association (ANA) 5–6, 11
Australian Republican Movement 163
Australian Settlement 13
Australian 'way of life' 107–8

B

Baker, Frank 82
Ball, George 88
Bandt, Adam 235, 236
Barnett, David 148
Barton, Edmund 6, 10, 11, 16–17, 23
Barton Government (1901–03) 17, 19, 23
Bartonites 14, 16
Battle of Britain 77
Beasley, Jack 80, 83
Beazley, Kim (Jr) 148, 186
 2001 election campaign 192–3, 204, 206
 on 2004 election loss 249
 on asylum seeker policy 214–15
 background 190
 on border protection 215
 leader's debate with Howard 206
 leadership of Labor 189, 198–200, 211, 220
 opposition to involvement in Iraq war 210, 212
 response to *Tampa* affair 198–200
Beazley, Kim (Sr) 190
Benson, Sam 125
Bishop, Bronwyn 205
Bjelke-Petersen, Joh 134, 138–40, 143, 146, 150, 153
Blainey, Geoffrey 140
Blair, Adair 83
Bligh Government (Qld) 233
Bond, Alan 145
border protection 197–8, 207, 215, 216
Bourke, W.M. (Bill) 98, 110–11
Brown, Bob 236
Brown, John 54
Brown, Tom 14, 16, 19
Bruce, Stanley Melbourne
 1929 election campaign 57–8, 59
 as Australia's high commissioner in London 64
 campaign for industrial relations reform 54–5, 59
 leadership of Nationalists 46
 loss of seat 48, 62–3, 220
 patrician hauteur 48, 49, 50–1
 political career 51
 as prime minister 49, 51, 54–6
Bruce–Page Government (1923–29) 46, 50, 52, 54–6, 58, 60
Bryce, Jeremy 35
Bryce, Quentin 235
Bulletin 33
Bunning, G.E. 16
Bunton, Cleaver 134
Bury, Les 119
Bush, George W. 219

C

Cain Government (Vic) (1952–55) 120
Cain, John (Jrn) 120
Cairns, Jim 115, 121
Calwell, Arthur 113–15, 119–20
Cameron, Clyde 130
Cameron, Rod 148
Canberra Air Disaster 70–2, 73, 89, 92

INDEX

Carlton, Jim 146, 148, 151
Carr, Bob 147
Cass, Bettina 145
Cassidy, Barrie 223
Chamberlain, Neville 77, 89
Charlton, Matthew 46, 53
Chifley, Ben 83, 91–2, 93, 101, 104
Chifley Government (1945–49) 91–2, 194–5
'children overboard' scandal 203–4, 207–8, 213, 216
Chinese, restrictions on voting 7
Chipp, Don xiii, 135
Churchill, Winston 69, 76–7, 79, 89
civic republicanism xii–xiii
Cold War 94, 95, 104, 107, 111–12, 122
Coles, Arthur 69, 84, 85, 86, 87, 91, 92
Colston, Mal 181
Commonwealth Electoral Act 1902 256–7
Commonwealth Electoral Act 1918 258, 272, 273
Commonwealth Electoral Act 1924 261
Commonwealth Franchise Act 1902 23, 255
Commonwealth Leagues 6
Commonwealth Liberal Party 25, 32–3, 35
communism 92, 95, 96, 98, 100, 107, 109, 111, 121–2
Communist Party of Australia (CPA), attempts to ban 92, 98, 104–5
communitarianism xii–xiii
compulsory voting xi–xiii, 46, 261–4
conscription referenda 45
consensus values 104
conservatism, of Australian voters 112, 161, 162, 185
Constitution, 5
   see also referenda
'Contingent Vote' 9
Cook Government (1913–14) 257–8
Cook, Joseph 25, 29, 45
Costello, Peter 152, 171, 179, 184, 191, 192, 204, 206, 220, 250
Country Party
   1940 election campaign 80–1
   coalition with Liberal Party 126
   coalition with Nationalist Party 46, 51
   coalition with United Australia Party 66, 68, 72, 74, 85
Crabb, Annabel 227
Crean, Simon 205, 210, 219
Crisp, L.F. 5, 13, 125–6
Crook, Tony 235
culture wars 186
Curran, James 75
Curtin, John 101
   1940 election campaign 77–80
   commitment to imperial cooperation 75, 77, 88–9
   on 'complete democracy' 78–9
   death 90, 91
   declaration of war on Japan 75
   leadership of Labor 66
   as prime minister 69–70, 87, 91
   refusal to form unity government 70, 72, 79, 86
   wartime legacy 89–90

D

Dawson Government (Qld) (1899) 28
Deakin, Alfred
   1901 election campaign 11, 12
   1910 election campaign 40–3
   on 1910 election loss 36
   anti-socialism campaign 35, 36
   and Liberal Party 32–3
   as prime minister 23–5, 32, 45
   retirement 45
   on 'three elevens' 13, 23
Deakin government (1903–04) 17
Deakinites 14
defence policy 39
democracy
   in Australia xiii–xiv, 112
   disillusionment with xiv
Democratic Labor Party (DLP) 236
   Catholic support for 111
   declining relevance 126
   formation 111, 113
   loss of all seats 134

preferences directed to coalition 113, 114, 124, 125–6
splitting of Labor vote 109, 111
Democrats 135, 136, 157, 159, 181, 209, 236
Denning, Warren 61, 62
Dickson, James 11
Don's Party (Williamson) 117
double-dissolution elections 27, 45, 92, 126, 133, 134, 135, 136, 142
Downer, Alexander 152, 160, 171
Drake, James 11

E

Edwards, Cecil 55
election campaigns
    personalisation of 224
    presidential style campaigns 224
    single issue campaigns 48, 59, 87
    'small target' campaigns 161, 180, 185
    see also federal election campaigns
elections
    applying significance in retrospect 94–5
    hung parliaments 68, 69
    importance xiv–xviii
    results *see* federal election results
    single issue elections 48
    that stall history rather than make it 117
    timing of 70, 72, 73
electoral administration, as institution of governance 278–82
electoral candidates, eligibility criteria 19
electoral roll management 269–71
electoral system *see* Australian electoral system
Elliott, John 158
emissions trading scheme (ETS) 221, 227, 230
environmental policy 155, 159, 220
Evans, Walter 80
Evatt, H.V. ('Doc') 77, 83
    1954 election campaign 101, 102, 108, 109
    at Royal Commission on Espionage 96–7, 110, 112
    defence of Communist Party in High Court 105, 110
    hostility of Catholic Right towards 98, 106, 110–11
    leadership of Labor 93, 95, 101, 113
    leadership style 96, 97, 98, 110
    and Petrov defection 95
    retirement from politics 113
Evidence Amendment (Journalists' Privilege) Act 2010 (Cth) 237
executive council, appointment in 1901 10–11

F

Fadden, Arthur 69, 71, 82, 87, 91, 107
Fairbairn, David 126, 128–9, 131
Fairbairn, James Valentine 71
federal election campaigns
    1901 10–15, 16–18
    1906 53
    1910 27, 33, 37–43, 44
    1925 46
    1929 47, 56, 57–62
    1940 75–81
    1954 100–1
    1969 122–4
    1972 116
    1993 160, 163
    1996 161, 176
    2001 203–8
    2007 47, 211–12
    2010 229–34
federal election results
    1901 1–10, 15, 18–19, 21
    1903 23, 31
    1904 27
    1906 24, 31
    1910 31–3
    1913 27, 45
    1914 45
    1919 46
    1922 46
    1925 46

INDEX

1928 46, 54
1929 62–3
1931 66, 74
1934 66, 74
1937 66–7, 74
1940 68, 69, 70, 81–5, 90
1943 91
1946 92
1949 92, 99
1951 92–3, 99
1954 99–100
1955 112, 113
1958 113
1961 114
1966 115, 117, 119–20, 121
1967 (half-Senate) 121
1969 117–18, 125–8, 132–3
1970 (half-Senate) 126
1972 116
1974 126, 134
1975 135
1977 135
1980 135
1983 136, 155
1984 136, 141, 156
1987 149–56
1990 156, 159
1993 160
1996 180–4
1998 186, 189
2001 208–9
2004 219, 249
2007 220, 226
2010 226, 232–3, 234–7, 240
2013 234, 234–7
2016 133, 239
Federation Conventions 6, 9
Federation Leagues 6
female politicians, treatment of 225, 246
Field, Patrick 134
Fightback! 137, 160, 163, 164
film industry 50, 52, 57
Fisher, Andrew
    background 28, 29
    defeat of Deakin 40–3
    election campaign strategy 30–1, 37–40
    Gympie 'policy speech' 37, 39–40, 44
    internationalism 29, 43
    leadership of Labor Party 30–1, 32, 36, 43
    as prime minister 25, 28, 33, 45
    retirement from politics 33, 45
    use of party power 37–40
Fisher Government (1908–09) 28, 32
Fisher Government (1910–13) 44, 27, 36
Fisher Government (1914) 27, 45
Fitzgerald Royal Commission 153
Forde, Frank 91
Forrest, John 11
franchise, in colonies 7
Fraser Government (1975–83) 138, 195
Fraser, Malcolm 107, 118, 132, 135–6
free trade 12–13, 14, 19–20
Free Traders 13, 14, 15, 23, 24
Freeth, Gordon 121–2
Freeth statement 121–2, 124, 127

G

Gair, Vince 122
Garrick, Horrie 125
gender politics 225, 247
George, Henry 14
Gillard Government (2010–13) 221
    alliance with Greens 235–6, 239
    budgets 238
    legislative record 237–8
    scandals 238–9
Gillard, Julia 69
    2010 election campaign 229–31
    agreement with Greens 235–6
    background 228
    calling of 2010 election 222–4, 234
    as deputy-leader of Labor 220
    as first female prime minister 225, 240–1
    leadership of Labor 221, 228–9
    misogyny speech 247
    negotiations with Independents 236–7
    on optional voting xi

personal scrutiny by media 246
as prime minister 221, 229–30, 238
sexist abuse of 223, 246–7
support among women voters 241–3
targeted for being childlessness 242, 245–6
Global Financial Crisis 47
Goods and Services Tax (GST) 160, 165, 186, 189
Goot, Murray 208
Gore, Mike 138
Gorton Government (1968–71) 121–2, 127
Gorton, John
   1969 election campaign 122, 123–4
   background 118
   challenges to his leadership 128–9, 131–2
   leadership of Liberal Party 118, 119
   leadership style 119, 128
   as prime minister 118
Gotto, Ainsley 128
Grattan, Michelle 150–1
Gray, Gary 149, 182
Great Depression 47, 64, 80
Greens 159, 181, 209, 235–6, 239
Gullett, Henry 71, 89, 92
Gullett, Jo 84, 92

H

Hancock, Ian 101, 118
Haneef, Muhamed 216
Hanson, Pauline 161–2, 178–9, 180, 186, 206, 216
Harradine, Brian 181
Harrison, Eric 107
Hartcher, Peter 242
Hartley, Bill 120
Harvester Judgment 38
Hasluck, Paul 119, 121
Hawke, Bob
   1984 election campaign 148, 152
   1987 election campaign 144–5, 148, 150
   on 1993 election result 165
   calling of 1987 election 142–3

challenge to Hayden's leadership 135
challenges to leadership 159
consensus politics 140
election to parliament 135
leadership of Labor 136
leadership style 171
popularity 152
Hawke Government (1983-91)
   economic policy 142
   environmental policy 155
   links to big business 144, 145
   pragmatism 167
   Prices and Income Accord 140, 155
   reforms 154–5, 158–9
   social policy 144–5
   US alliance 147–8
Hawker, Charles 63
Hayden, Bill 135, 136, 148
Hayman, Christopher 84–5
Haywood, Arthur 84
health policy 151, 155, 179
Heffernan, Bill 245–6
Henderson, Gerard 147
Hewson, John 159–60, 163, 164–5, 171
Higgins, Henry Bourne 18, 18n37, 38
higher education reform 154
Hinze, Russ 138
Hirst, John xii
Hollis, Colin 198
Holloway, Jack 62–3
Holman, W.A. 36, 44
Holmes à Court, Robert 145
Holt, Harold 114, 115, 116, 118, 119
House of Representatives
   1901 election results 15
   original composition 4, 9–10
Howard Government (1996–2007)
   asylum seeker policy 195–6, 199–200, 213
   border protection policy 197–8, 207
   'children overboard' scandal 203–4, 207–8, 213
   economic policy 184, 186
   education policy 186
   gun laws 186
   health policy 186–7

INDEX

intellectual exhaustion 211
introduction of GST 186
as 'mean', 'tricky' and not listening to voters 191
national security policy 202, 206–7
Pacific solution 201, 213, 215
policy back-flips 191–2
reforms 211
refugee policy 195–6
social policy 184
spending spree 192, 205
Tampa affair 187, 193–4, 195–8, 199–200, 213
and US invasion of Iraq 210, 219, 220
wedge politics 199
WorkChoices 48, 219–20
Howard, John xii
  1987 election campaign 143, 146–7, 148, 151, 158
  1996 election campaign 176–7
  2001 election campaign 190, 203–4, 205–7
  on Bjelke-Petersen 138, 140
  'headland' speeches 172
  on immigration 174
  leadership of Liberals 136, 141, 158, 160, 171–4
  loss of leadership to Peacock 152, 153, 158
  loss of seat 48, 185, 220
  as opposition leader 171
  policy agenda 141
  policy back-flips 191–2
  as prime minister 184, 210–11
  relationship with Costello 192, 206, 220, 250
  response to Pauline Hanson 180, 186
  and September 11 terrorist attacks 202
  social conservatism 158, 173
  as treasurer 171
  vision of Australian society 172–4
Howe, Brian 145
Hughes, Alan 117, 124, 127
Hughes, Jack 80

Hughes, W.M. (Billy)
  as Labor candidate in 1901 14, 19–20
  leadership of Nationalist Party 45–6, 51
  leadership of United Australia Party 56, 74, 87, 91
  opposition to Bruce's Maritime Industries Bill 55, 56
  parliamentary flair 34–5
  split with Labor over conscription 45
  support for free trade 14, 19–20
hung parliaments xv, 68, 70, 214, 222, 224, 235, 237

I

immigration policy 59, 158, 162–3, 216, 217–18
  Asian immigration 140, 159, 178–9
  asylum seekers 194–8, 195–6, 199–200, 213–15, 220, 228
  mandatory detention 194, 195, 196, 201, 213, 215, 216
  refugees 194
  White Australia policy 2, 16, 17, 59
incumbency advantage 10–11, 188, 189, 217
incumbency strategy 148
indentured labour 4, 5, 6, 11, 17
Independents MPs, influence of 68, 69, 70, 86–7, 236–7
Indigenous Australians
  1967 referendum 5n10
  and Commonwealth laws 5
  national apology to Stolen Generations 220
  voting rights 7, 8, 46
Indigenous policy 38, 123, 123n16, 167–8
Indigenous reconciliation 167–8, 181, 182–3
individualism 102, 104, 109
industrial actions 54
Industrial Groups 98
industrial relations 47, 48, 59, 103
internationalism, of Fisher 29

Iraq, US-led invasion 210, 219, 220
Isaacs, Isaac 18

J

Joh-for-PM campaign 138–40, 141, 143, 147, 150, 152
John Singleton Advertising 143–4
Johnson, Carol 167
Jones, Alan 247
Jones, Barry 204

K

Katter, Bob 235, 236
Keating Government (1991–96) 160, 161, 162, 164–70, 194
Keating, Paul
   1993 election campaign 165–6
   1996 election campaign 176, 182–3
   'big picture' policy agenda 164, 165, 167, 169, 171, 174, 176
   and calling of 1987 election 142–3
   campaign for Indigenous reconciliation 167–8
   challenges to Hawke's leadership 159, 163–4
   character 183–4
   leadership of Labor 159
   on national identity 169
   as prime minister 164–5, 164–70
   relationship with ALP organisation 182–4
   republicanism 163, 169–70
   as treasurer 145, 146
   vision for nation 164, 172–3
Keegan, Des 153
Kelly, Paul 149, 164, 167
Kelly, Ros 176
Kennett, Jeff 179
Kerr, John 134
Keynes, John Maynard 51, 64
Keynesianism 102, 106, 108–9
King, William Lyon Mackenzie 89
Kingston, Charles 11, 12, 18
Knowledge Nation policy 201, 204
Kyoto Protocol 210, 220

L

Labor Party see Australian Labor Party
labour movement, women's role in 38
labourism, promotion of 29
Lane, Albert 83
Lane, Bill 147
Lang, Jack 66, 67, 80, 83, 92
Langtry, John 82
Latham, John 58
Latham, Mark 219, 242–3, 249
Lawrence, Carmen 179
Lawson, John 83
Lenin, V.I. 44
Lewis, Tom 134
Ley, Sussan 209
Liberal Party (anti-Labor fusion) 25, 32–3, 35
Liberal Party of Australia
   1954 election campaign 101
   1987 election campaign 146–7, 151, 153–4
   1996 election campaign 162, 177
   coalition with Country Party 95–6, 126
   coalition with National Party 138–9, 151, 181
   disendorsement of Pauline Hanson 178, 180, 180n55
   factionalism 141, 152
   formation 92
   Fraser era 152–3
the Lodge, Canberra 49
Loveday, Peter 2
Lyne, William 10, 11, 12
Lyons, Enid 91
Lyons Government (1932–39) 66
Lyons, Joseph 63, 66, 74

M

Mabo decision 167–8
McAllister, Ian 208, 233
McClelland, Hugh 84
MacDonald, Ramsay 53
McEwen, John ('Black Jack') 118, 119, 122, 129

INDEX

McGowen, J.S.T. 18
MacKellar, Michael 125
Mackerras, Malcolm 126, 127–8
McKinlay's case 272
McLachlan, Ian 140
McLeay, George 72
McMahon, William 118–19, 129, 131–2
McMullan, Bob 148, 149
Macphee, Ian 152
Mahon, Hugh 19, 20
manhood suffrage, in colonies 7
Manifold, J.C. 14
Manne, Robert 95, 112
marginal seats, targetting of 148–9
Maritime Industries Bill 1928 55
Mathews, Race 130
Medicare 151, 155, 179
Megalogenis, George 168, 242, 243
Melville, Leslie 52
Menzies Government (1949–66) 92–3, 95–6, 99–100, 101, 113–14
Menzies, Robert
   1940 election campaign 76–7
   1954 election campaign 100–1, 102, 103–4, 106–7, 108–9
   announcement Australia was at war 74–5
   announcement of Petrov's defection 94, 95, 96–7
   calls for unity government during war 70, 72, 76, 79
   on Canberra Air Disaster 71
   decision to call 1940 election 72–3
   'Forgotten People' broadcast 104
   leadership of United Australia Party 72, 74, 92
   and Liberal Party of Australia 92
   as prime minister 69, 73–5, 86–7
   race patriotism 74–5, 76
   relationship with Earle Page 72, 74
   resignation from prime ministership 87
   retirement from politics 114
Milliner, Bert 134
Mills, Stephen 148
Ministerialists 13–14, 15
minor parties 250

minority governments 28, 32, 223, 224–5, 237–40
misogyny factor, in Australian politics 225
Montgomery, Edward 82
Morgan, Charles 92
Morgan, Hugh 140
Mulcahy, Dan 83
multiculturalism 162, 163
Mungana affair 58
Murdoch, Walter 43
Murphy, John 105, 107
Murphy, Lionel 134

N

National Farmers' Federation 140, 143
National Liberal and Protectionist League 17
National Party 209
   coalition with Liberal Party 139–40
   and Joh-for-PM campaign 138–9
nationalisation 39
Nationalist Party 46, 74
native title 168
Nelson, Brendan 221
'New Deal' 79
'new protection' 35, 38
New Right 137, 138, 140–1, 153, 156
Newman, Campbell xi
Nixon, Peter 152
Nock, Horace 82

O

Oakes, Laurie 145, 229
Oakeshott, Rob 235, 237, 250
O'Connor, P.J. 17
O'Connor, Richard 11
O'Malley, King 19
One Nation 209
optional voting xi, xii
O'Reilly, David 150

P

Pacific solution 201, 213, 215
Packer, Kerry 145

Page, Earle 46, 51, 52, 57–8, 61–2, 72, 74
Palmer, Clive xi
parliamentary government 30
party government 30
party identification 175
Peacock, Andrew 136, 141, 152–3, 158
Petrov, Evdokia, defection 100
Petrov, Vladimir, defection 94, 95, 96–7, 100, 107
plural voting 3
PNG solution 213, 214, 215
political advertising 49–50
Pollard, Reg 82
preferential voting 9, 10
press role in election campaigns
   1901 4, 14
   1910 33
   1929 49–50
   1940 79–81, 86
   1987 147
Prices and Incomes Accord 140, 155
prime ministers
   appointment of first prime minister 10
   power of 43
proportional representation for Senate 264–9
protectionism 11, 14, 23, 51–2
Protectionists 13, 16, 17, 23, 24, 32

Q

Queensland
   indentured labour 4, 5, 6, 11, 17
   voting system 3, 9
Quick, John 5, 11

R

race, and White Australia policy 2, 16, 17, 59
race politics 161–2, 182, 216, 217
radical liberalism 18, 19
Rau, Cornelia 216
Reagan, Ronald 141
referenda
   on Aboriginal policy and civil rights 5, 123
   on banning Communist Party 105–6
   on Commonwealth industrial powers 59
   on conscription 45
   Fisher Government proposals 36
   on republic 163, 184, 187
refugee policy 194
Reid, Alan 114, 128, 129
Reid, George 12, 17–18, 19, 24, 32–3
Reid Government (NSW) 17–18
Reith, Peter 192
Representation Act 1905 271, 272
republicanism 163, 169–70, 184
responsible government 42
Richardson, Graham 155
Robb, Andrew 177
Robertson, John 53–4
Robinson, Arthur 59
Roosevelt, Franklin D. 79, 89
Rosevar, Sol 83
Roxon, Nicola 245
Royal Commission on Espionage 95, 96–7, 98, 110
Royal Commission on the Moving Picture Industry 50
Rudd Government (2007–10) 220–1, 226–8, 249
Rudd, Kevin 226–8
   2007 election campaign 185, 220
   in 2010 election campaign 231
   apology to Stolen Generations 220
   on asylum seeker policy 213, 228
   background 226–7
   challenge to Beazley's leadership 220
   and emissions trading scheme (ETS) 221, 227
   leadership of Labor 220
   loss of leadership 221, 224, 228–9, 249
   popularity 227
   as prime minister 69, 220–1, 226–8
   resumption of Labor leadership 69, 233, 250
Ruddock, Phillip 196

INDEX

S

St John, Edward 125
Sawer, Marian 244
Schultz, George 148
Scott, Rose 4
Scullin Government (1929–32) 20, 47, 49, 64–5, 80, 83
Scullin, James
    1929 election campaign 57, 58–9, 60–1
    background and character 52–3
    leadership of Labor 46, 66
    as Opposition leader 46
    political career 53
    as prime minister 62
Senate
    1901 election results 15, 21
    character of 21
    original composition 4
    proportional representation 264–9
September 11 terrorist attacks 202, 208
Serle, Geoffrey 90
Shanahan, Denis 242
Sheehan, Tom 83
Shorten, Bill 235, 239
Sinclair, Ian 139, 152, 158
Singleton, John 143, 148
Slipper, Peter 238, 247
'small target' campaigns 161, 180, 185
Smyth, Brendan 176
Snedden, Billy 119, 134
social policy 39, 102–3, 106, 144–5
socialism 38–9, 43, 106
Solon, Vivian 216
South Australia, electoral administration 6
sovereign debt crisis 52
Sparkes, Robert 139
spatial politics 174–5
Spence. W.G. 44
Spender, Percy 84
stagflation 131
state aid to non-government schools 121, 126, 128
State Labor Party (SLP) 80
states' rights 4

Stolen Generations, apology to 220
Stone, John 146
Stone, Shane 191
Street, Geoffrey Austin 71
Summers, Anne 225, 242
Swan, Wayne, on optional voting xi

T

Tampa affair 187, 188, 193–8, 213, 214, 215, 216–17
Tangney, Dorothy 91
Tanner, Lindsay 235
terrorism 202, 208, 213
Thatcher, Margaret 141
Theodore, E.G. 57, 58, 60
Thomas, Josiah 19
Thomson, Craig 238
Tink, Andrew 89
trade unions, Communist leadership 98, 102
Trenwith, William 5
Tsokhas, Kosmas 50
Tudor, Frank 17, 46
Turnbull, Malcolm 133, 163, 221, 227, 234, 239, 250, 251
Turnbull, Reg 127
Turner, 11
two-party system, birth of 27, 32–3

U

United Australia Party (UAP) 77, 79, 80
    1940 election campaign 77, 79, 80
    1940 election results 84, 85
    coalition with Country Party 66, 68, 72, 74, 85
    electoral success under Lyons 66, 74
    formation 66, 73–4
    infighting and instability 71, 74, 81
US alliance 147–8, 202, 204, 210

V

valence politics 175–6
Victoria, women's suffrage 3–4
Victorian Labor Party 120–1, 126, 129–30

Vietnam War 114–15, 124, 127, 128
voter decision making
    competence of parties to manage salient issues 175
    explanations for 174–6
    party identification 175
    spatial politics 174, 175
voting rights 224
    Aboriginal Australians 8, 46
    compulsory voting xi–xiii, 46, 58–9
    exclusion of certain 'races' 4–5, 7, 8
    extension of xiv
    franchise laws of colonies 3–4, 6–8
    franchise laws of Commonwealth 5, 23, 255–6
    optional voting xi, xii
    women 3–4, 23
voting systems
    alternative vote 256–61
    in colonies 6–8
    compulsory voting xi–xiii, 46, 261–4
    'Contingent Vote' 9
    for first federal election 3–4
    first past the post 7
    Hare-Clark (or Spence) system 7, 8–9
    plural voting 3
    preferential voting 9, 10

W

Wall Street Crash 47, 49
War on Terror 213
Waterside Workers' Federation 105
Watson Government (1904) 27, 32
Watson, J.C. (Chris) 17, 18, 19, 24, 27, 30, 32
wedge politics 182, 199
Weinberger, Casper 148
Westminster system 68, 70, 73, 224, 234
Whingeing Wendy 144
White Australia policy 2, 16, 17, 59
White, Cyril Brudenell 70
White, Richard 108
'white shoe brigade' 138–9
Whitlam, Gough
    1969 election campaign 122–3, 124, 127
    background 119
    deputy-leadership of Labor 113–14, 119–20
    dismissal 134
    leadership of Labor 115, 120, 121, 127, 135
    reform of party 129–30
    relationship with party 120–1
    Victorian Labor Party 120–1
Whitlam Government (1972–75) 130–1, 134, 143, 194
Wilkie, Andrew 235, 236, 237
Willesee, Geraldine 128
Williamson, David 117
Willis, Ralph 179
Wilson, Alexander 84, 85, 86, 87, 91
Windsor, Tony 209, 235, 237, 250
Wise, B.R. 14
women
    and labour movement 38
    right to stand for political office 6
    voting patterns 241–4
    voting rights 3–4, 23
WorkChoices 48, 219–20, 220, 232
World War I 45–6
World War II 68, 69, 74–6

Y

Young, Mick 130

Milton Keynes UK
Ingram Content Group UK Ltd.
UKHW011958040823
426353UK00005B/242